Personal Relationships Across the Lifespan

Patricia Noller, Judith A. Feeney and
Candida Peterson

 **Psychology Press**
Taylor & Francis Group
HOVE AND NEW YORK

First published 2001
by Psychology Press
27 Church Road, Hove, East Sussex BN3 2FA

http://www.psypress.co.uk

Simultaneously published in the USA and Canada
by Taylor & Francis inc.
325 Chestnut Street, Philadelphia, PA 19106

Psychology Press is part of the Taylor & Francis Group

Reprinted 2001 and 2004 by Psychology Press
27 Church Road, Hove, East Sussex BN3 2FA
29 West 35th Street, New York NY 10001

© 2001 Patricia Noller, Judith A. Feeney and Candida Peterson

Typeset in Times by Keystroke, Jacaranda Lodge, Wolverhampton
Printed and bound in Great Britain by Biddles Ltd, King's Lynn, Norfolk

British Library Cataloguing in Publication Data
A catalogue record for this book is available from the British Library

Library of Congress Cataloging in Publication Data
Noller, Patricia.
    Personal relationships across the lifespan / Patricia Noller,
Judith A. Feency, and Candida Peterson
        p. cm. — (International series in social psychology)
    Includes bibliographical references and index.
    1. Interpersonal relations. 2. Intergenerational relations. I. Feeney, Judith.
II. Peterson, Candida C. (Candida Clifford) III. Title. IV. Series.
HM1106 .N65 2000
302—dc21

                                                                      00–040311

ISBN 0–415–18647–1 (hbk)
ISBN 0–415–18648–X (pbk)

Personal Relationships Across the Lifespan

Personal Relationships Across the Lifespan presents a comprehensive and up-to-date account of the role of personal relationships in people's lives.

Highlighting areas of special significance and research interest at each major life stage, Patricia Noller, Judith A. Feeney and Candida Peterson examine how close relationships develop over time and influence individual adjustment. They explore a wide range of relationships, including some that are often neglected, such as those with siblings, adult children and elderly parents. They also look at alternative family forms, such as single-parent families and step-families, and address important themes such as intimacy, conflict and power.

With insightful discussion of the theory and methods typically used by researchers working in this area, *Personal Relationships Across the Lifespan* is an ideal resource for students of both relationships and lifespan development. It will also be of interest to practitioners, such as social workers and family therapists, working with clients with relational concerns and anyone wanting to learn more about the nature of relationships.

Patricia Noller is Professor of Psychology, **Judith A. Feeney** is Senior Lecturer in Psychology and **Candida Peterson** is Professor of Psychology. They are all based at the University of Queensland, Australia.

INTERNATIONAL SERIES IN SOCIAL PSYCHOLOGY
Edited by W. Peter Robinson
University of Bristol, UK

This series provides a showcase of original contributions of the highest quality, as well as thorough reviews of existing theories suitable for advanced students and researchers. Many will be useful as course texts for higher level study; applied topics are well represented and social psychology is defined broadly to include other psychological areas like social development, or the social psychology of abnormal behaviour. A reflection of contemporary social psychology, the series is a rich source of information for dissertations, new research projects and seminars.

Recent books in the series:
Adjustment of Adolescents
Cross-cultural similarities and differences
Ruth Scott and W. A. Scott

Adolescence: From Crisis to Coping
A thirteen nation study
Janice Gibson-Cline

Children as Consumers
A psychological analysis of the young people's market
Barrie Gunder and Adrian Furnham

Understanding the Older Consumer
The grey market
Barrie Gunter

The Economic Psychology of Everyday Life
Paul Webley, Carole B. Burgoyne, Stephen E. G. Lea and Brian M. Young

Changing European Identities
Social psychological analyses of social change
Glynis M. Breakwell and Evanthia Lyons

Making Sense of Television
The psychology of audience interpretation (2nd edition)
Sonia Livingstone

Social Groups and Identities
Developing the legacy of Henri Tajfel
Edited by W. Peter Robinson

Stereotypes during the Decline and Fall of Communism
György Hunyady

Also available in the Routledge Research International Series in Social Psychology:
Cooperation in Modern Society
Promoting the welfare of communities, states and organizations
Edited by Mark van Vight, Mark Snyder, Tom R. Tyler and Anders Biel

Youth and Coping in Twelve Nations
Surveys of 18–20-year-old young people
Edited by Janice Gibson-Cline

Responsibility
The many faces of a social phenomenon
Hans-Werner Bierhoff and Ann Elisabeth Auhagen

Contents

Figures

Tables

1

Introduction

There is no doubt that most individuals see relationships as a central part of their lives, and that relationships have important implications for health and well-being. People engage in many relationships throughout the lifespan, with some of these being relatively superficial and others being very close.

Although we all participate in relationships, we seldom think about what the term really means. Perhaps the most obvious point is that relationships 'involve a series of interactions between two individuals known to each other' (Hinde, 1979, p. 15). This definition focuses on the overt behaviours occurring within the dyad. However, as Hinde points out, a relationship is much more than this. The behaviours that can be observed within a relationship context are accompanied by less visible emotional and cognitive processes, which are likely to affect the course of the interaction. For example, Peter and Jane may be discussing how they will spend their weekend. He may be concerned about some work he needs to finish, and she may be anxious because they have not visited her mother for several weeks. Some of these concerns may not be openly expressed, but will nevertheless shape this interaction, and the future interactions of this couple. As this scenario illustrates, interactions involve both relationship partners, and each brings their own individual needs and concerns to the interaction and the relationship in which it is embedded.

Kelley (1983) defines relationships in terms of the concepts of impact and interdependence. That is, people are in a relationship if they have an impact on one another and are 'interdependent in the sense that a change in one person causes a change in the other and vice versa' (p. 12). According to Kelley and his colleagues, the extent of interdependence is revealed in four properties of the relationship: frequency of impact, strength of impact, diversity in range of joint activities, and duration of interconnection over time.

Relationships in which the impact is frequent and strong, and in which the partners engage in varied activities together and the sense of connection is long-lasting, would generally be described as 'personal'. For example, marriage, parent–child relationships and friendships would all be considered as personal relationships. These relationships will be the primary focus of this book, although we will also consider processes such as social support and group interaction, as these bear upon the nature of personal relationships.

The term 'close' is sometimes used as a substitute for 'personal' in the relationship context, although this term is fraught with difficulties. For example, some marriages are much closer than others, and, in most relationships, feelings of closeness wax and wane over time. For these reasons, we generally prefer to use the term 'personal', unless we are referring specifically to the closeness or intimacy of a relationship, or to previous research which has used the term 'close'.

Stages of the Lifespan

The chapters of this book are organized sequentially around major stages of the lifespan, beginning with infancy and childhood and moving through adolescence and adulthood to the relationships of the elderly. This organization is designed to highlight the particular themes that are salient in relationships within specfic age groups, and to draw out the changes that link relational processes earlier in life with their subsequent developmental outcomes.

It is important to acknowledge, however, that there is ongoing debate about the extent to which there is continuity of individual development, and whether there are discrete stages that differ qualitatively from one another (Baltes, Reese and Lipsitt, 1980). Of course, we recognize that individuals do not always fit neatly into the stages as we describe them in this book. For example, we discuss marriage in the chapter on early adulthood, although it is obvious that some individuals marry during adolescence, and others marry much later in life. Similarly, we discuss divorce in the chapter on middle age, even though some couples divorce in early adulthood.

Important Themes in Relationship Development

Although we discuss relationships using a life stage framework, there are a number of recurring themes which need to be highlighted. These themes include attachment, intimacy, communication, conflict, and issues of power and control.

Attachment, for example, has been a cornerstone of our understanding of relationship development in infancy and childhood for at least four decades. As Feeney and Noller (1996) pointed out, however, it is now widely recognized that attachment processes have important implications for intimate relationships throughout the lifespan. Attachment principles have been used to explain both the normative processes involved in couple relationships, and the origin of individual differences in relationship attitudes and behaviours.

Similarly, intimacy (which is generally seen as involving affection, cohesion and emotional expressiveness) has its roots in our earliest relationships with our primary caregivers. Intimacy is an equally important feature of many friendships and sibling bonds in childhood, and also figures prominently in later relationships, including romantic relationships, marriages and adult friendships. However, intimacy manifests itself in very different ways depending on the developmental stage of each partner and the length of their relationship. The type of relationship (e.g., friendship versus marriage), and the characteristics of the particular individuals, also affects the ways in which intimacy is expressed.

It is impossible to think about relationships without considering the important role of communication. It is through communication that relationship partners develop a shared understanding, work out the rules of their relationship, express caring and affection, make decisions and resolve conflicts. In fact, it has been argued that good communication is almost synonymous with effective relationships (Montgomery, 1988).

The importance of partners' communicating about their differences and disagreements highlights the need to consider the nature and consequences of relationship conflict. Conflict has been defined as any instance of disagreement, difference of opinion or incompatibility (Cahn, 1990). If we think about this definition, it is clear that conflict is almost an inevitable consequence of involvement in a personal relationship. However, relationships vary greatly in terms of frequency and intensity of conflict, and in terms of the processes used to deal with conflicts. In this book, we explore the varied influences of conflict on individual and relationship development.

Many instances of relationship conflict are really about who has the right to make decisions and who can be told what to do – in other words, conflict is often about issues of power and control. In the context of close relationships, power has been defined by Huston (1983) as the ability to influence the partner when one wishes to do so. Power issues tend to arise out of conflicts of interest such as incompatible goals, different ideas, and contrary preferences about when and how to attain goal outcomes. The balance of power in specific relationships will vary according to developmental stage; for example, children gain greater power and control relative to parents, as they progress from infancy through adolescence. However, there are also individual differences and gender differences in strivings for control and modes of expressing dominance and submission, and these patterns can be observed fairly consistently from one life stage to the next.

Cultural and Subcultural Issues

In this book, our aim is to emphasize those features of human relationships which apply widely, irrespective of cultural background, historical cohort and other contextual factors. Nevertheless, owing to the disproportionate focus on relationship research in English-speaking countries, and especially North America, much of the data we report comes from these countries, and much of it involves contemporary populations. Where sufficient cross-cultural data are available, the major findings are mentioned. In addition, we report contrasts between different ethnic and subcultural groups within western societies, and also mention changes in demographic profiles over recent history as these bear on the conduct of personal relationships.

A more thorough treatment of cultural issues in relationships can be found in several volumes devoted to these issues, such as Goodwin (1999), and Hatfield and Rapson (1996).

The Effects of One Relationship on Another

As well as examining the ways in which particular relationships develop over the lifespan, we also explore the implications of experiences in one relationship for an individual's functioning in other relationships, and for the quality of those relationships. For example, we look at evidence suggesting that young children's interactions with their parents affect childhood friendships and adult romantic relationships. These effects have been explained in terms of a variety of mechanisms, including direct teaching, attachment processes and social learning. Even later in the lifespan, we explore the implications of early parent–child relationships for the adult child providing care to an elderly parent.

Methodological Issues

A wide range of methodologies can be used to study relationships. Marital conflict, for example, can be studied by asking spouses to complete questionnaires assessing general attitudes and behaviours, or to record aspects of specific interactions using structured diaries. Another approach to studying marital conflict involves bringing the couple into a laboratory setting to discuss a marital problem in front of a video camera. The data obtained in this manner can be treated in various ways. For instance, couples themselves may be asked to make global ratings of the interaction on specific scales, or trained observers may be asked to code the videotape using a systematic coding scheme, or to perform a content analysis on the transcript of the interaction.

The contrast between the ratings of trained observers and those of the participants themselves raises the issue of the different kinds of data obtained from 'outsiders' and 'insiders', and the unique perspectives that each brings. Trained observers are able to provide an objective account of the actual behaviour of the participants, but do not have access to relevant dyadic factors such as the history of the relationship or the interpretations of the behaviour being made by the members of the couple. On the other hand, a participating couple have access to these 'hidden' factors, but may be less objective about the behaviour, owing to their affective investment in the relationship (Sillars and Scott, 1983).

Another important methodological issue is that relationship development can be studied either cross-sectionally (using different groups of participants for each age group), or longitudinally (by following the same individuals over a long period of time). There are advantages and disadvantages to each of these approaches. There are undoubtedly difficulties, for example, associated with inferring development from cross-sectional studies: particular birth cohorts in a population are likely to differ, not only in terms of age but also in terms of education and more subtle factors such as the formative influences of societal attitudes while they were growing up. On the other hand, the cross-sectional methodology has the advantage of enabling the study of large and representative samples of members of widely spaced age groups in an efficient and economical manner. As Glenn has commented:

> All too often, students of aging now fail to recognize that cross-sectional data, properly analyzed and supplemented with information from other sources, can often provide more nearly conclusive evidence about the effects of aging than can any other kind of data.
>
> (1981, p. 362)

Longitudinal studies have the important advantage of allowing within-subject comparisons, with each participant serving as their own control. This feature can be particularly important in the study of relationships, which are influenced by individual differences in variables such as attachment history, family background and personality. A disadvantage of longitudinal studies, however, stems from the rapid progress of social change, particularly in areas of family and relationship functioning; thus, the experiences of the cohort taking part in a study over several decades may have little generality to more recent cohorts in the same population. Societal attitudes at a particular testing point are also confounded with subjects' age at that test, in longitudinal designs.

To overcome this problem, sequential methodologies (Schaie, 1994) have been developed. In this approach, age groups from several different cohorts are tested cross-sectionally and then followed longitudinally over time, enabling both cohort differences and time-of-test differences to be teased apart from age-related change. However, owing to their ambitious, expensive and time-consuming nature, these designs have as yet seen relatively little application to relationship research.

Organization of this Volume

In the next five chapters, we take a chronological perspective on the development of relationships. Specifically, these chapters explore the experiences of relationships in infancy and childhood, adolescence, early adulthood, middle age and old age. In the final chapter, we summarize the major research findings, and draw together the integrative themes outlined earlier in this chapter. Throughout the book, we aim to show how particular relationships shape the cognitive, social and emotional development of the individual, how they impact on interactions in other contexts, how they are influenced by major developmental tasks, and how they contribute to the individual's sense of well-being.

2

Infancy and Childhood

This chapter explores the growth of relationships from birth through early and middle childhood to pre-adolescence. This roughly ten-year period spans a remarkable amount of developmental change. Relationships and their social-psychological underpinnings are transformed as infants progress from entry into the social world of the family through a wealth of formative interactions with their parents, siblings, and other members of their immediate social groups. Gradually, new kinds of close relationships are forged with friends and peers, as children move beyond the confines of the family into friendship networks and age-segregated groupings in preschool, at school and in the neighbourhood.

To explore these important patterns of developmental change, we adopt an approach which is partially chronological and partially relationship-centred. We begin by examining the growth of infants' first social interactions with their parents, siblings and other household members. We then follow the growth of parent–child interaction from the infant's perspective, beginning with the process of attachment in which a special bond of affection to a particular caregiver is forged. The progress of the parent–child relationship is also examined through the social developments that follow from the child's gains in linguistic and conversational fluency during toddlerhood, and from increasing levels of biological, cognitive and social maturity throughout childhood. We also explore parenting practices, and how differences in a family's communication, teaching, discipline and conflict-management styles can shape differences in children's development outcomes.

The development of relationships with brothers and sisters during childhood is also explored, along with some of the variations in sibling relationship quality that are likely to arise as a function of family composition, parenting and the child's modes of interacting with siblings. The chapter concludes with a brief look at the growth of peer relationships during childhood, in preparation for a more detailed examination (in Chapter 3) of how older children and adolescents gradually shift their relationship focus from family members to members of the peer group.

Before the First Relationship: from General Sociability to the Threshold of Attachment

Newborn babies are sociable. But the quality of their social investment in others differs importantly from that observed in the close relationships that preoccupy and guide social behaviour and psychological development of older children and adults. Instead of singling out individuals, or showing awareness of particular people as relationship partners, very young babies are inclined to bestow their social responsiveness upon humans in general, without recognition of the distinct personalities of different individuals. Nor do relationship functions like feeding or soothing warrant special ties to particular caregivers during early infancy. For example, a baby only a few hours old is 'social', to the extent of preferring to look at, listen to, and touch, other human beings. But such a social preference generalizes to *all* human beings, not just the mother or father or other immediate family members. Indeed, close physical contact with a paediatrician or infant-health nurse who has extensive experience in holding and soothing neonates may be more gratifying than contact with an inexperienced new parent.

Experiments on auditory preference have shown that when newborns are given a choice of things to listen to, human voices stand out ahead of other pleasantly rhythmic and harmonious stimuli like orchestral music or birdsong (Brazelton, 1984). Very young babies also display their social inclinations through preferential reactions to human speech. The sound of a voice reading poetry calms the neonate's heart, soothes their distress, and motivates their non-nutritive sucking more effectively than any other type of non-human auditory stimulation (Brazelton, 1984; DeCasper and Spence, 1986).

Despite this general preference for human stimulation, newborn babies are not yet capable of taking an active and meaningful part in a specialized social relationship. To participate in a relationship in the true sense implies a selective awareness of partners as individuals, rather than as undifferentiated or interchangeable members of the human species (Hinde, 1992). Thus a very young infant who accepts comfort as readily from an unfamiliar caregiver as from the parent is displaying sociability, without yet having developed a clear indication of social relatedness.

The Maturation of Readiness for a Relationship

Another important characteristic of relationships, according to Schaffer (1996), is their anticipated continuity through time. As he explained:

> A relationship has characteristics of its own, such as faithfulness, involvement or devotion, none of which can be applied to any one specific instance of interaction. . . . We need to make a sharp distinction between the study of interactions and the study of relationships: The former are a here-and-now phenomenon, the latter imply continuity over time and are more than the sum of a series of interactions.
>
> (p. 99)

The development of the first truly social relationship is assisted by the maturation of the infant's locomotor, sensory and cognitive capacities over the early months of life. For example, a baby's visual acuity improves markedly over the first three months of postnatal life, assisting in accurate recognition of caregivers. In fact, even though newborn babies prefer to gaze at cartoon drawings of simple faces than at other symmetrical designs like bull's eyes and chequer boards (Fantz, 1961), their visual skills at birth are quite limited. The muscles which control eye movement are not completely under voluntary control, so the baby has trouble tracking moving objects or even keeping the two eyes oriented in the same direction. The ability to focus the lens is absent, causing objects at distances of greater than about 20 centimetres to appear blurry.

Even when focus improves, infants aged 2 months and under lock into the outer contours of a face, rather than the internal detail (such as shape of nose or eyes), that makes individuals distinctly recognizable. These skills improve with development and visual experience over the early months. Nevertheless, the ability to identify people by viewing their facial features alone does not emerge reliably in most infants until 3 months of age (Cohen, DeLoache and Strauss, 1979), and it is not until this age that babies can discriminate their own mother's photograph from those of other women of somewhat similar appearance (Barrera and Maurer, 1981). Without these perceptual capacities, the ability to relate socially to particular individuals is sharply curtailed.

Shapiro and Stern (1989) argue that infants' perceptual apparatus is 'pre-wired' to attend to such features as the mother's face and voice, and that the ability to regulate this attention develops over the first three months. For example, in a variety of observational studies, Stern (1976) has shown that the achievement of initiation and interruption of visual gaze at three months provides a template for later regulatory functions. In other words, infants come to regulate visual input by controlling whether or not they look at particular objects; they can also 'tune out' through changing the focus of their attention.

The forging of particular social relationships with individual people also requires maturation of the cognitive capacity to comprehend concepts of continuity and permanence (Piaget, 1970). The baby must come to the realization that the people whom he or she encounters remain the same individuals each time they come into, and recede from, sensory contact. According to Piaget (1952), infants under the age of 6 months lack such a notion of permanence with respect to people, as well as with respect to physical objects. Thus they appear to treat their sensory experiences as a series of changing parades of totally new and unrepeatable events. The old adage 'out of sight, out of mind' comes closest to epitomizing concepts of human beings at this stage.

Around the age of 6 months, many infants have overcome this cognitive limitation sufficiently to be able to search for a hidden toy in the place where it was last seen, and to anticipate a caregiver's return when he or she goes out of the room for a brief period. They begin to develop concepts known as *object permanence* (for physical objects) and *person permanence* (for caregivers and other familiar social stimuli). This cognitive milestone has crucial significance for the forging of a close relationship. Until the baby realizes that mother is the same person each time she disappears into another room and then re-emerges, or that the father who departed for work this morning is the same person now greeting the infant on his return home in the evening, no individualized social or emotional relatedness to a particular person is conceivable.

Stranger fear

Another developmental milestone that heralds the capacity to forge a personal relationship is the maturation of an emotional phenomenon known as *stranger wariness* (or stranger fear). From the age of 2–4 months, when the art of social smiling is mastered, most babies are a sociable delight for strangers to meet and greet, as well as for familiars. The approach of a smiling human face reliably evokes an answering grin from the infant unless he or she is extremely drowsy or distressed. But the baby's social responsiveness at this stage is largely indiscriminate. A smiling woman encountered for the first time in a supermarket can evoke just as friendly a greeting as the caregiver from whom the baby has rarely, or never, been separated.

Between the ages of 7–10 months, this social attitude of generalized friendliness is likely to give way to a new and more discriminating social approach. Starting at about 24 weeks, as shown in Figure 2.1, and peaking between the ages of 28 and 40 weeks, most babies display wariness in response to the social overtures of people outside their familiar circle of everyday contacts. Thus a 10-month-old girl, instead of grinning, cooing and raising her arms when a smiling stranger looms over the shopping trolley, may look stern and uncomfortable. If the welcoming 'stranger' (who may be a visiting aunt, neighbour or grandparent, not just the kind of complete stranger who might reasonably evoke wariness in an older child) persists in her approach, or intensifies her expressions of positive emotions, the typical baby at 7–10 months will withdraw, pucker, cry, and display other manifestations of distress. As illustrated in Figure 2.1, sociability towards people in general has given way to a rejection of those who are unfamiliar.

Separation anxiety

Negative emotional reactions to being parted from familiar caregivers are also likely to develop at about the same time, as part of a related social system known as separation protest or *separation anxiety* (Thompson and Limber, 1990). Emotional distress over having to part from a caregiver, even while being soothed by a substitute, emerges in many infants around 6 months of age, is clearly present in most 8-month-olds, peaks at about 14 months, and then gradually subsides. Though an important indicator of social maturity and the readiness to forge a special relationship, separation anxiety can pose practical difficulties for parents,

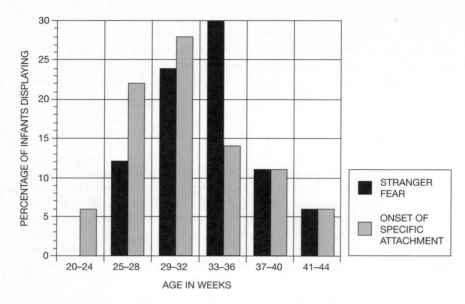

FIGURE 2.1 Developmental changes in social and emotional reactions during infancy

particularly if regular separations (to attend childcare or visit relatives) are a normal part of the baby's routine.

Mothers whose infants have reached the stage of separation anxiety may wonder if it is still appropriate to leave their unhappily protesting baby in the care of a grandparent or babysitter who would have been greeted enthusiastically during the less mature phase of generalized sociability. From a practical point of view, parents can minimize the distress of temporary partings during this phase by forward planning. If brief separations and regular reunions are made a familiar part of the baby's daily routine before the age of 6–8 months, subsequent distress at separation is reduced. In addition, during the period when wariness of strangers peaks (see Figure 2.1), a parent can further facilitate the baby's adjustment by getting ready for each brief parting with a relaxed and friendly period for saying goodbyes, incorporating plenty of warm reassurance. In contrast to abrupt and melancholy farewells, or stealing away in a shroud of secrecy, these relaxed and open tactics are found to ease the temporary pain infants experience through separation anxiety (Thompson and Limber, 1990), while also paving the way for the first genuine relationship, known as a *specific attachment*.

Defining Attachment

One-year-old infants' negative emotional reactions to approaches from strangers and to separations from parents are signs of social maturity. These emotional developments, though superficially negative, are actually positive achievements that signal the baby's readiness for becoming attached to people in a special way. As generalized sociability declines in favour of a particular regard for one chosen person, the first genuine relationship can be said to develop. This relationship is known as an *attachment* (Bowlby, 1969). As Schaffer (1996, p. 127) defined it, an attachment is 'a long-enduring, emotionally meaningful tie to a particular individual'. Sroufe and Waters (1977) describe attachment as 'an insubstantial psychological tether which binds the infant and caregiver together' (p. 1186). In other words, the development of an attachment implies the growth of a true social relationship. This bond is experienced by infant and target alike as:

- specific and selective (attachments are confined to particular dyads and involve feelings and behaviours not expressed in interactions with other people);
- emotionally supportive and satisfying;
- continuous through time and separation (like an invisible cord);
- evocative of separation protest and physical proximity seeking.

These features can be summarized in terms of the major functions of infant attachment behaviours. That is, attachment behaviours are designed to keep the infant close to a nurturing adult (proximity-seeking and separation protest), to provide a source of comfort in times of danger and stress (safe haven), and to provide a base from which the infant feels confident to explore and master the environment (secure base).

The Roots of Attachment in Mother–Infant Interaction

According to Butterworth and Jarrett (1991), the ability to read the mother's gaze develops early in human infants, progressing through a series of stages over the first two years of life. They tested this proposition in a series of experiments, using a controlled looking procedure, as illustrated in Figure 2.2. The mother and infant were seated in a face-to-face position. As the mother followed the tester's instructions to look at predetermined points in the room, the infant's gaze behaviour was carefully recorded. From as early as 6 months of age, most babies were able to use the social cue embodied in a full maternal head turn to redirect their attention towards the object the mother was looking at. However, if she merely held her head still and glanced at the object by moving her eyes, no consistent evidence of the ability to locate the focus of her attention emerged in infants under one year old.

By the age of 18 months, the capacity to follow the mother's gaze was so sophisticated that most of the infants in Butterworth and Jarrett's study could track the mother's gaze to locate an object that was initially outside their own range of sight. At least implicitly, they appeared to be aware that their mothers could attend to things that they themselves were unaware of, opening a new avenue of social understanding that extended beyond the boundaries of immediate perceptual experience. These developmental milestones are illustrated in Figure 2.2.

The use of the mother as a reference point for exploring the world of people and objects may contribute to the infant's early understanding of human beings as distinctive social stimuli and, consequently, to the formation of a special relationship to one particular person. This bond of attachment, in its turn, can facilitate cognitive exploration and the further growth of social understanding, as we will see in a later section of this chapter.

According to Trevarthen (1992), a specific attachment to a caregiver reflects the culmination of two distinct social developments in the infant's involvement with the person (for example, the mother) to whom they have become attached. Over many months of interacting and communicating prelinguistically before attachment reliably emerges (see Figure 2.1), a wealth of emotional information has been exchanged. This process happens imperceptibly, through the many daily encounters between mothers and infants. Trevarthen used the term *primary intersubjectivity* to describe the infant's increasingly conscious awareness of the mother as a distinct person, especially in relation to emotion.

The give and take of emotional communication responsible for this increased awareness is evident in experimental demonstrations. In a typical test (Butterworth, 1994), mother and baby come to the laboratory and are seated in front of a closed-circuit television camera. They are positioned so that the image of the mother's face, along with the sound of her voice, are relayed to the baby's eyes via the camera, rather than directly. Once the baby acclimatizes to this fact during preliminary interaction, a time lag is introduced by delaying the closed-circuit picture. When this happens, infants are likely to become puzzled. They may cry and display other signs of distress. Although the video image of the mother interacting responsively is a live one, its delay by a few seconds poses a challenge to the infant's social consciousness. According to Trevarthen, the baby's development of social related-ness, via primary intersubjectivity, relies upon synchrony between the infant's emotional states and social cues as to the corresponding emotional states of the familiar partner.

Secondary intersubjectivity, for Trevarthen, is achieved when the infant achieves *joint visual attention*. This developmental acquisition enables the baby to appreciate the physical and social world as mediated through the mother's mind and feelings. According to Butterworth (1994), by the age of one year the average infant 'achieves secondary intersubjectivity, based on jointly construed meaning, the negotiation of conventional knowledge, common purposes, and communication through symbols' (p. 122). These inner cognitive attributes can be observed overtly in the infant's special attention to the mother's face, voice or pointing cues.

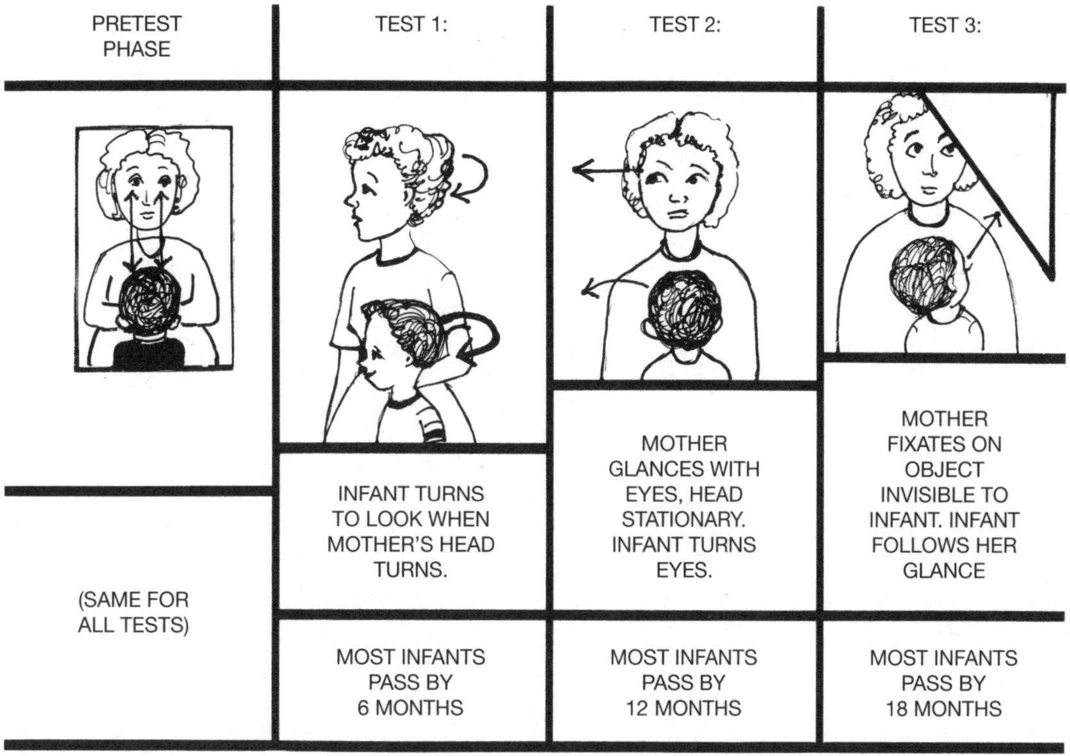

FIGURE 2.2 The growth of gaze communication

PRETEST PHASE	TEST 1:	TEST 2:	TEST 3:
(SAME FOR ALL TESTS)	INFANT TURNS TO LOOK WHEN MOTHER'S HEAD TURNS.	MOTHER GLANCES WITH EYES, HEAD STATIONARY. INFANT TURNS EYES.	MOTHER FIXATES ON OBJECT INVISIBLE TO INFANT. INFANT FOLLOWS HER GLANCE
	MOST INFANTS PASS BY 6 MONTHS	MOST INFANTS PASS BY 12 MONTHS	MOST INFANTS PASS BY 18 MONTHS

Attachment as an Integrated Behavioural System

John Bowlby, a pioneer in the study of infant attachment, viewed the attachment process as 'a way of conceptualising the propensity of human beings to make strong affectional bonds with others' (1977, p. 201). He suggested that the quality of the close bond forged between infants and their primary caregivers during the first years of life continued to shape social relationships across the lifespan, a proposition which we examine in detail in later chapters of this book. Bowlby also postulated a biological basis for the human propensity to develop attachments, rooted in species genes selected through evolutionary history. The survival value of being able to summon and cling to a caregiver is obvious for a species in the wild which is subject to threat from roaming predators. In modern human society, the risk of an attack by a wild animal may no longer be a probability, but the same evolutionary link is reflected in the activation of the attachment system by threat, danger or distress. Thus human infants seek attachment targets more strenuously when stressed by ill health, unfamiliarity or perceptions of danger. Through social perception (via gaze-following and intersubjectivity), the caregiver may then supply cognitive and emotional reassurance, as well as providing comfort through physical contact.

Bowlby (1973) postulated that the attachment system in humans is an integrated behavioural unit comprising several interlocking subsystems. One of these, known as *proximity seeking*, involves the desire to maintain closeness to the caregiver. Proximity seeking itself can be viewed as an integration of behaviours like looking, following and crying, each of which can interchangeably serve this goal, depending on the infant's maturity and physical situation. *Secure-base exploration* (the facilitation of physical or cognitive exploratory activity when in the presence of the caregiver) is another component of the attachment system. Thus an infant gains the readiness to learn and to cope with cognitive challenges through the presence of a caregiver to whom he or she is attached.

Bowlby proposed that expectations about the availability and responsiveness of caregivers develop over the first three years of life. Further, these expectations are subject to important individual differences, a proposition we will examine in more detail in terms of research on the role of situational variables (like day care) and caregiver attributes (like responsiveness) as contributors to infants' attachments. In addition, Bowlby (1969, 1973, 1980) argued that the developmental course of attachment formation can be described by the four-stage sequence shown in Table 2.1.

Naturalistic and Laboratory-based Assessments of Infant–Parent Attachment

Another pioneer in the study of infant attachment, Ainsworth (1973), examined the growth of infants' attachments to their mothers through three converging lines of empirical inquiry. Initially, she conducted a naturalistic-observational investigation

TABLE 2.1 *Steps in the infant attachment process according to Bowlby*

Stage	Age range (average)	Principal characteristics
Pre-attachment	0–2 months	Indiscriminate sociability
Attachment in the making	2–7 months	Maturation of readiness through visual recognition of familiar people, concepts of person permanence, etc.
Clear-cut attachment	7–24 months	Separation protest, stranger wariness, clinging, proximity seeking
Goal-corrected partnership	2 years onwards	Relationships are mutual; child recognizes parent's needs

in Uganda, of tribal infants' developmental patterns of expressing needs for proximity-seeking, exploration and comfort-gaining (Ainsworth, 1967). She then extended the observational study of attachment cross-culturally by undertaking a longitudinal study of mothers and their first-born infants in Baltimore, USA (Ainsworth and Bell, 1969). Eventually, her insights were drawn together into the development of a laboratory-based measure of attachment (the Strange Situation; see Ainsworth, 1973) that we will examine in detail in a later section of this chapter.

Ainsworth's (1973) studies identified a number of indicators demonstrating the replacement of generalized sociability by a specific attachment to a familiar caregiver. Depending on the baby's maturity of motor control and cognitive development, these may include the following:

- crying to attract the caregiver's attention;
- smiling more at the caregiver than at other people;
- vocalizing more in the caregiver's presence than when alone or with strangers;
- crying when the caregiver leaves the room or puts the baby down;
- reaching towards or following the caregiver;
- looking at the caregiver, or in the direction of the caregiver's voice;
- enthusiastically greeting the caregiver by grinning, crowing and general excitement after a separation, while showing less enthusiasm in the greeting of strangers;
- lifting arms to be held by the caregiver when approached;
- clapping hands, grabbing or scrambling over the caregiver;
- burying the face in the caregiver's lap;
- embracing, hugging or kissing the caregiver more than other people;
- making eye contact with the caregiver or attending to his/her emotional cues when frightened or perplexed;
- fleeing to the caregiver as a haven of comfort;
- accepting comfort from the caregiver while rejecting the comforting overtures of others;

- clinging physically either to the caregiver or to one of the caregiver's familiar possessions, such as a handbag or cardigan.

Some of these manifestations of attachment occur more frequently than others. A few cannot occur at all until necessary skills (such as locomotion) have developed. Furthermore, no single manifestation is sufficient to show that a baby has developed a personalized attachment. Babies may smile as a gesture of affiliation with caregivers to whom they are attached, but smiling can also be evoked by successful problem-solving, by the relief accompanying a nonthreatening interaction with a stranger, or as part of an exploratory inspection of a visual display. Nevertheless, when seen in combination, these behavioural and expressive responses provide a telling picture of attachment as a complex social system. This system involves multiple cognitive, affective and behavioural channels, and guides the growth of later social relationships in myriad ways.

As the above examples show, there are many manifestations of attachment behaviour in the everyday lives of 1-year-old infants. For example, a visit to a doctor's surgery may evoke crying and clinging; these behaviours may be followed by exploration of the toys and people in the waiting room as the baby becomes more relaxed, using the mother's responses for cues that the situation is safe, and her presence as a secure base around which to orient these exploratory activities.

Behaviours like these are available for empirical investigation through naturalistic observation (Ainsworth and Bell, 1969). But in order to obtain a more standardized measure that is comparable across different environments and cultures, researchers frequently employ specially structured observations in a controlled laboratory setting.

The Strange Situation

In contemporary attachment research, a widely used instrument for studying the formation of attachment is Ainsworth's (1973) Strange Situation. According to Bretherton (1992), this is 'a 20-minute miniature drama with eight episodes' (p. 765). The procedure begins when the mother brings her infant to an unfamiliar laboratory room, equipped with a one-way mirror. Researchers (who are hidden from sight behind the screen) record the infant's responses to a series of brief episodes designed to evoke such components of the attachment system as exploration and proximity seeking. As shown in Table 2.2, some episodes involve the mother staying with the baby; others involve separations or reunions with the mother or a female stranger.

As scored by Ainsworth (1979), the Strange Situation procedure enables researches to measure the nature and quality of the infant's social interaction with the mother (or other primary caregiver). In addition, a comparison of the baby's social behaviour with the mother and with the stranger enables differential regard to be teased apart from generalized sociability. Furthermore, the infant's emotional

TABLE 2.2 *Strange Situation Test*

Episode number	Participants	Duration (approx.)	Brief description of behaviour measured
1	Mother, baby and researcher conducting test	30 seconds	Tester guides mother and baby to the experimental room, then leaves. (The room contains an appealing range of toys.)
2	Mother and baby	3 minutes	Mother sits quietly while baby explores; if necessary, play is stimulated after 2 minutes.
3	Stranger,* mother and baby	3 minutes	Stranger enters. *First minute*: stranger is silent. *Second minute*: stranger converses with mother. *Third minute*: stranger approaches baby. After 3 minutes, the mother leaves unobtrusively.
4	Stranger and baby	3 minutes or less	*First separation episode.* Stranger remains in the room and responds to the baby's initiatives.
5	Mother and baby	3 minutes or more	*First reunion episode.* Mother returns and greets baby, comforting if necessary. She then tries to settle the baby into play. Mother leaves when play is established, saying 'bye-bye'.
6	Baby alone	3 minutes or less	*Second separation episode.* Baby remains alone in the room until a reaction is noted; then stranger arrives.
7	Stranger and baby	3 minutes or less	*Continuation of second separation.* Stranger enters and gears her behaviour to that of the baby.
8	Mother and baby	3 minutes	*Second reunion episode.* Mother enters, greets and cuddles infant while stranger departs unobtrusively.

Note: *An unfamiliar female research assistant of about the same age as the mother.

reactions to separations from, and reunions with, the mother are carefully noted, along with the feelings and nonverbal behaviours the baby displays during each episode. How quickly infants regain their composure after upsets, along with the mother's skill in comforting them, are additional important elements in this structured observation.

When all of this information is put together, a picture emerges of infant attachment style which can fall into one of three broad categories. Ainsworth labelled these attachment patterns: Type A, Type B and Type C. They can be briefly characterized as follows:

(1) *Type A* 'Insecure avoidant': Babies with this attachment classification show relatively little upset when the stranger approaches them or the mother leaves

them alone. However, they are often reluctant to contact or cling to the mother. Relative to infants in other classifications, they display indifference to the mother throughout all phases of the procedure, generally showing no particular attention to her, and little delight in reunion with her.

(2) *Type B* 'Securely attached': Babies with this classification usually display their secure bonds of affection and attachment for the mother by protesting vigorously when she departs, actively searching for her during her absence, and displaying intense delight in reunion with her. These reactions are stronger than their social approaches to the stranger.

(3) *Type C* 'Anxious/ambivalent-insecure': These babies often cling or hover near their mother and show severe distress when she leaves. Yet they are likely to give little evidence of joy upon reunion with her, and may continue crying when she tries to soothe them. Their behaviour generally appears disorganized, anxiety-ridden and emotionally negative.

More recently a fourth attachment style, Type D, has also been identified (Main and Solomon, 1990). Infants with this 'disorganized' classification display negative emotion and immaturely overwhelmed reactions to the entire Strange Situation procedure, often spending the entire sequence of episodes as if frozen in a trance, or engaging in stereotypic motions such as rocking or head-shaking throughout the test.

The Strange Situation measure has been shown over several decades of intensive research to be a reliable index of the quality of individual babies' attachments to their caregivers (Sroufe, 1985). It appears to function well as a measure of the normality of the attachment process in societies like the United States, Australia, New Zealand and Canada, where most infants are familiar with such analogous real-life situations as being left in the care of a babysitter. In these populations, roughly 60 per cent of infants emerge with a secure Type B classification and the remainder are approximately evenly divided between the two insecure classifications, Type A and Type C. But the cross-cultural validity of the Strange Situation is open to question. Japanese babies, who traditionally are almost never left with babysitters, and who usually remain in the mother's arms or lap when she talks to strangers, appear to find the Strange Situation far too strange to cope with. In one study, approximately 38 per cent of Japanese infants were classified as Type C, as compared with only 15 to 20 per cent typically so classified in the USA. This appeared to be mainly because Japanese babies became so upset by the unfamiliar separation that they refused to accept comfort when the mother returned (Miyake, Chen and Campos, 1985). With cultural cautions like these in mind, however, the Strange Situation has generated a wealth of evidence about the process whereby babies forge social ties to their mothers.

Most research that has used the Strange Situation to measure attachment has focused exclusively on the mother–infant relationship (Field, 1996). When the mother is the primary caregiver (staying with the infant throughout the day while other family members are at work or school), it may seem natural that the baby's first specific attachment would be to the mother, and that affection may only gradually extend to other family members. However, owing to the importance of caregiver behaviours such as primary intersubjectivity and sensitive responsiveness in inspiring infant attachment (as discussed earlier), this assumption is not necessarily correct. Indeed, the results of a longitudinal study that pre-dated the Strange Situation and involved naturalistic observations of infants and caregivers in spontaneous family situations (Schaffer and Emerson, 1964) provided some empirical counter-evidence.

Schaffer and Emerson's sample consisted of 60 Scottish infants and their parents and siblings. These families were observed regularly across the first two years of the babies' lives during their normal interactions at home. The results were intriguing. Even in homes where the mother was the primary caregiver, some babies attached themselves first to their fathers, contradicting the intuitive hypothesis outlined above. Other infants formed their first specific attachment to a grandparent or an older sibling who lived in, but did not spend as much time with baby as the mother did. Still others failed to single out any one person, but instead seemed to form multiple attachments to a number of family members simultaneously. As time went on, the tendency towards multiple attachments increased, so that by the age of 18 months, 87 per cent of this group of babies had more than one attachment. But this spreading of love did not detract from the strength of the initial bond to the first attachment figure. The onset of a first attachment to a caregiver who is only available outside of working hours suggests that it is the *quality* of the interaction with the baby, and not its sheer *quantity*, that is important.

What Determines a Secure Parent–Child Attachment?

The primary factor that determined these Scottish babies' choice of an initial attachment target has been highlighted as a primary determiner of a secure attachment, using the Strange Situation Test: this is the caregiver's sensitive responsiveness to the infant's changing moods, needs and physiological states. According to a recent research study (NICHD, 1997), the parent's sensitivity is a multidimensional construct which can be observed during free play and caregiving activities in behaviours like those illustrated in Table 2.3.

A wealth of research over many years has linked secure attachment with indices of parental sensitivity (see NICHD (1997) for a recent review and summary). Infants whose parents lack these elements of sensitivity in their caregiving are likely to emerge as Type A or Type C when tested in the Strange Situation (Ainsworth *et al.*, 1978). However, it is relatively rare, as Schaffer and Emerson's (1964) pioneering study showed, for home-reared infants to grow up in a household where *none* of their caregivers possesses this crucial attribute of sensitive responsiveness. The reciprocal role of mothers and fathers in inspiring secure Type B attachments was revealed by the results of 14 separate investigations in which infants' attachments to mother and father in the same intact family had been assessed

TABLE 2.3 *Components of sensitive parental responsiveness to infant behaviour*

Category	Example
Parent's positive involvement	'Parent's tone of voice conveys positive feeling towards child'
Parent's affection	'Parent kisses or caresses child'
Absence of parental negativity	'Parent does not shout at child'
Parent stimulates cognitive development	'Parent talks to child during play'
Parent is sensitive to distress	'Parent picks crying child up and soothes child'
Parent is not intrusive	'Parent tones down the level of play when infant shows discomfort or over-excitement'
Parent displays appropriate affect	'Parent displays positive and negative feelings appropriately during play' (as contrasted with flat affect)
Parent is involved, not detached	'Parent plays peekaboo with child'

Source: Based on data in NICHD, 1997, pp. 864–865

using the Strange Situation. The results of this meta-analytic comparison are shown in Table 2.4.

The results revealed that most infants (83 per cent) had a secure attachment to a least one parent. Further, being securely attached to the father (64 per cent) was just as frequent as being securely attached to the mother (63 per cent). Of course, these results do not tell us about the temporal order in which these attachments to each parent were forged. The important lesson conveyed by Van Ijzendoorn and DeWolff's (1997) meta-analysis, however, is that attachment can be protectively compensatory in families where both parents are present and actively involved with their infants. Although a total of 354 infants (37 per cent) in this large sample had an insecure attachment to their mother (replicating proportions commonly reported in Strange Situation studies with smaller samples), only 17 per cent had an insecure attachment to *both* parents. According to attachment theorists (Bowlby, 1969), only the latter small minority are likely to be at risk for later adjustment problems as a result of an impaired early social relationship. The fact that secure attachments to the other parent were forged in more than half the cases where a baby's attachment

TABLE 2.4 *Security of infant attachment to each parent in two-parent families*

Attachment to father	Attachment to mother		
	Secure	Insecure	Total
Secure	428 families	188 families	616 families
Insecure	174 families	166 families	340 families
Total	602 families	354 families	956 families

Source: Based on data in Van Ijzendoorn and DeWolff, 1997

to one caregiver proved insecure suggests that the attachment process is a powerful motivator for affection and bonding for parents and infants alike.

Day care is another influence that many parents worry may interfere with the development of a secure attachment. This concern is understandable. Indeed, a scientific debate has raged for several decades over the likely effects of the regular separation of infants from their parental caregivers to attend day care. Does day care weaken the bond of attachment to the primary caregiver, either through the stress of continual separation or through curtailing the time that infants and parents spend together? The results of an ambitious longitudinal study completed recently in the United States (NICHD, 1997) have supplied a more conclusive answer to this vexing question than have the many small-scale studies that had previously been conducted. A total of 1,153 infants and their mothers were studied intensively by the NICHD team. Maternal and infant behaviour was measured at regular intervals from the age of 1 month to 1 year 3 months. The quality of the infant's attachment to the mother was assessed in the Strange Situation at the age of 15 months. Based on data from this large and varied sample, the US researchers concluded that: 'There were no significant main effects of child-care experience on attachment security or avoidance' (p. 860).

Only when the mother was insensitive and unresponsive in her caregiving did day care seem to make a difference. A significant interaction effect revealed that poor-quality childcare combined with poor-quality mothering exacerbated the insecure attachments associated with insensitive parenting. But when mothers were sensitive and responsive to their babies' needs, neither the amount of time spent in day care, nor the quality of the childcare environment itself, made any discernible difference to attachment security. In this study, as in Schaffer and Emerson's (1964) pioneering investigation, quality of interaction was far more important than the sheer quantity of interaction as the key determiner of a baby's attachment style.

Relationship with Parents during Childhood: Long-term Consequences

As they progress through childhood and adolescence, youngsters with a secure (Type B) attachment classification are likely to enjoy a number of cognitive and social advantages over their insecurely attached peers. Attachment security has been linked, during toddlerhood, with intellectual curiosity and exploratory behaviour. Thus infants and older children who have a confident, secure relationship with a primary caregiver are equipped to learn effectively about their physical and social environment (Siegal, 1997; Siegal and Peterson, 1994). Each successful new venture into learning (for example, a toy that yields its secrets to the infant's manipulative efforts) can foster feelings of confidence, skill and the motivation to engage in more challenging feats of exploration and problem-solving. Consequently, the cognitive growth that has its basis in secure attachment is likely to spiral throughout childhood. A study of the long-term consequences of secure attachment revealed that securely attached children displayed higher levels of cognitive performance from childhood through adolescence than those who had insecure attachments (Jacobsen, Edelstein and Hofmann, 1994).

Having forged a secure attachment to a parent in infancy also confers social benefits for children. Research findings have consistently linked secure parent–infant attachments with the following variables, measured during childhood:

- high self-esteem;
- confident social overtures to peers and adults;
- popularity with playmates and within established social groups of friends in nurseries, day care, preschool or the neighbourhood;
- curiosity and enthusiasm for learning;
- mature independence from parents;
- skills for imaginative social problem-solving.

For example, in a study designed to test how secure attachment to the mother may influence a child's social learning through collaborative problem-solving, a team of Canadian researchers (Moss *et al.*, 1997) tested two groups of preschoolers on a series of realistic planning tasks, such as developing a shopping list for a visit to the grocery store. One group of youngsters had secure attachments to their mothers, whereas the other was insecurely attached. In interaction with their own mothers, secure children displayed better problem-solving skills and a more sophisticated, metacognitive understanding of the social and pragmatic elements of the tasks. However, the mothers themselves were at least partly responsible for this effect. When they performed the grocery-planning task with their securely attached infants, these mothers displayed more collaboration and goal orientation than mothers with an insecurely attached child. They were more in synchrony with the child's level of involvement and understanding, supporting the notion that sensitivity and synchrony in parents' caregiving are elements of a secure attachment pattern during childhood as well as infancy.

To test the magnitude of the mother's independent contribution to children's efficient problem-solving, the researchers included a second condition. This time, mothers whose own infants were securely attached were asked to perform the grocery-planning task with an unfamiliar child who had an insecure attachment to his or her own mother. Similarly, the mothers of the insecurely attached children planned shopping lists with secure preschoolers. In these interactions among unfamiliar dyads, the child's own contribution to successful problem-solving became clearly evident. The security status of the adult stranger's child did not influence the way each mother behaved with her child partner. Securely attached children, however, continued to display better problem-solving skills, greater goal orientation and more advanced levels of metacognitive awareness of the task than the insecurely attached children (Moss *et al.*, 1997). It seems that the cognitive and social benefits of a secure attachment style generalize to children's interactions with adults outside the family, and that insecurity can diminish the likelihood of successful problem-solving, even with a partner who has no history of a troubled relationship with the child.

Social Intelligence: Growth of a Theory of Mind

As children develop through early childhood, social cognitive growth is facilitated by conversations both with parents and with adults outside the family. In everyday situations at home, at preschool, in the supermarket, or in the neighbourhood, children have numerous opportunities to converse with their parents, siblings and family friends. In informal play and interaction, they likewise accumulate countless opportunities to observe other people's behaviour, to speak with them, and to try to anticipate their actions and motives. Between the ages of 3 and 5 years, an important transformation takes place in children's consciousness of others, which has come to be known as the development of a *theory of mind.*

This important cognitive attribute, which most 5-year-olds possess and most 3-year-olds lack, is central to social intelligence. A theory of mind enables its possessor to predict and make sense of other people's thoughts, feelings and actions. Without realizing it, older children and adults who have a well-functioning theory of mind are able to practise 'naïve psychology'. This helps them understand people and predict what they will do, and makes them aware that human behaviour is governed by covert mental states that do not always correspond to objective reality. For example, a 5-year-old in a supermarket queue might experience momentary bafflement when he sees a customer in the line ahead of him withdraw from the line with her full trolley and walk away, after having waited patiently for several minutes. The child's theory of mind, however, would soon suggest a number of conceivable explanations. Maybe the woman has forgotten something important that is on her shopping list and has gone to find it. Maybe she has lost patience with the slow pace of the queue and has decided to come back and do her shopping another time. Maybe she has an urgent appointment and cannot afford to wait any longer, and so on. To a skilled 'mindreader' (Baron-Cohen, 1995), the varying mental states that can be ascribed to account for seemingly irrational human behaviour are almost limitless.

A theory of mind confers the ability to impute mental states (beliefs, intentions, memories and desires) to self and others (Wellman, 1990). As such, its development is an important cornerstone of social, communicative, cognitive and affective life. A practical understanding of mental states enables children to appreciate that their own and others' behaviour may be shaped by cognitive abstractions that are not a part of the immediately perceptible world. A concept that beliefs may be false is crucial to sophisticated engagements with others, including empathy, joking, pretending and the meeting of minds in intimate reminiscence, self-discovery and mutual insight (Mitchell, 1997). Children who are 'mindblind' (Baron-Cohen, 1995), through the lack of an awareness of the possibility of false belief, are not only socially handicapped when it comes to the pleasures to be gained through the meeting of minds, but are also defenceless against the manipulation of their thoughts by those who would deceive or betray them.

Links between the growth of a theory of mind and the child's attachment style were discovered by Meins *et al.* (1998), when they studied a group of 4-year-olds whose security of attachment to their mothers had been assessed during infancy. Using a standard false belief test, the children's theory of mind was measured by questioning them about the probable search behaviour of a story character whose toy had unexpectedly been shifted. Success on this task demands an awareness that the naïve protagonist, unlike the child being tested, will not know that the object has been moved, and hence will be led by a false belief to search in the wrong place. In the absence of a theory of mind, younger children typically state that the character will search for the object where it really is, as they seem unable to imagine the possibility of being misled by a belief that is discrepant from reality.

The results of the Meins *et al.* (1998) study indicated that attachment security during infancy predicted the rapid development of a theory of mind during early childhood. Four-year-olds were more likely to pass the unexpected transfer test of false belief when they had been scored as securely attached as infants. In addition, from as early as 31 months, toddlers who had been securely attached were better able than their insecure peers to incorporate an experimenter's imaginative suggestions, testifying to their early awareness of mental states like pretending as a basis for behaviour. Yet there were no overall differences in cognitive ability between the children who had been securely and insecurely attached to their mothers during infancy. In other words, the cognitive advantages the secure group enjoyed were specific to social understanding, apparently reflecting their expectation that human behaviour is inherently predictable.

Observations of maternal behaviour during infancy and childhood support these suggestions. Meins *et al.* found that, in contrast to mothers of insecurely attached babies, the mothers of the secure group had a propensity to treat their children 'as individuals with minds'. This process was reflected in the Moss *et al.* (1997) Canadian study, in the more sensitive and engaging tutoring strategies that mothers of secure children employed when instructed to teach tasks to their offspring in naturalistic situations. In addition, when mothers of the secure children with advanced theories of mind were asked to describe their children in interviews, they frequently made reference to their children's mental characteristics – a good memory, intellectually curious, vivid imagination, and so on.

Opposition and Negotiation in the Parent–Toddler Relationship: The Phenomenon of Negativism

One potent reminder that people have minds of their own arises during interpersonal conflicts and disagreements. When an adversary expresses a viewpoint that is in direct opposition to one's own, this forces recognition of a counter-intuitive mental state. During toddlerhood and early childhood, young children are confronted on a daily basis with actual and incipient disagreements with their parents. Indeed, the phenomenon popularly known as the 'terrible twos' (or more accurately as the *negativism of toddlerhood*) highlights, through its name, the frequent oppositions and verbal disputes that are likely in households with children between the ages of two and three years (Wenar, 1982). As children become independently mobile and gain enough skill in manipulating devices like doorknobs and electric power points to pose hazards to their own safety and that of the family's possessions, the word 'No!' becomes a frequent component of parental vocabulary. Negation is also a concept over which children themselves rapidly gain semantic and pragmatic mastery. As Charles Wenar (1982) explained:

> 'No' [represents] the first conquest of an abstraction. It contrasts with the concrete global words of the period between the 15th and 18th months of life by conveying the specific concept 'I do not want this'. The process underlying this abstraction consists of distinguishing essential elements from unessential ones; specifically the toddler abstracts the common element of prohibition from the many situations in which the caretaker says 'No'. The shift from situational physical resistance of infancy to the 'No' of the toddler is a shift from action to symbolic representation of action. Thus freed, the symbol can be employed at will and with considerably less expenditure. Because of its availability, 'No' is more conscious and volitional than the reactive resistance of infancy . . . the toddler now has entry to the arena of semantic communication. Discussion and negotiation – those uniquely human achievements – become possible.
>
> (pp. 19–20)

Observational studies of interactions between parents and young children suggest that the phenomenon of negativism, which can be defined operationally as 'the toddler's intentional noncompliance to adult requests, directives and prohibitions' (Wenar, 1982, p. 5), reaches a peak between the ages of 18 and 24 months. Infants who are much younger than this are unlikely to have developed the cognitive skills to be aware of alternatives to simple compliance. Similarly, they may have only a hazy awareness of the boundary between self and other. After the third birthday, most children's skills for verbal negotiation and persuasion have developed to a point where verbal debate, compromise and conciliation can replace some of the blindly oppositional obstinacy that is seen in the negativistic 2-year-old's everyday interactions with parents. The child's rate of progress through this important developmental process may depend partly upon culture and childrearing strategies. In Australia, Goodnow *et al.* (1984) studied parents' socialization of verbal assertiveness skills in samples of families who came from either Anglo-Australian or Lebanese-Australian backgrounds. The results revealed several similarities between parents from the different ethnic backgrounds. For example, both groups believed that children should preface all requests to an adult with 'please', at least by the time they were 4 years old. But differences were also evident between the two groups of parents, as shown in Figure 2.3 which also displays the results of similar research on Japanese and North American parents of young children.

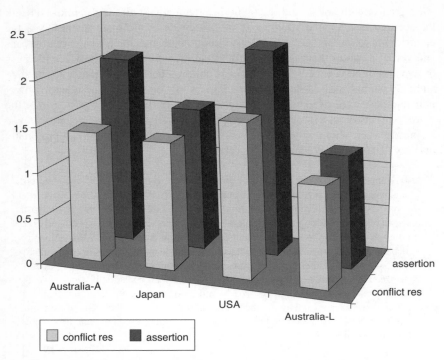

FIGURE 2.3 Mothers' expected timetables for the development of verbal self-assertion skills as a function of cultural background. Based on data in Goodnow *et al.*, 1984 Note: Australia-L = Lebanese-Australian mothers; Australia-A = Anglo-Australian mothers; 1= 6 years or older; 2 = 4 to 6 years; 3 = younger than 4

Lebanese-Australian mothers were less inclined than their Anglo-Australian peers to expect early mastery of skills for verbal self-assertion, persuasion and expression of independent opinions. Thus the child's acquisition of verbal skills for self-expression and conflict resolution may depend in part upon parental expectations and encouragement.

Acquiring Persuasion Skills

The opportunity to argue a case with a parent with an opposing viewpoint can also serve as a powerful stimulus to the child's linguistic and social-cognitive development. The arguments children put forward in their efforts to resist their parents' or teacher's directives, or to attract the adult to their point of view, display increasing versatility and sophistication over the period from 3 to 4 years (Tizard and Hughes, 1984). But there are interesting differences between the types of arguments children use in different social settings. The arguments children address to their teachers tend to be shorter and simpler than those that the same child will put forward in a debate with a parent at home. Indeed, children's powers of persuasion and reasoned argument when negotiating with their mothers are quite remarkable for their rationality, sophistication and overall maturity (Dunn and Munn, 1987). In contrast to their brief and simple responses to teachers' prohibitions and directives, debates with parents appear to draw out the best in children's negotiation skills. It would seem that the emotional investment of children's modes of relating to their family members combines with the security, familiarity and continuity of these family relationships to facilitate the growth of social cognition and the marshalling of reasoned argument.

The topic of parent–child debate also makes a difference to the level of sophistication that is expressed when children negotiate. Dunn and Munn (1987) found that 3-year-olds more often gave justifications for their positions when arguing with their mothers about personal rights and social conventions than when the disputes involved material damage, physical aggression, getting dirty, toileting, buying lollies, or being unkind to people or animals.

In addition, Dunn and Munn observed important developmental changes in the quality of children's disputes with their mothers over the period from 18 months to 3 years. As they grew older, children increasingly offered explicit reasons to justify their opposing points of view. Emotionality and parental reasoning both predicted frequency of justification at 36 months. Those issues that had been the source of the most emotionally heated disputes between 18-month-olds and their mothers were most likely to produce coherent justifications at age 3. The mothers who had used reasoning most often in disputes with their toddlers also received the most frequent reason, some 18 months later. These observations suggest that conflicts can serve a beneficial effect in families when they teach children how to communicate rationally and persuasively.

Through early childhood, children are likely to gain in the capacity to negotiate in ways that successfully overcome parental objections, displaying an increasingly sophisticated concept of the parent's mind. Axia (1996) studied a total of 88 Italian children aged 4 through 8 years while they were shopping with their parents in the toy section of a large department store. Using a hidden tape recorder, the children's spontaneous speech was recorded and later transcribed.

When the persuasive arguments that the children used to try to influence their parents to purchase a desired toy were mapped against their age in years, a clear developmental trend emerged. Four-year-olds adopted a relatively simple and direct approach, reminiscent of the negativism of toddlerhood. They were inclined to demand what they wanted, and often used physical tactics such as pushing, grabbing, or even hitting. They appeared to conceive of persuasion quite simply as a matter of using speech and action to gain the adult's attention and take control. There was little evidence in their spoken arguments of any awareness of the adult's resistance, countervailing desires or mental states. Nor did the very young children display the ability to modify their initial positions in response to their parents' reactions.

Six-year-olds were somewhat more sophisticated. Like their younger peers, they tried to gain control over the adult. However, they were better able than 4-year-olds to take account of their parents' objections. They also displayed a primitive bargaining strategy, though its tenor was primarily competitive. Threats were offered more often than enticements or promises as contingencies against parental resistance. The 8-year-olds displayed the highest levels of persuasive communication skill, and the clearest evidence of sensitivity to their listeners' points of view. In their spoken arguments, these older children appeared to be aware of their need to overcome the potential conflict between their own desires and those of their parents. They therefore oriented their conversational exchanges towards cooperation and compromise. In addition, their persuasive arguments displayed their sensitivity to the adults' objections and a willingness to accept the logic of such a point of view.

Family Dialogue and Household Work

When they converse with their parents and engage with them in play and household tasks, children come to master important communication and negotiation skills that they may later apply in their relationships with their friends, siblings and other social contacts both inside and outside the family. The domain of household work provides a particularly rich arena for the development of bargaining, cooperation, conflict-resolution skills and empathic social understanding (Goodnow and Bowes, 1994). Rheingold (1982) found that infants as young as 18 months often helped their parents perform a number of simple household tasks in a homelike laboratory setting where the families were observed naturalistically. Helpfulness increased with age from 18 to 30 months, partly as a result of increasingly skilled communication over this age period.

Lawrence (1984) used a laboratory that was fitted out to resemble a family home to observe parents' use of persuasion strategies, and to assess children's responses both to polite requests and to authoritative commands. Her subjects were 60 toddlers, who each came to the lab with one of their parents. Lawrence videotaped parent–child conversation and interaction during a series of prearranged tasks, in which parents had to try to involve the toddler in helping them perform simple household chores such as dusting, sweeping and picking up litter. The maturity of a child's language growth was a better predictor of compliance with parental directives than either sex or chronological age. In fact, Lawrence found that those toddlers who were speaking in simple sentences averaging three or more words in length were significantly less overtly defiant and also less passively negativistic than those whose speech was less mature. The typical response of these latter children was to defy requests or ignore them altogether. But children of the same age whose language development was more advanced generally acceded to the same requests.

Better language skills might conceivably have promoted compliance by enabling children to understand more fully the vocabulary and syntax of their parents' verbal requests. In fact, Lawrence did find greater compliance by all children to requests that were phrased simply and concretely ('Pick up those red books and put them on the table') than to grammatically complex and abstract expressions ('Would you mind helping me clean up?'). But another important feature of parents' interaction with offspring who had advanced language skills was their more extensive use of mutual discussion and negotiation. Lawrence noted that these children, in agreeing to comply with parental requests, often used their advanced command of language to negotiate a 'contract' with the parent that comprised explicitly agreed conditions and verbal guarantees acceptable to both parties.

Parental Discipline Strategies

The challenge of engaging in a verbal disagreement with a parent may stimulate a toddler's development of sophisticated cognitive and language skills. The progress of cognitive maturity and the widening of the child's social horizons may similarly enhance the motivation to negotiate. As children acquire persuasion skills, they are apt to gain more satisfaction with the outcomes of verbal disputes. This can happen during a wide range of parent–child conversations, including those that centre on the teaching and disciplining of the children. The methods parents select in their efforts to discipline children vary widely from family to family and culture to culture (Chao, 1994). Within the same family, discipline styles also change over time, in step with the child's increasing social and cognitive maturity. According to contemporary researchers, family discipline and decision-making patterns can be organized into three basic groupings (Silverberg, 1992). These can be outlined briefly as follows:

Authoritarian parenting. This is a strict style of discipline in which parents are high in authoritarian control and 'demandingness', and expect submissive obedience from their children in all important matters. There is minimal discussion of family rules, and parents are usually prepared to use force to compel obedience if necessary. Parents tend to be lower in warmth and acceptance than those using other styles, but also to be high in involvement and concern.

Democratic or authoritative parenting. Parents who use this style set limits and exert control, while at the same time allowing their children a moderate amount of autonomy and initiative. These parents tend to discuss rules with their children at length, offering rational explanations for the demands they make; however, these rules are firmly and consistently enforced. Thus this style combines a high level of control (including rule-setting, high expectations and monitoring) with warmth, affection and respect for the child's own decision-making competence.

Laissez-faire, permissive or indulgent parenting. In this style, parents tend to be warm and available as resources for their children to use or not, as they please.

However, permissive parents are inclined to behave rather passively when it comes to rule-setting and control. They may tolerate impulsive and immature behaviour, sometimes on the grounds of an ideological belief that adults have no right to interfere with children's natural inclinations. Some permissive parents are lax about monitoring their children's behaviour and disinclined to set limits. Whether through being a single parent, or because of work commitments or other reasons, these parents are often unaware of who their children's friends are, where they spend their time after school or at weekends, and how well they are doing in school. Furthermore, they may avoid confronting any problems their children might be having. Discipline, when practised at all, is apt to be inconsistent and erratic.

Maccoby and Martin (1983) distinguished two forms of permissive parenting. The first type is known as *indifferent-uninvolved*. Mothers and fathers who adopt this style typically do not establish rules or guidelines even when these would benefit the child, and are very low in monitoring. At the same time, their attitudes to their children are often rather cold and aloof. They are inclined to structure their lives around their own needs, with little or no consideration for the child's needs, wishes or opinions. In the extreme, such parents can be guilty of neglect. The other form of permissive parenting, known as *indulgent*, involves a low degree of control. Indulgent parents are fond of their children but, for a variety of reasons, make little or no effort to guide, control or monitor their behaviour. They set minimal limits which they enforce inconsistently, if at all.

Positive developmental outcomes have been observed during childhood and adolescence in the offspring of parents who use authoritative discipline strategies, as compared with permissive, neglectful or authoritarian styles. Children of authoritative parents have been found to have high self-esteem, to be maturely self-reliant, and to display friendliness and competency in their relationships with peers (Baumrind, 1975, 1991). Other research confirms that, through the primary school years and into adolescence, better social and academic outcomes are observed in offspring of mothers and fathers whose authoritative parenting practices combine warmth and openness to negotiation with firm expectations for socially appropriate behaviour (Lamborn *et al.*, 1991). Some of these results are illustrated in Table 2.5.

Permissive parents who are low in warmth as well as low in control (or exercise of discipline) have been described as 'neglectful' or as 'indifferent/uninvolved' (Maccoby and Martin, 1983). Children of these parents are at risk of delinquency and emotional disturbance (Baumrind, 1991). They are also likely to display disrupted peer relationships and school performance, and a strong sense of alienation from their families and society.

In a thoughtful and comprehensive analysis of the effectiveness of parents' disciplinary strategies, Grusec and Goodnow (1994) drew attention to the child's active role as a processor of disciplinary information. Children think about the lessons their parents offer and make reasoned decisions about whether or not to accept parental direction.

TABLE 2.5 *Frequent consequences for children of exposure to three distinct styles of parental discipline*

Authoritarian	Authoritative	Permissive
Poor-quality peer relationships	High academic achievement	Lacks self-control
Lacks self-confidence	High self-esteem	Academic underachiever
Socially withdrawn	Popular with peers	Socially immature
Obedient without an internalized conscience	Strong conscience	Poor impulse control
Lacks spontaneity	Mature internalization of moral rules	
Little intellectual curiosity	High level of social skills	
	Cognitively inquiring	

In addition to the child's own active role in the process, a number of other factors influence the effectiveness of parental discipline, according to Grusec and Goodnow. These include the quality of the early attachment bond between parent and child (see pp. 17–19), as well as the communicative effectiveness of the disciplinary message. When a child is securely attached to a parent, the threat of parental disapproval may carry more weight than if the attachment bond forged during infancy was insecure. Similarly, for a disciplinary message to be internalized, the child must notice it, understand it and feel motivated to comply with it. The interconnections among these factors, according to Grusec and Goodnow's (1994) model, are shown in Figure 2.4.

In other words, in order to be influential, a disciplinary message must be clear, meaningful, and suited to the child's present level of cognitive maturity. But this is not enough. The child must also want to comply. The motivation to do so can be boosted by the child's believing that the message is logical, important, and in his or her own best interests. Desire to please the parent, fear of punishment or parental displeasure, and recognition of how much the issue means to the parent, can also boost the child's motivation to behave in accordance with the parental directive.

Marital Conflict and Children's Development

As well as engaging in conflicts and negotiations with their parents directly, young children in most families have many opportunities to witness the disputes of others, and so to learn indirectly about how interpersonal conflict can be managed. Marital conflict between the child's mother and father provides one such source of observational input, and much early research suggested that the influence upon children of exposure to disputes between husbands and wives was uniformly negative (Porter and O'Leary, 1980). However, more recently, an imaginative series of experimental studies by Cummings and his colleagues (e.g., Davies and

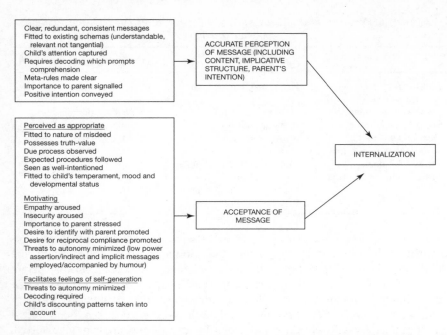

FIGURE 2.4 A model of effective disciplinary communication in the parent–child relationship. Source: Grusec and Goodnow, 1994. Copyright © 1994 by the American Psychological Association. Reprinted with permission.

Cummings, 1994) has suggested that it is the *mode* of resolution of couple disagreements, and not the existence of marital conflict *per se*, that determines child outcomes. When children bear witness to festering parental hostility, whether it is expressed as angry aggression or as icy withdrawal, the outcomes are likely to be negative. Children who are exposed to high levels of interparental hostility and destructive conflict management run a higher risk than those exposed to constructive marital conflict resolution, of such externalizing behaviour problems as delinquency, classroom disruptiveness and emotional disturbance. Destructive marital conflict has been found to spill over to disrupt children's social relationships with their siblings, peers and grandparents, while at the same time interfering with parent–child communication and attachment (Cummings and Davies, 1994).

To test whether parents' use of destructive conflict avoidance could have the same effect on children as overt verbal hostility, Cummings and his colleagues created a set of videotaped interactions between actors who, taking the roles of husband and wife, portrayed either (a) unresolved verbally hostile disputation, or (b) unresolved, nonverbally angry, conflict avoidance.

As an example of the former, the filmed husband and wife might be arguing about who should prepare dinner that evening. The disagreement could progressively escalate into angry exchanges of insults and hurtful remarks about one another's selfishness, exploitation, lack of cooking skills, lack of affection, and so on. By contrast, the hostile avoidance of overt conflict was depicted in the couple's exchanges of dirty looks, pained expressions and the 'silent treatment', in which negative feelings are expressed but no direct attempts are made to talk about or resolve the disagreement. As Cummings points out, this approach to conflict is epitomized in the following exchange, to which nearly all children bear witness at some point or other in their mothers' and fathers' interactions.

Husband: 'What's wrong?'
Wife: [looking pained and angry] 'Nothing!'

When exposed to videotaped portrayals of these approaches to couple disagreement, the children in Cummings and Davies' (1994) sample showed equivalent, and highly negative, emotional reactions to conflicts of both types. They became upset and angry while watching the videotapes and reported feeling upset, sad and powerless afterwards. It would seem that when unresolved conflict exists in the marital relationship, negative emotional consequences for the offspring may ensue, irrespective of whether the disputes erupt into angry fighting, or are held in check to fester through anxious conflict avoidance.

On the other hand, successful resolution of a marital dispute can bring benefits for the children who witness the episode, as well as for the disputing adult parties. Indeed, so strongly beneficial were the observed effects on child viewers that Cummings was led to describe constructive marital conflict resolution as a 'wonder drug'. He found that, when very high levels of anger and heated dispute preceded an agreed resolution in the videotaped debates, children reacted positively rather than negatively, as long as the final outcome proved satisfactory. Indeed, both the immediate and long-term effects of angry interparental conflict that culminated in an agreed resolution were just as positive as the effects of uniformly positive conversations.

In further research, Shifflett-Simpson and Cummings (1996) found that children as young as age 6 are sensitive to both verbal and nonverbal cues in couple disagreements. When these two types of information are discrepant (as when an adult apologizes verbally while retaining an angry facial expression), children incorporate both of them into their reactions. When estimating their own levels of post-conflict emotional distress, for example, the 6-year-olds focused more on the verbal message, whereas in suggesting interventions they were influenced more by the adults' nonverbal emotional expressions. The researchers concluded: 'Adults should be aware of the relative sophistication of young children in understanding adults' emotional communications. Even relatively young children are sensitive, not only to what is said, but to how it is said as well' (p. 447).

Siblings and Development

Children also gain cognitive and social skills through interacting with siblings. In a naturalistic observational study conducted longitudinally in the homes of families of preschoolers, Dunn (1994) kept track of the conversations and arguments that preschoolers engaged in with their parents and siblings. She was particularly interested in how these informal exchanges within the household can foster social understanding. As the children developed increasing language skills over the period from two and a half to four years, she noted numerous instances in which they were faced with contradictions between their own perspectives and those of older and younger siblings. She concluded that these disputes had a beneficial effect upon relationship development. The cognitive challenges created when a child struggled to appreciate the alternative viewpoints of a family member seemed to stimulate the growth of social cognition. For example, when children realized that their younger siblings were not yet mature enough to understand complex ideas or language, they were likely to engage in conversational accommodation strategies (simplifying speech, using gesture, assessing listener comprehension, etc.), in order to sustain a dialogue.

These skills, which are essential to the effective use of language as a social tool, are not likely to be as readily acquired through discussions with adults or peers, owing to the older conversational partner's more mature mind and language. At the same time, Dunn (1994) noted that dialogues between preschoolers and their mothers frequently revolved around the sibling's emotional or cognitive perspective. A sense that a younger sibling is receiving favoured treatment, or more privileges, may motivate the gathering of conversational insight into others' mental states. When she catalogued the queries that 3-year-olds addressed to their mothers, she discovered that many of them reflected an interest in the mother's intentions to be fair, as when a child said: 'I want some Rosehip. Why do we need to save it for the baby?' Similarly, when the child perceives a parent behaving in an unpredictable manner, resultant queries as to the adult's motives and feelings may boost understanding of the other person's mental states: 'Why don't you like to eat ice cream just before dinner?' a child asks. 'Why are you tired of reading me stories?' another inquires. Mothers' responses to queries like these may help children understand social points of view that contrast sharply with their own.

Consequently, dialogues with siblings and parents contribute to the growth of social understanding. The results of Dunn's longitudinal observational studies (Dunn, 1996; Brown, Donelan-McCall and Dunn, 1996) have shown that children who initially engage in the most conversation with family members about thoughts, intentions and feelings are the ones who subsequently develop the most sophisticated appreciation of others' mental states (as assessed using the 'theory-of-mind' tasks described on pp. 23–4). In addition, the children whose conversations with their parents displayed the strongest preoccupation with feelings, needs and beliefs were the ones who responded with greatest sensitivity to their younger siblings during play and caregiving activities.

Preschoolers who have older or younger siblings seem to develop a theory of mind at a faster rate than only children, whose opportunities for conversation at home are limited to their parents and adults (Jenkins and Astington, 1996; Perner, Ruffman and Leekam, 1994). Comparisons of 80 British children aged 3 to 4 years,

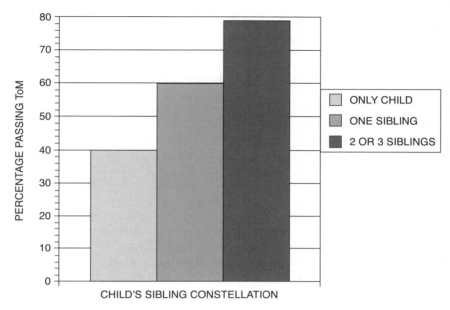

FIGURE 2.5 Children's accuracy on theory-of-mind tasks as a function of family size.
Based on data in Perner *et al.*, 1994

who had between 0 and 4 siblings at the time of being tested on a measure of theory of mind, can be seen in Figure 2.5. The children who had no siblings scored lower in social understanding than those who had one sibling, who in turn did less well than those with two or three.

It seems that the opportunity to exchange affection, intimate ideas and feelings with a sibling in the family adds to the benefits children gain from conversing with their parents when it comes to the development of an understanding of other people's points of view. In addition, the presence of siblings in the household may motivate children to think about how to manipulate others' thoughts for both benign and devious purposes. As Perner *et al.* (1994) suggested:

> Sibling conflicts also tend to elicit . . . much explicit reflection on motives, intentions and knowledge. Consequently, we might expect that children who have siblings to work and play with should have a noticeable advantage over only children, who are stuck with their parents as their only source of social entertainment.
>
> (p. 1229)

These researchers suggested that the advantage could assist, not only in the ability to pass theory-of-mind tasks, but also in advanced skills for deception and subterfuge. Children who have a sophisticated grasp of other people's mental states of belief and disbelief may, for example, 'be more able to make it appear that their sibling was at fault, which might lead their mother to exert control on their sibling' (p. 1234).

Differential Parental Treatment and Sibling Rivalry

While the sibling relationship exerts many positive influences upon an individual child's psychological development, adverse effects can also accrue through sibling rivalry and the perception of differential parental treatment. Indeed, the quality of the bond between brothers and sisters may be compromised by family dynamics in which parental affection and disciplinary control are unequally distributed. Siblings who perceive a brother or sister as gaining more favoured treatment than themselves may take this as a sign of parental hostility, or else as evidence of their own unworthiness for love (Brody *et al.*, 1998a). This process can be especially damaging to children who suffered insecure patterns of attachment to their parents during infancy (see pp. 17–20). Furthermore, the fact that there is often a link between problems in the parents' marriage and parents' tendency to treat siblings differentially (Brody, 1998) suggests that adverse consequences of differential affection and control for children's development may be compounded by the direct effects of family discord.

On the other hand, differential treatment by parents can also have positive effects on children and on their relationships with their siblings, when this treatment reflects parental sensitivity to children's individuality and special needs. Much depends, as in the case of many other aspects of development examined in this chapter, on how the differences in parenting are communicated. According to Dunn (1993), a focus on the parent–child relationships of siblings who, as members of the same family, share the same set of parents, teaches three important lessons:

(1) Each sibling has a different kind of relationship with the same parent.
(2) Children are highly sensitive to these differences (which can be described as 'differential parental treatment').
(3) Differences in the way a parent treats different siblings can exert considerable impact on children's development from infancy through adolescence.

Of course, it will come as no surprise that parents behave differently towards children of different ages. Our brief journey (earlier in this chapter) through the dramatic developmental changes of infancy and early childhood demonstrates how impossible it would be for a parent to treat an 18-month-old identically to her 4-year-old sister. One child is barely speaking; the other has many of the social qualities of an adult companion.

On the basis of longitudinal studies conducted with colleagues in Colorado, Dunn (1993) was able to demonstrate continuity in parental treatment, despite vast differences in the treatment of older and younger siblings at any given point in time. Her results showed, for example, that some mothers in her sample were highly infant-oriented. They displayed the greatest affection to each of their children at the age of 12 months. Relative to other mothers, they were cool and distant in their treatment of 3-year-olds. But because they retained these patterns throughout their offspring's growing up, differential treatment was relative to age (and not to any characteristic of the individual siblings). From the mother's point of view, this behaviour reflected utter impartiality. The mothers were fondest of each child when he or she was around one year old, becoming progressively less loving through the 'terrible twos' and the 'trusting threes'. But, from the perspective of the siblings themselves, such consistency in maternal behaviour is likely to give rise to unhappy perceptions of favouritism. The jealous 3-year-old who accurately perceives that her mother is presently fonder of her 12-month-old sibling than herself is unaware of the consistency in this maternal pattern in terms of the respective ages. Nor is she aware of the consistency in treatment of herself and her sibling when they were each just one year old.

Of course, in addition to age differences, differential parenting may be prompted by differences in siblings' gender, personality traits, or the family's circumstances at the time each successive sibling enters a given stage. Whatever their source, differences in parenting and siblings' own perceptions of differential parental affection and control are likely to exert very strong influences on siblings' relationships with each other and with their parents (Stocker and McHale, 1992). Furthermore, each child's own developmental outcomes are seen to reflect the extent to which their parents treated them differently (Dunn, Stocker and Plomin, 1990). Mothers' and fathers' differential displays of affection and control have been linked in longitudinal research to children's anxiety, self-concept, delinquency, depression, and difficult relationships with peers outside the family (Dunn, 1996).

For example, using a longitudinal methodology, Dunn (1996) assessed differences in maternal and paternal affection and control in a sample of British children, first at the age of 6 years and then again at the age of 9. Children who had been the recipients of relatively more affection than their siblings and less control from their mothers showed higher self-esteem and a stronger sense of competence at the testing points than those whose mothers had differentially favoured a brother or sister. Differential treatment by fathers exerted similarly significant effects at both times. Child temperament also contributed, as did the match between the child's personality and the parent's own. However, the links between parental favouritism and later self-concept were statistically independent of the differences that had existed in children's temperament patterns when they were 6 years old. This finding suggests a direct influence of parents' differential treatment of the siblings, over and above the effects of personality variation among family members.

In an earlier study, however, Dunn and Kendrick (1982) found that children who, as infants, had displayed difficult temperament qualities of negative mood and failure to accommodate were the ones who reacted least well to the birth of a younger sibling. Unlike children with cheerful, easygoing temperaments, they were apt to withdraw, to display mood swings, to suffer sleep disturbances, and to become immaturely 'clingy' and dependent when a younger brother or sister was born. As children grow older, temperament continues to play an important role. Sibling conflict is most frequent, intense and hostile in families where at least one sibling has a temperamentally high activity level, especially when this temperament is coupled with a predominantly negative mood tone (Brody *et al.*, 1994).

The parents' personalities also exert formative influences on the nature and quality of siblings' relationships with one another. Marital distress, hostility and unhappiness are associated with negativity and rivalry in siblings' interactions with one another. Along similar lines, depressed and emotionally unstable parents are found to behave in a more conflicted and distant manner to their offspring, possibly explaining the observation of impaired sibling relationships in the context of parental mental illness. As Brody (1998) explained:

> Prior experiences in the family are not erased by current ones, but are integrated into new relationship patterns and continue to influence the sibling relationship at subsequent points in time . . . An impressive consensus of research findings indicates that higher levels of parent–child relationship positively are linked with higher levels of positive affectivity and prosocial behavior in the sibling relationship. Similarly, sibling negativity is associated with overcontrol and intrusiveness in the parent–child relationship.
>
> (p. 7)

Humour can exert a positive influence on social relationships at any stage in life, and family relationships are no exception. The effects of differential parental treatment may be mediated by differences in humour among siblings in the family, or even the closeness of the match between what a parent considers funny and what the child does. Dunn (1994) analysed the jokes exchanged by a group of family members in Cambridge, England, when one of the children in the household had just turned three. The results showed that a majority of the jokes the family members found funny were either initiated by the 3-year-old, or else took this young child's behaviour as a central component in the family's exchange of humour and laughter. As well as contributing to warmth and social understanding, humour, like play, may enable the child to release tension and express feelings of sibling rivalry in a socially acceptable manner. Temperament also plays a role in these processes. Dunn (1993) cited the following description by a mother of differences between her relationship with her 5-year-old daughter, Caroline, and her 3-year-old son, Martin:

> I just don't have the same jokey time with Caroline as I do with him. She takes everything more seriously, and we can't seem to laugh off our disagreements the way Martin and I do. With him, everything is a riot – even when I'm trying to get him dressed. He's always been a joker. With her, I have to tread so carefully.
>
> (p. 39)

Sibling–Sibling Interaction and Individual Development

The *sibling tutoring effect* (Zajonc and Hall, 1986) refers to the explicit teaching by elder siblings of their younger brothers and sisters, and to the resulting cognitive gains that may emerge for both teacher and learner. In fact, even though the younger sibling may know less about a particular subject, elder siblings are seen to develop intellectually through being allowed to teach new skills to their younger family members. Large-scale comparisons between the intelligence tests scores of children from families of various sizes have shown that the eldest child in a family of two or three children scores consistently higher than singletons (only children) from similarly intellectually stimulating home backgrounds. Youngest children also lag behind the middle or eldest children in a family. The explanation seems to be that: 'Acting as a teacher helps a child's intellectual growth, but the only child never gets that opportunity' (Zajonc and Hall, 1986, p. 49).

Across diverse cultures throughout the world, older children gain nurturance and empathy by being allowed to care for their infant brothers and sisters (Dunn, 1983). Thus one observational study of tribal African children's caregiving strategies during their frequent periods of being in sole charge of their infant siblings revealed an even wider range of nurturant and teaching behaviours by these children than by parents or extended adult kin in the same families (Whiting and Whiting, 1975). Parents' and older siblings' rates of scolding, helping, and giving food and attention to the babies were quite similar. But brothers and sisters played with and teased the infants more, and were also more punitive than aunts, uncles, parents and grand-parents.

Vandell, Minnett and Santrock (1987) studied a group of 73 closely spaced sibling pairs between the ages of 4 and 11 years. As the pairs grew older, the younger sibling was seen to gain steadily in power and status relative to the older brother or sister. Thus, by the end of middle childhood, being the eldest was no longer very distinctive from being the youngest. Instructions, teaching and direct help of the younger by the older brother or sister all declined over time. But pleasurable companionship and the positive emotional tone of siblings' involvement together increased with age. The researchers suggested that the new companion role developed during middle childhood could potentially remain an important bond throughout the remainder of the lifespan. These issues will be explored in later chapters.

Peers as Playmates and Agents of Socialization

With the young child's transition out of the family into day care, preschool, or primary school, parental social influences are joined in a sometimes complementary, sometimes contradictory, and often completely independent fashion by social influences from the child's peer group. Peers, or other children outside the family who are about the same age, associate with one another in the neighbourhood, in the classroom and on the playground before, during and after school, although the child's goal in playing with peers may appear to be nothing more than sheer enjoyment. However, processes of psychological development are influenced by the peer group in myriad ways. Peers provide models of behaviour. They also offer direct coaching when they tell or show a friend how to do something, and teach important social lessons via their approval or disapproval of one another's actions. They offer rewards, ranging from smiling or verbal praise to gifts or the sharing of toys, and punishments, ranging from tears or hitting to verbal reprimand or ridicule. Above all, the child's membership in a social group of peers provides a source of companionship among equals, and lessons in the benefits that group belonging can provide.

Children's play in early childhood involves important social lessons. In their initial play experiences with peers, toddlers may learn simple social skills, such as attending to others and taking turns in speech and behaviour. They are also apt to practise simple physical modes of persuasion and influence, along the lines of the early negotiation attempts within the family that we explored earlier in this chapter, while at the same time learning to share objects and activities in simple play routines. Between the ages of two and five years, observers have noted the emergence of a concept of *intersubjectivity* in children's play (Rubin *et al.*, 1999). Compared to younger children, peers aged four and over engage in more negotiation and cooperative agreement. They may discuss what they will play and how their play sequences will unfold, taking account of one another's views. There is often a clear and explicit allocation of roles and functions (for example, who should be the mother when playing house, or who is 'it' in a game of hide-and-seek).

In addition, by engaging in pretend sequences and make-believe, toddlers create and share symbolic meanings and representational understanding. Pretend play involves the substitution of a toy or imaginary symbol for its real-life analogue. A child may pretend that a doll is a baby, or engage in dialogues or dramatic sequences with a fictitious playmate who exists purely in the imagination. By sharing the pretend worlds of others, children may be helped to acquire a theory of mind (Dunn, 1996; Wellman, 1990; see also pp. 23–4 and 34–6, this chapter).

Play patterns vary within the same society, as a function of such factors as presence of siblings at home, length of acquaintance and the child's attendance at day care (Howes, 1985). Some of these differences may persist past toddlerhood into later phases of the lifespan. Thus, when Smart and Smart (1980) contrasted the complexity of social play in American and New Zealand primary schools they found a higher rate of sophisticated social play in New Zealand. There were no differences between boys and girls, but Maori children played more complex social games than Pakeha (white) New Zealanders. The Smarts suggested that a lower rate of solitary television viewing might be one of the factors responsible for New Zealand children's superiority over Americans. The Maori children's advantage could also reflect infrequent television viewing, coupled with cultural norms favouring collective cooperation and mutual group activity.

Researchers have also observed relationships between high levels of imaginative play in preschoolers and their parents' child-rearing methods (Fein, 1981). Fathers of imaginative, intellectually competent preschoolers spend more time with their sons and daughters than other fathers. Though such a relationship could be due to fathers' delight in the company of offspring who stand out for their dramatic skills, an observed link between children's imagination and parenting during infancy suggests an alternative direction of causality. Fein (1981) noted that the security of an infant's attachment to the mother and/or father at the age of 18 months predicted the imaginative quality and variety of the child's make-believe play as a 2-year-old.

A link between social and cognitive development during early childhood is revealed in the finding that children who frequently engage in make-believe and fantasy play, display advanced levels of cognitive maturity for their age, and do exceptionally well in academic subjects at school (Singer and Rummo, 1973). In an experimental intervention study, a group of preschool children at the preoperational stage of cognitive development (i.e., able to construct internalized representations, but unable to formulate rules or concepts) was exposed to a series of deliberately engineered sequences of pretend play (Golomb and Cornelius, 1977). For example, the adult experimenter might involve the child in pretending that a chair was a car. Or she might take a pretend bite out of a chalkboard duster, exclaiming 'Good cake! Yum yum!' This play experience dramatically enhanced preschoolers' concepts of quantity and number, as assessed by Piaget's conservation tests (Piaget, 1970).

The Peer Group and Sociometric Measurement

By socializing with peers, children learn to exercise leadership or conformity, to play cooperatively or competitively, to make or break rules, and to cope with group acceptance and rejection. Researchers studying peer group relationships during the school years have often employed a method of assessing children's peer relationships that is known as the *sociometric technique* (Hymel, 1983). A researcher who uses this method to evaluate the individual child's status within a social network must first select a peer group for study (for example, a scout troop, a classroom of children in preschool or primary school, or a neighbourhood playgroup). Individual members of the chosen group are then interviewed individually to determine who they like and dislike. This question may be asked directly ('Name someone you really like to play with'; 'Who do you like best?'), or specific behavioural indicators of liking and dislike may be elicited instead ('Who would you like to invite to your next birthday party?'; 'Who do you usually sit beside at lunchtime?'). A child's discomfort at being asked to articulate dislike for a peer can be minimized by using the 'class-play' variant of the sociometric procedure. Here, pupils suggest members of their class to occupy various typecast roles, such as 'someone who is very bossy', 'someone who can't get along with others', or 'the loner'. Similarly, with very young groups of children, the problem of not knowing everyone's name can be overcome by using a photograph of the class and having children point to the faces of those they like or dislike.

Positive sociometric nominations are the votes a child gets when peers are asked who they like and want to play with. Negative nominations are choices of an individual in response to questions about dislike or antisocial behaviour. After all members of the peer group have been interviewed, the totals for positive and negative nominations earned by each child are added up. Based on these totals, children can be assigned to one of four distinct classifications: popular, neglected, controversial or rejected. Table 2.6 shows how these classifications are arrived at.

As Table 2.6 shows, being unpopular is not simply the reverse of being popular, or having lots of friends. There are rejected children who are unpopular, in terms of active dislike by many members of their peer group, and few or no liking choices. Another group earns few or no positive nominations: these children are unpopular, not through overt peer rejection but merely through being neglected. Though not actively sought after by others as playmates, they do not appear to be actively disliked either. With few or no choices as either a desired or an undesired companion, they are merely isolated or ignored. Perhaps an even more intriguing social situation is that of the controversial child, who earns an exceptionally large number of both 'like' and 'dislike' votes from peers. While some playmates actively seek this child out as a companion, others are equally adamant in their desire to avoid his or her company.

Extending from the 1930s (Moreno, 1934) when the first studies of children's friendships and sociometric popularity were conducted, researchers have amassed a considerable body of research using sociometric measures. The results of these studies demonstrate that a child's status as a popular, average, controversial, neglected or actively rejected member of the peer group is likely to remain stable over brief spans of time (Dodge, 1983; Hartup, 1970, 1987). Stability is greatest: (a) among older children as compared with preschoolers, (b) in well-established groups, as compared with temporary, *ad hoc* groups (for example, a school classroom versus a group thrown together for a one-week camping holiday); and (c) at the extremes of high popularity or consistent rejection. These results indicate that children recognize friendship hierarchies in their peer groups. They also suggest that the sociometric technique is a valid and reliable index of how children relate to one another in established groups. Perhaps a more interesting question, especially in light of the lasting influences that experiences of acceptance or rejection are likely

TABLE 2.6 *Sociometric status characteristics of children's peer groups*

	Positive nominations (likes)	
Negative nominations (dislikes)	*Many*	*Few or none*
Many	Controversial	Rejected
Few or none	Popular	Neglected (or 'socially isolated')

to have on individual children's happiness and developmental opportunities, is 'What determines peer popularity?'

Predictors of Popularity

Some of the correlates of children's social acceptance, rejection and neglect that have been uncovered using sociometric techniques may seem both unfortunate, unfair and largely irrational. It has been found, for example, that a child with an unusual first name (e.g., Archibald or Beryl) is less likely to be sociometrically popular than a peer whose first name (e.g., Steven or Alison) is common within the social cohort (McDavid and Harari, 1966; Perry and Bussey, 1984). Similarly, a child with a trim but muscular body build is more likely to score high in acceptance than one who is obese or abnormally thin. An attractive facial appearance is another observed correlate of popularity over which children themselves have little control (Langlois and Downs, 1979). Unpopular children (whether neglected or actively rejected) also display poorer academic performance than their popular peers (Van Lieshout and Van Aken, 1987).

On the other hand, many of the attributes that show the strongest and most consistent correlations with peer popularity make intuitive sense. Children who have outgoing, friendly temperaments and a good command of social skills are popular because they are skilled at participating in, and facilitating, harmonious social relationships within the peer group (Putallaz, 1983). When tested in novel social situations, children who are highly popular within their familiar group of peers are apt to display advanced skills for establishing contact with unfamiliar playmates. Having broken the ice, children who are popular are likewise exceptionally adept at maintaining friendly interaction within novel groups, through the use of social skills such as cooperative turn-taking, the volunteering of appropriate information, and expressing a friendly interest in others (Putallaz and Gottman, 1981). Some additional correlates of popularity and unpopularity in children's peer groups during early and middle childhood are shown in Table 2.7.

The consequences of sociometric popularity status for later psychological adjustment are strong, and are bolstered by children's tendency to retain the same popularity status as they grow older, even when the peer group judging their acceptance or rejection is itself subject to change (Dodge, 1983). For example, when Coie and Dodge (1983) followed a group of 8- to 11-year-olds in the USA over a five-year period, they observed a high level of stability in the children's sociometric classifications, even though the children had changed schools and passed through the dramatic physical and psychological transformations of puberty. Sadly, the highest levels of stability were observed amongst children with the least favoured initial statuses: rejected children and, to a lesser extent, those who were neglected. In another longitudinal study, Kupersmidt and Coie (1990) followed a group of 11-year-olds over a seven-year period to assess psychological and behavioural problems, as well as sociometric popularity. Children who were rejected by their

TABLE 2.7 *Correlates of children's peer status as popular, neglected, controversial or rejected*

Popular	Neglected
Outgoing, sociable, friendly	Shy
High levels of cooperative play	Prefers adults to peers
Frequent expressions of affection and approval	Frequent solitary activity, not a joiner
Effective leader, not aggressive	Not aggressive
Sound social-cognitive understanding	Withdraws in the face of others' aggression
Willing to share	Lacks skills for initiating or maintaining pleasant social interaction
Good group entry skills	

Controversial	Rejected
High levels of attention seeking	High in antisocial aggression
High activity level	High activity level
High rates of both prosocial and antisocial aggression	High in disruptive behaviour
Frequent prosocial behaviour	Lacks social understanding
Sound social understanding (though possibly Machiavellian at times)	Talkative, but inclined towards egocentric or argumentative speech

peers at the start of the study were significantly more likely than others to have: (a) been suspended from, or dropped out of school, (b) been in trouble with the law for truancy, shoplifting or other violations, and (c) received a clinical diagnosis for nonspecific behaviour problems.

Whether these difficulties are a direct consequence of rejection by childhood peers, or an indirect consequence of associated difficulties (e.g., high levels of aggressiveness or a negative mood tone), cannot be determined definitively on the basis of present research. Indeed, as we will see in the next chapter when we examine developmental changes in peer relations during pre-adolescence and adolescence, there are many complex and interacting effects of early social experiences on emotional and cognitive outcomes. However, the pain of peer rejection and neglect is a palpable entity in childhood, quite apart from its predictive significance for serious adjustment difficulties in later life. For this reason, it is important to note the success that has been achieved in intervening to overcome rejected and neglected children's difficulties with their peers, especially through programmes incorporating training in social skills and social cognition (Ladd, 1999).

Summary

In this chapter we have examined the development of social relationships from their earliest onset in the infant's formation of an attachment to a primary caregiver, through the many changes that punctuate relationships with parents, siblings and peers as children mature. We also explored individual differences in the nature and quality of early social relationships, in terms of their immediate and long-term consequences. Parental responsiveness was seen to be an important determinant of individual differences in infants' attachment styles. Infants with secure attachments tend to develop social-cognitive understanding more readily than those whose attachments to parents are anxious or avoidant.

Family discussions, dialogue and conflict also contribute to individual differences in relationship quality and children's developmental outcomes. Toddlers learn reasoning and social perspective-taking through persuasion and arguments with siblings and peers. Parents' discipline strategies also influence a wide range of developmental outcomes. Authoritarian parenting may lead to low self-confidence and problems in peer relationships, whereas overly permissive parenting may lead to social immaturity and lack of self-control. Optimal developmental outcomes are seen to be associated with an authoritative or democratic style of parenting.

Children also gain social and cognitive skills through interaction with their siblings. Dialogues with family members about motivations, desires and beliefs may be particularly useful in stimulating children's social understanding. It would seem that opportunities to exchange ideas and feelings with siblings add a dimension of social input that extends children's understanding beyond the level achieved when interacting purely with adults, thus explaining why children with siblings develop a 'theory of mind' at an earlier age than singletons. On the other hand, differential parental treatment can contribute to the development of children who have siblings in ways that can be both harmful and beneficial to subsequent social adjustment. The sibling tutoring effect refers to explicit teaching of younger brothers and sisters by older children in the family, who may benefit cognitively as a result of this experience.

Children's play with peers in childhood teaches important social lessons, and the peer group may also influence the individual child's social and emotional adjustment through processes of acceptance or rejection. Children who are popular with their peers generally display high levels of social skill and social understanding. Those who are neglected by the peer group may be shy and lacking in skill for initiating or maintaining cooperative interaction. Controversial children, who score high in both sociometric popularity and sociometric rejection, often have high activity levels which combine prosocial behaviour with antisocial aggression. Those who are rejected or unpopular are often both aggressive and less capable than their peers in understanding other children's perspectives.

3

Relationships During Adolescence

Adolescence is generally a time of rapid change, both physiological and psychological. In early research and theorizing, the emphasis was on the 'storm and stress' of adolescence, but later work has tended to show that adolescence is not always so stressful. Offer and Sabshin (1984), for example, found that very high levels of stress were characteristic of only 21 per cent of the adolescents in their sample. Nevertheless, even for the placid majority, adolescence is a developmental turning point that marks the passage to maturity. Working through this stage demands psychological adjustment to a dramatic and far-reaching sequence of changes, including important changes in the nature and quality of personal relationships. In this chapter, we deal with three different sets of relationships during adolescence: relationships with parents, with peers and with romantic partners.

Parent–Adolescent Relationships

In addition to the dramatic physical growth and developing sexuality of this phase of the life cycle, adolescents increase their capacity for abstract reasoning, and hence for entertaining and exploring alternatives. Erikson (1968) suggested that the central task of adolescence was the establishment of a clear sense of personal identity, including the resolution of the question of future career, and the formation of values and beliefs. It is within this context of dramatic physical and cognitive change that adolescents face their central social challenge: balancing the paradox of independence and dependence, of autonomy and connection, in a broadening context of relationships with both family and peers. For these reasons, parent–adolescent relationships have been of great interest to researchers.

In their cross-sectional study of family relationships across the life cycle, Olson and his colleagues (1983) showed that marital satisfaction, family satisfaction, family cohesion and family strengths were all seen as lower in families with adolescents than in families at other stages of the life cycle; parents of adolescents also saw their quality of life as lower. These findings suggest that, even if life for the adolescent is not as tumultuous as has been thought in the past, adolescence can be a fairly stressful time for parents, and for the family as a whole. Stone and

Church (1968) summed up the reasons for problems in parent–child relationships during adolescence when they suggested that 'readiness for adulthood comes about two years later than the adolescent claims and about two years before the parent will admit' (p. 447).

Attachment issues in adolescence

Parent–adolescent relationships also tend to be problematic because of the changing patterns of relationship with parents and peers. Although the attachment functions we described in Chapter 2 are equally important for adolescents, there is likely to be a transfer of these functions from parents to peers, especially romantic partners. In fact, one way of understanding the development of close relationships in adolescence is to chart this transfer of attachment functions to those outside the immediate family.

To explore this issue, Hazan and Zeifman (1994) interviewed a sample of children and adolescents ranging in age from 6 to 17 years. These young people were asked to name the people they would turn to in various situations (e.g., 'Who do you turn to for comfort when you are upset, feeling down, etc.?'). Responses to these questions were used to quantify the extent to which parents and peers were used to meet different attachment needs. These researchers found that a marked shift in targets of attachment occurred between 8 and 14, with peers coming to be preferred over parents as persons to spend time with, and as sources of emotional support and comfort (safe haven). For the 11- to 14-year-olds, and even for the 15- to 17-year-olds, parents were still performing the secure base function. These findings suggest that adolescents tend to try out peer relationships from the vantage point of the secure base provided by their relationships with their parents. Figure 3.1 illustrates this pattern of change over time.

Of those in the late adolescent group who considered a peer to be their primary attachment figure, the overwhelming majority saw a romantic partner as performing attachment functions. It is interesting to note that the majority of these adolescents were insecure in attachment style (either avoidant or anxious-ambivalent), suggesting that, as Hazan and Zeifman note, insecure attachments to parents may lead to early romantic attachments.

Hazan and Zeifman (1994) also carried out a study of adults with romantic relationships of varying lengths, and including some participants who were not in romantic relationships. They concluded that the process of transferring attachments from parents to peers takes about two years. Most of these young adults who were in relationships of two years or more reported that they relied on their romantic partners to fulfil all attachment functions.

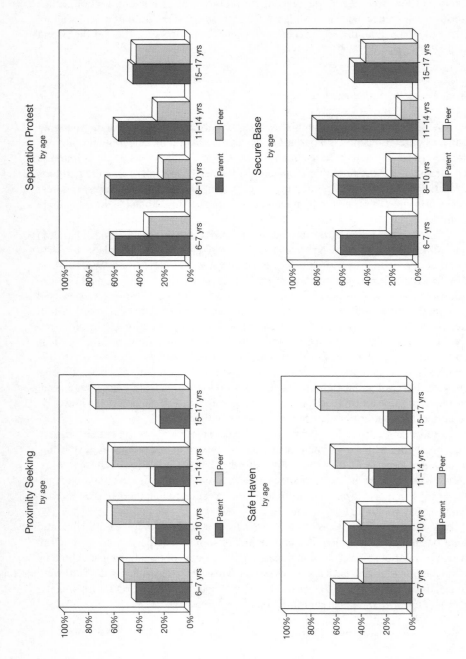

FIGURE 3.1 Parents and peers as targets of the four components of attachment, by age group. Hazan and Zeifman, 1994.

Changing relationships with parents

One of the most important tasks of adolescence, as Grotevant and Cooper (1986) have pointed out, involves the renegotiation of the parent–child relationship to reflect the adolescents' growing independence. Adolescents look for a more adult–adult relationship based on mutual respect, rather than a hierarchical relationship based on authority and power. They want to make many of their own decisions and to be in charge of their own lives, as far as possible.

Noller and Callan (1986) had parents and adolescents report on their family in terms of Olson's dimensions of cohesion and adaptability. Family members rated both the current state of their family and the way they would like that family to be. Compared with parents, adolescents of all ages were less satisfied with the levels of adaptability in the family, judging the present state of the family as more inflexible and resistant to change than their parents did. Parents saw the family as more cohesive than the adolescents, but even the adolescents reported fairly high levels of cohesion. Overall, adolescents seemed to want flexibility and openness to change, within a cohesive and supportive family system; that is, they wanted to be able to do as they pleased but with the full support of their parents. Table 3.1 shows adolescents' reports of current and ideal levels of adaptability and cohesion. It is clear from this table that adolescents wanted higher levels of both adaptability and cohesion than were currently present in their families, although levels of both current and ideal cohesion decreased with adolescents' age. The finding for adaptability fits with the comments by Stone and Church (1968), reported earlier, in that adolescents were clearly wanting more control over their lives than their parents were willing to give them. It is interesting to note, however, that the adolescents also wanted higher levels of cohesion, indicating that parental support was very important to them.

In some ways, as Larson and Richards (1994) point out, the changes in family relationships that come about at adolescence are very difficult for both the parent and the child. The adolescents are experiencing 'a pile-up of personal changes that

TABLE 3.1 *Reports by adolescents of current and ideal levels of adaptability and cohesion in their families*

	Adaptability		Cohesion	
Age of adolescent	*Current*	*Ideal*	*Current*	*Ideal*
13 years	42.1	51.12	59.4	65.1
14 years	41.4	52.3	58.6	66.3
16 years	40.9	52.75	53.9	63.1
17 years	39.3	50.35	49.8	59.5

Note: The maximum possible score for adaptability is 70 and for cohesion is 80.
Source: Adapted from Noller and Callan, 1986

intensify their emotional lives, [and] a mother finds herself caring for an adolescent who is more withholding, more prone to negative moods, and who sometimes directs the brunt of his displeasure at her' (p. 131). In addition, given that many problem behaviours (smoking, alcohol, drugs, early involvement in sexual activity) can begin during adolescence, parents tend to be very concerned about their adolescents.

Communication in families with adolescents

In their comprehensive study of affect and parent–adolescent relationships in middle-class American families, Larson and Richards (1994) provided family members (mother, father and an adolescent) with an electronic pager, with the goal of obtaining 'an emotional photo album of their family life' (p. 9). Family members were beeped about eight times per day for seven days. They were also given a set of forms on which they were asked to record what they were doing and how they were feeling when their pager beeped.

Larson and Richards (1994) found that mothers tended to spend more time with adolescent offspring than did fathers, although only about an hour a day was spent in joint activities. In addition, adolescents talked to mothers more than to fathers, especially about more intimate topics, such as friends and family. Noller and colleagues (Noller and Bagi, 1985; Noller and Callan, 1990) also found that adolescents talked more with mothers than with fathers, with politics being the only topic about which young people talked more with fathers than mothers. Collins and Russell (1991) have reported similar findings.

The emotional highs and lows experienced by the adolescent participants in Larson and Richards' (1994) study were only too evident. Adolescents tended to be much more emotional than their parents, even when dealing with the same issues (such as the death of the family cat), and they reported both more euphoric highs and more intense lows.

In addition, the adolescents reported social discomfort on a wide range of dimensions: self-consciousness, embarrassment, awkwardness, loneliness and nervousness. Whereas younger children were more likely to hang out with the whole family in the living room, family room or kitchen, adolescents in the sample spent a lot of time alone in their rooms feeling weak, lonely and sad. On the brighter side, they tended to use this solitary time as a time of restoration, and would generally come out of their rooms feeling better.

In parent–adolescent relationships, the childrearing 'task' of mothers (to care for and be responsible for their children) and the developmental 'task' of adolescents (to break away and become their own person) are often in conflict. Mothers in this study tended to want more engagement with their children and more involvement in their lives, whereas teenage children wanted to spend more time with peers, more time alone, and more time away from home and family. As Larson and Richards explain:

They may close their bedroom doors, expressing a desire for privacy that excludes parents. Girls will fill pages of a diary or spend hours conversing with a girlfriend as they dissect the intricacies of personal relationships. Boys may absorb themselves in playing computer games alone or shooting baskets with friends. Such activities are a way for growing teenagers to establish a personal sense of who they are, a private self separate from parents and family.

(1994, p. 133)

Of course, it is important to keep in mind that the families in Larson and Richards' study were middle class and that, in working-class families, children may not have the luxury of a room of their own.

According to Erikson's (1968) theory of lifespan personality development, a central psychological task for late adolescents involves resolution of an identity crisis, revolving around concepts of self. The personal sense of 'who they are', that Larson and Richards view as a focus for solitary reflections, is bound up with the search for identity resolution, according to Erikson's theory. Progressively, as identity develops, teenagers gain a firmer sense of themselves as independent individuals, with personally chosen goals, values and future directions. Identity development also includes plans for future relationships, which Erikson sees as crystallizing with the young person's transition into the next developmental crisis. That is, in early adulthood, there is a tension between the striving for intimacy and the drive for private self-sufficiency and isolation from others. (See Chapters 4 and 5.)

In line with these ideas, the older adolescents in Larson and Richards' (1994) study tended to report feeling less friendly and less close towards their mothers than did the younger ones. In addition, the older adolescents perceived their mothers as being less friendly and less warm towards them.

With regard to relationships with fathers, it is not uncommon for adolescents to report that their fathers are less sensitive than their mothers to the various things that are going on in their lives. Daughters, in particular, are likely to describe their fathers as cold and distant (Collins and Russell, 1991). In fact, Larson and Richards (1994) found that, although many fathers believed they were close to their children, the children were less likely to agree. These differences in perception may have arisen because of the limited time fathers had to spend with their children, and because work activities tended to take precedence, even at weekends. It is interesting to note that the fathers and adolescents also disagreed about when they were together, and the amount of time fathers spent alone with their adolescents was quite small (about 12 minutes per day on average).

Larson and Richards found that fathers mostly engaged their adolescents, and especially their sons, in leisure activities related to television and sport. Time was also spent eating together, doing household tasks or helping with homework. Fathers' participation with their adolescents, however, seemed more voluntary than that of mothers, with fathers tending to withdraw if they did not feel like being involved. As we noted earlier, conversation with fathers was not often personal in nature. Almost half the fathers in the sample reported that their child hardly ever talked to them about their feelings.

Adolescents' self-esteem tends to be affected by the quality of the family environment (Noller *et al.*, 1992). These researchers found that adolescents in families where intimacy was high and parents used a democratic parenting style were high in self-esteem, whereas those in highly conflicted families tended to be low in self-esteem. Burt and his colleagues (Burt, Cohen and Bjorck, 1988) also found that where adolescents perceived the family environment as conflictual and controlling, they were more likely to have low self-esteem and high levels of depression. However, a six-month follow-up showed that perceptions of conflict and control at the earlier time were not related to self-esteem or depression at the later time.

Conflict in families with adolescents

Many studies (e.g., Steinberg, 1991) have shown that conflict with mothers increases during adolescence, even though adolescents tend to report that their mothers understand them better and are easier to talk to than their fathers. One of the reasons for the increased conflict with parents during adolescence is that young people come to see their parents' rules and demands as less legitimate and more arbitrary (Smetana, 1988). For example, they tend to think that they, and not their parents, should decide how often they go out, where they go, who they go with, and what time they should come home.

This issue of parental authority versus adolescent autonomy has been studied by Smetana and Asquith (1994). Parents and adolescents (aged 12 to 16 years) rated the legitimacy of parental authority across a wide range of issues, including moral, conventional, friendship and personal issues. Parents and adolescents agreed that the parents should retain authority in moral and conventional issues, but they disagreed about the other types of issues, with adolescents wanting more say in these areas than parents thought appropriate.

Flannery, Montemayor and Eberly (1994) examined the relation between parents' affective expression in interactions, and their adolescents' perceptions of their relationships with those parents. They collected self-report data from the adolescents on their physical maturation, the amount of conflict in their relationship with each parent, and their perceptions of parenting behaviours. The more physically mature the adolescents were, the more negative communications they reported with their parents, in line with the findings of Larson and Richards (1994) reported earlier. It is interesting to note that the higher levels of negativity were confirmed by the parents' expressions of negative affect in their interactions with their adolescents. Fathers' negative affect seemed to be particularly salient for both sons' and daughters' perceptions of communication quality and psychological autonomy. In fact, the more negative their fathers' affect, the more autonomous these young people perceived themselves to be. These findings seem to support the view that conflict between parents and adolescents is an integral part of the process of breaking away from the family and gaining independence, although such conflict may produce negative outcomes when parents are highly controlling.

In general, conflicts between parents and adolescents tend to be about the minor details of everyday life, such as household chores, getting along with other family members, social activities and homework (Smetana *et al.*, 1991). However, young people tend to argue about different issues with each parent. Arguments with both parents are about household responsibilities, but arguments with mothers tend to be about personal manners, and choice of friends and clothes; arguments with fathers, on the other hand, tend to be about money, use of leisure time, and attitudes to school and school work (Ellis-Schwabe and Thornburg, 1986; Montemayor, 1983).

Learning conflict patterns in the family

Noller *et al.* (1996) tested the possibility of links between marital, parent–child and sibling relationships, in terms of the way conflict was dealt with in families with adolescents. They used a self-report measure which assessed conflict patterns in each relationship type: coercion (when each tries to get his or her own way by force), mutuality (when each seeks to understand the other's point of view), demand–withdraw (when one tries to raise an issue and the other refuses to talk about it) , and the level of distress (e.g., guilt or resentment) present in the relationship after the interaction. They found strong links between marital and parent–child conflict patterns for all four relationships (mother–daughter, mother–son, father–daughter, father–son), and these links were generally present, albeit weaker, even when a different family member reported on the marital and parent–child relationships. Table 3.2 shows the correlations between parents' reports of marital and parent–adolescent conflict for each parent–child dyad.

Links between parent–child and sibling conflict patterns were less strong, but were still present, especially for interactions involving sons, and the more negative patterns of coercion and demand–withdraw. Few links were found between marital and sibling conflict patterns. This finding suggests that offspring do not model the way they handle sibling conflict on how their parents deal with conflict in their marriage, but, rather, learn these conflict patterns in interaction with their parents.

Parenting style and parent–adolescent relationships

Researchers have compared families in terms of the styles of discipline and care employed by the parents (see also the section on parental discipline strategies in Chapter 2). Lamborn *et al.* (1991) compared adolescents from four types of families: authoritative (high on both acceptance and strictness), authoritarian (low on acceptance and high on strictness), indulgent (high on acceptance and low

TABLE 3.2 *Correlations between marital and parent–child conflict*

Couple conflict	Mutuality	Coercion	Demand–withdraw
Mutuality			
Mother–daughter	0.48*	−0.23†	−0.26†
Mother–son	0.24	−0.06	−0.21
Father–daughter	0.55*	−0.34*	−0.30*
Father–son	0.49*	−0.33†	−0.23
Coercion			
Mother–daughter	−0.05	0.34*	0.20†
Mother–son	−0.44*	0.58*	0.46*
Father–daughter	−0.22†	0.34*	0.09
Father–son	−0.32†	0.36†	0.37†
Demand–withdraw			
Mother–daughter	−0.17	0.21†	0.47*
Mother–son	−0.38†	0.20†	0.55*
Father–daughter	−0.32*	0.23†	0.41*
Father–son	−0.23	0.41*	0.54*

Note: * $p < 0.01$; † $p < 0.05$
The respective parents reported on marital conflict and the respective adolescents reported on parent–child conflict.
Source: Adapted from Noller *et al.*, 1996

on strictness), and neglectful (low on both acceptance and strictness) as described more fully on pp. 29–31. The clearest difference was between those from authoritative and neglectful families. Adolescents raised in authoritative homes were more socially competent, performed better academically, experienced less internalized distress and engaged in fewer problem behaviours than other young people. In contrast, those from neglectful homes were less socially competent, performed worse academically, experienced more internalized distress and engaged in more problem behaviours than other adolescents.

In a one-year follow-up of this sample, Steinberg *et al.* (1994) found that adolescents from authoritarian homes showed increased levels of psychological and somatic stress over the 12-month period; this finding fits with other research showing the problems created by overcontrolling parents (e.g., Stark *et al.*, 1990). Over time, those from indulgent homes reported more positive academic self-conceptions and less somatic distress, but, on the negative side, they became less oriented towards school and engaged in more misconduct at school. Again, however, the contrast between authoritative and neglectful families was most clear. Adolescents from authoritative homes maintained their high levels of adjustment, and the gap between them and those from neglectful families became even larger. Adolescents from neglectful homes showed continuing declines in functioning: they became markedly less oriented towards work and school, and engaged in more delinquent behaviours and use of alcohol and drugs. Steinberg *et al.* (1994) described these youngsters as

'on a downward and troublesome trajectory characterized by academic disengagement and problem behaviour' (p. 765).

Parent–adolescent relationships and the development of problem behaviours

As suggested by these findings, adolescence is not only a time of rapid change but
also a time when young people are particularly likely to become involved in problem
behaviours. These potential problems can be a source of serious concern for parents.
Problems such as substance abuse (including both alcohol and illegal drugs),
antisocial or delinquent behaviour, high-risk sexual behaviour and academic failure
(Metzler *et al.*, 1998) are all likely to develop at this stage. There is evidence that
high parental conflict is associated with poor family relations and inadequate
parental supervision (see Table 3.3). This lack of parental supervision seems, in
turn, to be associated with young people being involved with peers who engage
in deviant behaviour (Ary *et al.*, in press; Ary *et al.*, 1999).

This group of researchers also found that inadequate parental monitoring
was associated directly with involvement in deviant behaviour (Biglan *et al.*, 1995).
In other words, the involvement in deviant behaviour may occur either before
or after the involvement with delinquent peers. For example, a young person
may decide to use marijuana, go looking for a source for the drug, and become
involved with other drug users through that action. Of course, involvement in the
deviant group is likely to reinforce or even expand the young person's involvement
with drugs. The role of inadequate parental monitoring in the development of
problem behaviours fits with the findings of Lamborn *et al.* (1991) and Steinberg
et al. (1991), showing that children raised in neglectful families are more likely to
engage in problem behaviours.

There is also clear evidence that inept parental discipline contributes to children's
antisocial behaviour (Patterson, Reid and Dishion, 1992). Inept discipline, from
this perspective, involves parents failing to establish clear rules for their children,

TABLE 3.3 *Correlations between parenting constructs and measures of adolescent problem behaviour*

Construct	Association with deviant peers	Antisocial behaviour	Substance use
Parent–child conflict	0.36	0.87	0.59
Positive family relations	−0.43	−0.67	−0.40
Parental monitoring	−0.47	−0.91	−0.40
Parental rule-making	−0.33	−0.46	−0.31
Consistent enforcement of rules	−0.24	−0.39	−0.30
Positive reinforcement	−0.21	−0.35	−0.23

Note: all correlations are significant at p< 0.05.
Source: From Metzler *et al.*, 1998

and failing to enforce those rules. Parents also need to be aware of the importance of providing positive reinforcement for good behaviour, rather than just punishing bad behaviour. Programmes designed to teach parents and adolescents positive reinforcement, rule making and consistent rule enforcement have been shown to increase positive behaviour and decrease antisocial behaviour in adolescents (Irvine *et al.*, 1998).

Although neglectful and inept parenting are risk factors for problem behaviours, coercive family interactions can also contribute to the development of antisocial behaviour in young people (Patterson, Debaryshe and Ramsey, 1989; Patterson *et al.*, 1992). These researchers argue that parents who use aggressive means of control are more likely to produce aggressive children, particularly if conflict with the child is frequent, if there is little positive involvement with the child, and if parents fail to monitor how their children behave outside the home and family. (See section on authoritarian parents in Chapter 2.)

Barrera and Stice (1998) tested the possibility that the effects of family conflict would be moderated by whether the adolescent received high or low parental support. They found that conflict between parents and adolescents was more strongly related to adolescent problem behaviour when parental support was low, rather than high. These researchers also included a group of families where the father was an alcoholic, and found that conflict between parents and adolescents was related to adolescent problem behaviour for children of alcoholics, but not for children from other families. Based on these findings, these authors emphasize that the effects of parent–adolescent conflict on adolescents need to be studied in the broad family context.

The importance of broad family context is illustrated by the work of Brody and his colleagues (Brody *et al.*, 1998b), who explored how children's norms about alcohol use develop. Brody and colleagues looked at a number of factors including children's temperaments, parents' and siblings' norms for alcohol use, and parent–child discussions. They found associations between other family members' norms for alcohol use and those of the target child (aged 10 to 12 years), and these associations were particularly strong for those whose temperament put them at risk for early alcohol use. In addition, in families where there were frequent discussions between parents and children on the issue, children's norms tended to be less liberal and more conventional.

Adolescents' responses to parental conflict

There is increasing evidence that adolescents' responses to their parents' marital conflict have an impact on their later adjustment (Grych and Fincham, 1990; Kerig, 1995). Davis *et al.* (1998) carried out a longitudinal study assessing the effects of adolescents' responses to conflict between their parents on later aggression. Assessments were taken at two points in time, approximately one year apart. Later levels of aggression were higher for boys who responded aggressively to the mother when she initiated marital conflict, and for girls who responded aggressively towards the mother when the father initiated marital conflict. In addition, both male and female adolescents who responded aggressively towards the father when the mother initiated marital conflict were more likely to be aggressive at the later time.

In their review of the effects of marital conflict on children, Grych and Fincham (1990) emphasized important variables such as whether the conflict was child-related or not, whether the conflict was seen to be resolved or not, how the conflict was dealt with, and the level of stress the conflict caused for the offspring. Noller *et al.* (1999) followed up this work by conducting an analogue study of marital conflict in families with adolescents. Parents and adolescents listened to a set of tapes portraying four different types of marital conflict: mutual negotiation (which involved constructive interaction), mother demand/father withdraw (where the mother tried to resolve the issue but the father avoided dealing with it), father demand/mother withdraw (where the father tried to resolve the issue but the mother withdrew), and coercive (where both partners blamed and threatened each other).

Following each tape, all three family members rated how typical the interaction was of conflict interactions between their own parents, how stressful it was to listen to, how likely the issue was to be resolved, and the extent of positive and negative emotion they experienced while listening to the tape. There were very strong effects of conflict style, with the mutual style being rated as more typical, more likely to be resolved, and as inducing more positive and less negative emotion. The coercive style, on the other hand, was rated as less typical, more stressful, and as inducing more negative emotions. These findings emphasize the importance of constructive approaches to conflict in minimizing the impact of that conflict on family members.

Leaving home

An important goal of socialization in the family is to raise individuals who are able to manage on their own and take control of their own lives. Part of this process is leaving home, which must occur at both a physical and a psychological level. At the psychological level, the process of leaving home involves the transfer of attachment functions from parents to peers, as noted earlier (Hazan and Zeifman, 1994).

At both the physical and psychological levels, young people may need to leave home to study or find work, to establish more independent lives, and to form their own close relationships and their own families. The need for independence is an important motivation for leaving home (Young, 1987), particularly in families where parents tend to be very controlling and the young person's desire for independence creates conflict between them and their parents (Noller and Callan, 1991).

Unfortunately, some young people are forced to leave home because of abuse and conflict in the family. Seventy-three per cent of homeless adolescents who participated in a study by Pears and Noller (1995) reported leaving home because of abuse in the family. This abusive behaviour was often quite serious in nature, ranging from hitting and slapping to having a broken nose, broken arms, having one's head split open or being raped. Almost half of these young people (48 per cent) reported that the abuse occurred on a daily basis, and 23 per cent reported weekly abuse. These abused adolescents were more likely to engage in high levels of self-harm and other self-destructive behaviours such as smoking and drug use.

Having the adolescent leaving home, and becoming more focused on peers, can be quite difficult for parents. As Ekstein (1991, p. 531) notes:

> The most complex act of true parental love is the one that permits the child to move away towards his own life. This act of letting go is an act of love. Frequently we think of love in terms of 'forever, until death us do part'. Parental love, however, suggests that if we are to love forever, love must include letting go, separation and giving up.

Developments in Peer Relationships

The child's transition through the years of primary school into adolescence entails extensive exposure to the social world of peers. Given the growing significance of friendships and other forms of peer interaction, and the cognitive advances of adolescence, a number of important developmental changes take place in relationships with friends and peers. For example, friendship as a process is increasingly understood and appreciated for its emotional and psychological attributes (intimacy, trust, mutual support, and so on). Interactions with peers become an increasingly high priority, and a forum for questioning and resolving the issues of personal identity that play a central role in adolescent personality development, according to Erikson's (1968) theory. The peer group itself changes in predictable ways through the teenage years and, in its development, propels its members forward from the playful associations of childhood to the threshold of adult couplehood.

The growth of social cognition and peer relationships from childhood to adolescence

As children develop an understanding of people and social relationships their thinking about friends and friendship becomes progressively more sophisticated. Older children have the cognitive skills to consider multiple items of information simultaneously, and to go beyond concrete and superficial characteristics of friends to consider abstract and implicit ideas (Piaget, 1970). At the same time, the skills and motivation to consider the perspective of the other person in a close relationship develops markedly in pre-adolescence (Selman, 1981). These cognitive skills assist teenagers to develop realistic expectations of friends, to consider their friends as complex psychological entities, and to understand both the immediate and the long-term implications of friendship in terms of commitment, trust and reciprocal responsibilities.

Beginning several decades ago, a number of classic research studies have provided empirical support for the predicted changes in 'philosophizing' about friendship (Selman, 1981) that can be derived from cognitive theory. Interviews with cross-sectional samples of children, pre-adolescents and teenagers have revealed that the ability of friends to understand or think about each other in psychological terms increases abruptly during early adolescence. Thus Duck (1973) found that only 5 per cent of the 12-year-olds he studied made use of psychological or personality qualities such as 'eager', 'uncertain', 'shy' or 'caring' in descriptions of their friends. But the figure rose to 25 per cent among 14- and 15-year-olds and to 63 per cent among 18-year-old students.

Similarly, when Douvan and Adelson (1966) asked the 3,000 girls in their sample to name the quality they valued most in a friend, clear age differences emerged. Those aged 11 to 13 offered relatively superficial characteristics: the friend should have good manners, be amiable and cooperative, should play fairly, and not be grouchy or a show-off. In other words, for girls whose main purpose in friendship is the sharing of activities, the principal demand upon playmates is that they not disrupt the working or playing endeavour. In adolescence, on the other hand, friendship was sought in its own right, and the qualities looked for in a friend reflected this new emphasis. The older girls, aged 13 to 17, wanted a friend they could confide in, who would be loyal, sensitive and a source of support in an emotional crisis.

This new meaning of friendship in early adolescence appears to come about partly as a result of the growth of self-awareness, shared understanding of new sexual feelings and the desire for personal acceptance and social support. But another important factor in the growth of adolescent friendship is the greater cognitive capacities emerging with formal operational thought (Piaget, 1970). These new cognitive skills enable the adolescent to see beyond the superficial and obvious qualities of people into their deeper personalities.

Thus, young adolescents, aged 13 to 14, who are sensitive to personality attributes among individuals, come to choose best friends with some of the same discerning selectivity that they will later apply to their choice of a marital partner. The sensitivity of older children to those qualities that make individual peers unique was brought out in an English study asking a group of 8- to 15-year-olds to describe their best friends and to say why they liked them (Livesley and Bromley, 1973). The younger children's descriptions tended to focus on superficial attributes like possessions and appearance, or on irrelevant details which revealed nothing about their friends' true characters. Thus one child's portrait of his friend was limited to the statement that he had been to France for his holidays. Another said of a girl: 'I used to like her but I don't now because her dog bit me.' By contrast, the young British adolescents in the sample produced sensitive descriptions which revealed an acute appreciation of their friends' unique personalities, including their motives, values, aspirations, needs and private idiosyncrasies.

Similar results were obtained in the USA by Peevers and Secord (1973), when they asked children and adolescents to describe three of their friends. Young children tended to give global descriptions which failed to draw a line between the person and his or her situation, and so told nothing about what the friend was like as an individual ('John lives in a big house'). Adolescents more often described their friends' specific personal characteristics ('John is a good athlete'), and some also included personality dispositions which predicted the person's behaviour across a wide range of situations ('John is talkative').

Selman (1981) interviewed children extensively about their approaches to friendship and their cognitive appreciation of the meaning of friendship as a social relationship. On this basis he came up with a developmental progression describing the evolution of a 'philosophy' of friendship from childhood into adulthood. His model can be briefly outlined as follows:

- Momentary companions of convenience: friends are defined as playmates who happen to live near by and play together often.
- A one-way partnership: this level involves the idea that a friend is a special playmate who is willing to engage in one's own favourite form of play (such as dolls or rocket ships).
- 'Fair-weather cooperators': here, friends are seen as partners whose material likes and dislikes are known and accommodated, without any genuine understanding of the underlying basis for such preferences.

But Selman found that, by the age of 12 or 13, friendship philosophizing came into full flower. Most prevalent between the ages of 12 and 15 was a style of thinking about friends that Selman called 'intimate and mutually shared relationships'. Numbering this new acquisition Stage 3, to distinguish it from fair-weather relationships at Stage 2, and one-way partnerships at Stage 1, Selman (1981) gave the following description of the adolescent's more advanced understanding of the meaning of friendship:

> At Stage 3 there is the awareness of both a continuity of relation and affective bonding between close friends. The importance of friendship does not rest only upon the fact that the self is bored or lonely; at Stage 3, friendships are seen as a basic means of developing mutual intimacy and mutual support; friends share personal problems. The occurrence of conflicts between friends does not mean the suspension of the relationship, because the underlying continuity between partners is seen as a means of transcending foul-weather incidents. The limitations of Stage 3 conceptions derive from the overemphasis of the two-person clique and the possessiveness that arises out of the realisation that close relations are difficult to form and to maintain.
>
> (p. 251)

This last point led Selman to identify a fourth stage of thinking about friendship that did not emerge clearly until after age 14 or 15. This model of friendship, once acquired, is likely to persist throughout the lifespan. Selman (1981) described Stage 4's 'autonomous interdependency' as follows:

The interdependence that characterises Stage 4 is the sense that a friendship can continue to grow and be transformed through each partner's ability to synthesise feelings of independence and dependence. Independence means that each person accepts the other's needs to establish relations with others and to grow through such experiences. Dependence reflects the awareness that friends must rely on each other for psychological support, to draw strength from each other, and to gain a sense of self-identification through identification with the other as a significant person whose . relation to self is distinct from those with whom one has less meaningful relations.

(p. 251)

The levels of friendship reasoning that Selman identified also help to explain how children and adolescents think about such specific relationship issues as friendship formation and group exclusion. Their thoughts about how friends should deal with the conflicts and disagreements that inevitably arise in close relationships are shaped, to a large extent, by the highest level of friendship reasoning of which they are capable. Table 3.4 shows an example in which the levels of friendship reasoning predict young people's ideas and advice for dealing with conflicts and disagreements between peers.

TABLE 3.4 *Strategies for dealing with conflict as a function of levels of reasoning about friendship*

Stage 0: Momentary physical interaction
1 Conflict resolution through non-interaction
2 Physical intervention to force the issue
3 Forget and escape the conflict

Stage 1: One-way assistance
1 Negating the action of an adversary
2 Appeal to other's outlook

Stage 2: Fair-weather cooperation
1 Resolutions which appeal to both parties' sensibilities
2 Taking back *true* intent along with reparation
3 Forget in order to forgive
4 Friendship can weather disagreement

Stage 3: Intimate sharing
1 Conflicts arising in the relationship need mutual resolution
2 Conflicts of personality can express themselves in many ways and are no one's 'fault'
3 Working through conflicts strengthens the friendship (continuity of friendship is possible through thick and thin)
4 Superficial conflicts can be dealt with when deeper bonds hold the relationship together
5 Talk it out until a mutually acceptable solution is reached

Stage 4: Autonomous interdependence
1 Relation of complex personalities and complex conflicts
2 Level of communication between friends is central to conflict resolution
3 Disagreements may reflect a lack of communication between friends

Friendship and attachment to parents

Children's friendships differ from peer popularity in that friendship involves a close and mutual exchange of liking, whereas peer popularity (as measured by group belonging or by sociometric indices; see Chapter 2) reflects wider acceptance by group members. Popularity may or may not include mutuality of choice. When pairs of children select one another as mutual friends, this type of relationship may confer special developmental benefits during childhood (Parker and Asher, 1987).

In his pioneering theoretical contributions to the understanding of children's peer relationships, Sullivan (1953) put forward a notion of *chumship* to describe such mutuality. He suggested that children's friendships take on a new psychological meaning during middle childhood, with the growth of a close bond of affection for a special friend or 'chum'. Chums, or 'mutual friends' (Ladd, 1999), are close companions who share one another's affection and regard for one another. (They would be likely to pick one another ahead of other classmates on a sociometric test.) In addition, chums communicate more intimately than casual childhood friends. Sullivan suggested that pre-adolescents who are fortunate enough to have a chum are likely to develop unique social skills in the context of this relationship. Dealings with the chum teach the benefits of trust, egalitarianism and cooperation, while at the same time providing vivid lessons in the social costs of hostile domination, self-centredness, betrayal or insensitivity.

Sullivan argued that, as a consequence of these emotionally and socially significant attributes, children's mutual friendships contribute in important ways both to personality development and to the readiness for forming an intimate couple relationship during late adolescence or adulthood. The reciprocal regard that is likely to develop between mutual friends serves the developmental benefit of bolstering each individual child's self-esteem and teaching the realistic appreciation of areas of personal worth and deficiency that will foster identity development in later years (Erikson, 1968). By exchanging intimate information and ideas through conversation, chums likewise challenge and validate one another's beliefs and plans, while at the same time teaching the skills of trust and self-disclosure that will be important for later couple relationships (see Chapter 4). In addition, and most importantly from Sullivan's psychoanalytic point of view, the forging of a close relationship with a same-sex chum enables the child to loosen some of the bonds of dependency and emotional attachment to parents that kept the child tightly focused within the family during infancy and early childhood.

Lieberman, Doyle and Markiewicz (1999) measured the quality of children's same-sex mutual friendships in terms of closeness (e.g., 'I miss her when away'), security (e.g., 'If I have a problem I can talk to her about it'), helpfulness ('My friend would help me if I needed it') and companionship ('We spend all our free time together'). They found an association between these positive characteristics of mutual friendships and the security of children's attachments to their parents. Children aged 9 to 11 years who felt close to their parents and relied on them in times of stress reported higher levels of similarly positive qualities in their same-sex friendships. However, among the subgroup whose mothers were highly available and supportive, those who reported lower levels of dependency on their mothers had the highest levels of positive qualities in peer friendships.

It seems that secure attachment to a parent may serve as a starting point for the formation of a friendship. Based on the attributes distinguishing secure from insecure parent–child attachments (see Chapter 2), the friendships these children forge are likely to be characterized by similar qualities of trust, security and closeness. As securely attached children gain these emotional supports from close friends, they may feel able to relax their bonds of dependency upon their mothers, particularly when the mother has been highly available as a secure base during the earlier years. As Lieberman and her colleagues explained:

> The present findings are consistent with attachment theory that better adjustment, especially as indexed by positive social relationships with close peers, would be associated with those children who viewed their parents as highly available and themselves as capable. As expected, it was found that more secure attachment was related to lower conflict in friendship relations. This finding suggests that children who are more secure in their relationships with parents may learn better conflict resolution skills and may be better at controlling their negative affect and expressing positive affect.
>
> (1999, p. 210)

As we saw earlier in this chapter, the child's development across the school years results in a gradual shifting of their targets of emotional attachment from parents to peers (Hazan and Zeifman, 1994). For example, when children aged 6 to 7 years are asked 'Who do you miss most when you are away from them?', a large majority name a parent and only a few suggest a friend. By age 16, peers are named as often as mothers or fathers as the prime target for this separation protest dimension of attachment. When it comes to the safe haven component, the shift is even more pronounced, with about 80 per cent of 16-year-olds claiming they would turn first to a peer for comfort when distressed (see Figure 3.1).

Peers and peer-conformity: positive and negative influences

As young people increasingly move out of the confines of the family into the wider social world their dependency upon parents and other family members gradually decreases. More time is spent in contact with peers, whose opinions and values come to play an ever greater role in the individual adolescent's thinking and decision-making. Conformity to the peer group in values, behaviour, preferences (for music, clothes, etc.) and, occasionally, antisocial activity, increases steadily from late childhood to the middle teens, as shown in Figure 3.2. This increasing orientation towards the peer group for guidance, opinion formation and social support may assist adolescents to become less dependent (practically, emotionally and socially) on their parents. Peers may also be used as a refuge from conflict

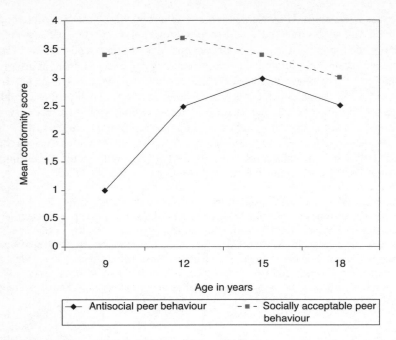

FIGURE 3.2 Children's and adolescents' peer conformity as a function of age and
behaviour domain. Based on data in Berndt, 1979

within the family, and as a resource in the adolescent's bids for greater independence
(Connell *et al.*, 1975).

However, the increases in peer conformity and peer group exclusiveness that
arise during early adolescence can also have adverse consequences. The pain of
group rejection is poignant, and the struggle to conform to peers may undermine
independent decision-making and self-reliance. Indeed, the results of one ambitious
longitudinal study (Epstein, 1981), conducted over a one-year period with young
people aged 12 to 18 years, revealed that those with mutual friendships suffered
certain psychological disadvantages, even compared with peers who were unable
to acquire or maintain any friendships that were reciprocated. For example, students
who had no friends scored higher in self-reliance after a year than those who
had managed to maintain stable friendships (controlling for initial levels of self-
reliance). Similar effects were observed for plans to attend university. Epstein
concluded that the drive to conform to friends' opinions may undermine developmental outcomes during early adolescence, especially if the values and goals of
the peer group itself are problematic.

More recent research has also highlighted the importance of solitude and
self-reliant independence from peer group influences for adolescent growth
and adjustment. For example, when Larson (1997) studied a sample of almost
500 Anglo-American children aged 10 to 15 years, he found that students' deliberate

wishes to spend time alone, rather than to be with friends, increased significantly as they progressed through the early teens. Furthermore, for early adolescents (aged 13 to 15), though not for younger children, time spent in solitude exerted a positive influence upon emotional state. When signalled with a pager at random intervals throughout the day and asked to record their feelings and behaviour, higher mood scores were earned by teenagers who were alone, or had been recently, than by those who were immersed in interactions with their friends.

From a developmental standpoint, the most striking result of this study was the discovery that moderate exposure to solitude had a beneficial effect upon psychological adjustment. Compared with their classmates who spent large amounts of time in interaction with friends, those who regularly spent between one-third and one-half of their spare time alone were lower in depression and higher in parents' and teachers' ratings of their social and psychological adjustment. It appeared that spending too much time in peers' company may have undermined adolescents' self-reliance, initiative and coping skills, in line with Epstein's (1981) earlier findings. As Larson (1997) explained:

> Solitude might provide a needed opportunity to relax and step back from the demands of enacting a public self with peers. In relationships with family, solitude may play a role in the developmental task of negotiating greater autonomy.
>
> (p. 91)

However, moderation in solitude, as well as companionship, seemed to be the guide to optimal adjustment. Teenagers in the sample who had few or no friends and spent more than half of their free time alone tended to have as many problems as those who were constantly socializing. Figure 3.3 shows the inverted U-shaped

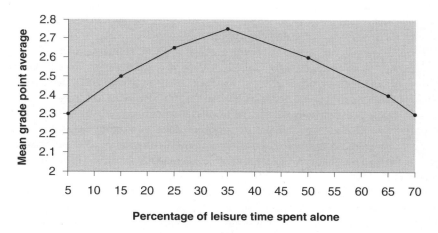

FIGURE 3.3 Relationships between proportion of time alone and academic achievement in teenagers aged 13 to 15 years. Larson, 1997, fig. 2, p. 88. Copyright © Society for Research in Child Development: reproduced by permission of SRCD.

curve that emerged when Larson plotted academic achievement (as indexed by grade-point average in school) against the proportion of their time that teenagers aged 13 to 15 spent alone as compared with their companions.

Understanding the peer group

During the pre-adolescent and adolescent years, peer relationships continue to exert important influences over the child's development. The peer group helps to shape the psychological growth of its individual members, over and above the dyadic influences of friendship and associated cognitions that we have examined so far. Indeed, during the teens, the peer group itself develops as its members grow older, with important ramifications for the development of social skills and social understanding. Concern about conformity, a heightened need to fit in with the social and sexual standards endorsed by the peer group, and worry over losing status if dating is delayed, all highlight how the peer group shapes its members' development during adolescence. In addition, peers and close friends regulate the pace of development, both of sexuality and of heterosexual friendship. Peers put pressure on each other to achieve a level of boy–girl intimacy which corresponds to the group average. Young people who are too far behind or too far ahead of the rest of the group are subject to disapproval.

The adolescent's popularity among peers of the same sex has much to do with his or her popularity with peers of the opposite sex, but the relationship between these two factors is complex. It depends on the adolescent's age and status within the group, and on the degree of boy–girl intimacy the group considers appropriate at each stage. Thus, the goalposts for peer acceptance during the teenage years are ever shifting ones that serve to propel the young person forward along a developmental path that leads from single-sex friendships, through co-ed groups, to dating and romantic relationships as a couple.

These interesting facts about the developmental and social functions of adolescent peer groups were first noted by Dunphy (1963) in a study which took place in clubs and milk bars, on the beaches and street corners, at parties and in teenagers' homes in suburban Sydney, between 1958 and 1960. Owing to its innovative and original findings and its unusual and ambitious methodology, this study has earned a special place in the research literature on adolescence. Furthermore, despite being gathered some four decades ago, its results continue to provide an accurate description of the social dynamics and important developmental functions of adolescent peer groups today.

Dunphy used the research method of participant observation to explore how adolescent peer groups function. In order to probe beyond what adolescents might say in order to make a good impression on an interviewer, and to uncover aspects of peer relations that teenagers might not be fully aware of themselves, Dunphy decided it would be useful as a researcher to become a 'fly-on-the-wall'. By watching and joining in with the groups of teenagers when they got together at weekends or after school, Dunphy gathered a rich pool of insights that could not have been gleaned using the techniques more commonly employed by researchers (such as interviews or self-report questionnaires).

Dunphy discovered important developmental changes in the adolescent peer group from age 13 to 20. Most older adolescents belonged simultaneously to two structurally different kinds of groups: the clique and the crowd. Cliques were small, close-knit groups of three to nine members, and crowds were aggregates of two or more complete cliques (they averaged a membership of 20). Clique members usually lived near one another and often met during the week to share secrets, to plan and analyse crowd functions, or just to talk. Crowds usually assembled only at weekends for more structured social functions like dances, parties and movies.

Membership in a crowd required membership of one of its cliques, and the boundaries of cliques themselves were rigidly enforced. To gain entry, the adolescent had to express an active desire to belong, and had to conform to the basic outlook and interests of the rest of the group. However, entry into a clique or crowd did not guarantee continuing membership. In order to escape the peer group rejection that looms large in many adults' memories of being a teenager, adolescents had to conform to the norms of their group in two important ways.

First, they had to obey the clique's or crowd's implicit leader. (Even though many of Dunphy's subjects stated that their group was leaderless and completely democratic, his observations revealed that all peer groups had a member who assumed the leader's role and directed much of the functioning and communication within the group, as well as being a channel for communication with other adolescent peer groups in the neighbourhood.) Followers who challenged the leader's authority risked exclusion from the group.

As shown in Figure 3.4, adolescent peer groups followed their own course of developmental change as their members grew older and shifted their interests from unisex leisure pursuits to co-ed parties and dating. At age 13, most of the teenagers in the study belonged to small all-boy or all-girl cliques, but as they moved through their teens, heterosexual cliques formed within the overarching crowd structure. By the end of adolescence, young men and women who had left school began pairing off as couples. Then the crowd slowly disintegrated, leading eventually to the social developmental processes of adult couple relationships that we will explore in more detail in Chapter 4.

In addition to following the leader, the other prerequisite Dunphy observed for teenagers maintaining their group membership was that members had to keep pace with the level of social development set by the leader and accepted by other members of the group. An individual who failed to keep pace with the peer group's progression through these stages of increasing heterosexual involvement risked social exclusion. Dunphy (1969) cited the experience of a girl called Kay who told him:

> I used to go around with Gay's crowd and in fact I was very friendly with Gay. But I was just dropped out of the group, I don't know why, for no reason at all that I

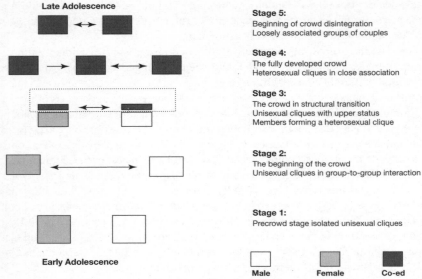

FIGURE 3.4 Stages in the development of adolescent peer groups. Dunphy, 1969,
fig. 4.1, p. 61

could see. They're like that; you're not spoken to or invited out with the crowd, they just ignore you. They all seem to have their boyfriends with them in the group and they don't care about anyone else.

(p. 77)

The leader of her group, Gay, confirmed that Kay's exclusion had resulted from her failure to keep up with her peers' increasing interest in boys. As Gay explained:

Well, we've all grown up a lot lately and we go out a lot with boys. But Kay never had anyone to go out with. She seems a bit young to us now, though she's about our age. Our interests have changed a lot really.

(p. 77)

The role of adolescent peer groups in the progression of individuals from unisex cliques through heterosexual peer groups to dating was also highlighted in a more recent study by Richards *et al.* (1998). Using the 'pager' methodology described earlier in this chapter, a longitudinal analysis over a four-year period revealed a steady increase in the amount of time teenagers spent socializing with members of the opposite sex. Across two cohorts of teenagers, the time spent with opposite-sex friends increased more than fourfold from age 13 to age 18, while the average amount of time socializing with same-sex peers remained relatively constant. These results are in line with Dunphy's (1963) suggestion that the same-sex peer group serves as a base and source of motivation for individuals to develop heterosexual attraction and dating.

During pre-adolescence, the North American teenagers who took part in this study resembled the Australian teenagers Dunphy (1963) had studied some three decades earlier, in being almost exclusively preoccupied with friends of their own gender. Less than 2 per cent of their time was devoted to thoughts about peers of the opposite sex. But a developmental change in thought patterns preceded the shift to mixed-sex interaction. By the age of 14, these teens were spending an average of 4 to 6 hours per week thinking about opposite-sex friends, but only about half an hour actually interacting with them. As time went on, the balance between thought and behaviour shifted. Adolescents aged 17 and 18 spent most of their leisure time with companions of the opposite sex. This involvement had a positive effect on moods and feelings: when in the company of the opposite sex, adolescents reported feeling 'more attractive, great and important' than when they were socializing with friends of their own sex. These heightened positive feelings may lead to the development of romantic love, as we will see in the next section.

Romantic Relationships

At the start of this chapter we discussed Hazan and Zeifman's (1994) research into the targets of children's and adolescents' attachment behaviour. Their results clearly showed that young people gradually increase their reliance on peers as sources of intimacy, comfort and support. Although close friends are an important part of this network of peer support, the exploration of romantic relationships represents a new and exciting challenge at this point in the life cycle. This challenge requires the adolescent to deal with a number of interrelated issues and tasks, including dating and courtship, the beginnings of sexual expression, and the development of romantic attachments.

Dating and courtship

Dating and courtship patterns depend on the cultural context in which they take place. Further, they tend to be heavily influenced by historical factors. For this reason, it is useful to consider some of the changes in these patterns over the last 40 to 50 years, focusing primarily on western cultures. Over this period, 'youth culture' has become an increasingly important phenomenon, with young people tending to see and define themselves in ways distinct from those of their parents. 'Youth' as a life stage has also become extended over time, with sexual maturation occurring earlier, and increased levels of education delaying the transition to adulthood. It is not surprising that these trends have been accompanied by changes in patterns of dating and courtship. Specifically, dating has become less bound by formal rules and customs, and young people now have less sense of a clear progression of relationships from first meeting to marriage (Cate and Lloyd, 1992).

Age of first dating has not changed markedly over the last 40 to 50 years, although adolescents do start dating earlier than they did in the first half of this century. The average age of first dating in western countries is generally around 14 to 15 (Cate and Lloyd, 1992; Kelley, 1995), and most adolescents have been involved in at least one dating relationship by the end of high school (Dowdy and Kliewer, 1998). Age at first dating is influenced by variables such as sex and place of residence: girls generally begin dating slightly earlier than boys, and those in urban centres tend to begin dating earlier than those in rural areas (Kelley, 1995). Although adolescents develop 'steady' relationships somewhat earlier than they did in the past, informal interactions between the sexes are also increasingly common (Cate and Lloyd, 1992).

As well as considering global changes in dating patterns, it is important to think about the role of dating relationships in the individual's development. According to Sarantakos (1992), dating relationships generally serve one or more of the following functions: recreation and relaxation, socialization into the world of intimate relationships, status achievement, learning of roles relevant to future marital relationships, assessment of compatibility, and provision of a context for affection and sexual experience.

Several researchers have studied dating relationships from the perspective of developmental (or life) tasks. For example, Sanderson and Cantor (1997) conceptualize social dating as an age-graded task which involves an interplay between the adolescent's personal goals and daily life experiences. According to this perspective, dispositional, situational and subcultural factors influence the extent to which adolescents pursue intimacy goals in their dating relationships. For example, those who have largely resolved their identity issues are likely to emphasize intimacy goals, as opposed to identity goals. These different goals, in turn, are associated with different preferences for dating: adolescents with strong intimacy goals prefer to be in steady dating relationships, whereas those pursuing identity goals prefer a series of casual relationships. Satisfaction and effective regulation of behaviour depend on being in a context conducive to goal fulfilment; hence, adolescents with strong intimacy goals generally report satisfaction in steady relationships, even if they have little experience of specific intimacy promoting situations (e.g., time spent alone with the partner).

Dowdy and Kliewer (1998) argue that the way in which adolescents deal with specific developmental tasks (such as dating) has implications for family conflict patterns and for the development of autonomy. These researchers examined the links of adolescent dating status, grade (10th and 12th graders, who were approximately 16 to 18 years of age), and gender to the frequency and intensity of parent–adolescent conflict and to adolescents' autonomy in decision-making. Higher levels of parent–adolescent conflict were reported by those who were currently dating, and this effect was stronger for females, for younger adolescents, and for those in relationships of shorter duration. Autonomy was higher for males and for those currently dating, with the latter effect being stronger for older adolescents. These results suggest that dating is a salient development that affects both adolescent and parent. Parents may try to increase their control over their offspring at this point, especially if dating activity is seen as involving a strong element of risk or a threat to parental authority. In this way, the increase in conflict over mundane matters seems to reflect underlying issues about power and control, together with parents' concern about the potential consequences of dating behaviour.

Becoming sexually active

From the perspective of dating as a developmental task, an important aspect of the task concerns establishing a sexual identity; that is, exploring one's sexual attitudes and standards, and negotiating one's involvement in sexual activity. These negotiations now take place in a different world from that of previous generations; there has been a lot of change in sexual attitudes and behaviours, related to such developments as improved contraception and increased concerns over sexually transmitted diseases. Data from several western countries indicate that first inter-course tends to occur at an earlier age than in the past, with the majority of young people becoming sexually active while still in their teens (Hartley and de Vaus, 1997; Small and Luster, 1994). Consistent with these figures, at least 80 per cent of male and 65 per cent of female college freshmen report some sexual experience (Cate and Lloyd, 1992). Recent Australian studies (e.g., Rosenthal and Moore, 1991) show similar results. The timing of first sexual experience has also changed in terms of its place in relationship development. Previously, premarital intercourse was likely to be restricted to engaged couples; now, it is likely to occur within 'steady' relationships.

Of course, not all adolescents begin sexual activity at the same relationship stage. Christopher and Cate (1985) identified four types of dating couples, defined by their retrospective reports of speed of involvement in mutual sexual activity. Rapid-involvement couples (7 per cent) had sex very early in the relationship, often having intercourse on the first date. Gradual-involvement couples (31 per cent) reported a steady increase in sexual involvement from first date, to casually dating, to 'becoming a couple'. As suggested by the descriptor, delayed-involvement couples (44 per cent) delayed engaging in high-involvement sexual activity until they perceived themselves to be a couple. Finally, low-involvement couples (17 per cent) were still not very intimate sexually, even when they regarded them-selves as a couple.

There are also gender differences in the point of sexual involvement: female teenagers tend to report that their first coital partner was a steady partner, but male teenagers are likely to report that their first intercourse occurred while dating casually (Christopher, 1996). For African-American and white adolescent females, involvement in sexual activity is related to the desire to please the 'steady' partner, to the inability to say 'no' to sexual overtures, and to the belief that sexual inter-course is expected of them. Further, adolescent females are more likely to engage in intercourse when their male partner makes the decisions as to whether intercourse will occur and what type of birth control (if any) is to be used (Christopher, 1996). In other words, females seem to be more vulnerable than males to the perceived role demands of the steady relationship.

This finding is part of a broader picture, in which consistent sex differences emerge across measures of sexual behaviour, attitudes and norms (De Gaston, Weed and Jensen, 1996). De Gaston *et al.* assessed sex differences in these measures among a sample of adolescents aged 12 to 15 years. Compared with males, females in this age group were less likely to report ever having had sex. They had less permissive sexual attitudes, reported greater commitment to abstinence, saw sexual activity as more detrimental to future goal attainment, saw teen parenthood as more of a problem, and were more likely to believe that sexual urges can be controlled. They also perceived less peer pressure for sex and more support for waiting, and viewed their parents as less approving of their potential involvement in sexual activity. In addition, females were more likely than males to discuss sex and dating practices with their parents.

There is also some evidence of ethnic and racial differences in sexual involvement. For example, in the United States, African-American and Hispanic adolescents in urban areas tend to show high levels of early sexual activity (Smith, 1997), although it is important to note that social class may be confounded with race and ethnicity. For adolescents in these samples, substance use and family stress were linked not only to earlier sexual activity but also to more risky sexual behaviour.

Sexual behaviour: decisions and dilemmas

Studies of differences in age of first sexual involvement raise questions about how adolescents decide when they are ready to have sex. Young people who are sexually inexperienced report different reasons for not having sex. Some believe that sexual intercourse should be reserved for marriage; that is, they endorse an abstinence standard that is often associated with family beliefs or with religious convictions. Others are open to the possibility of having sex, but report that they have not found the right partner, or have not been in the right situation. Similarly, young people cite different reasons for deciding to have sex for the first time. These include feelings of positivity and affection for the partner, physical arousal, obligation and pressure (from partner or from social norms), and contextual factors (involving alcohol or drugs, or perception of a 'special' event) (Sprecher and McKinney, 1993).

Given the problems associated with HIV/AIDS and other sexually transmitted diseases, many recent studies have explored the correlates of safe and unsafe sexual practice. Together, the results of these studies suggest that most young people are quite knowledgeable about sexually transmitted diseases (especially HIV/AIDS), but that knowledge is a poor predictor of safer sex behaviour. This finding can be explained by the fact that safe sex practice involves a complex decision-making process which requires skills in resisting peer pressure and in communicating with relationship partners. In other words, safe sex involves a sequence of behaviours, in which the learning of safe sex information has to be followed by involvement in presex discussion and negotiation with the partner (Boyer, 1990; Fisher and Fisher, 1992).

A study of adolescents aged between 14 and 19 years has revealed a variety of strategies used to promote sexual encounters (Eyre, Read and Millstein, 1997). In this study, both sexes reported using strategies that communicated commitment and investment. However, males were more likely to mention strategies involving coercion (pressuring, raping), and manipulation (lying, getting a partner drunk or high), and females were more likely to mention strategies signalling sexual avail-ability. There appear to be developmental trends in the strategies used to promote sexual encounters, with adolescents mentioning fewer strategies than adults usually report.

The types of coercive strategies discussed by Eyre *et al.* have been the focus of a large amount of research. There is evidence that the incidence of 'date rape' among adolescents is similar to that among college students, and higher than in other age groups (Koss, 1993). In addition, data from several western countries (e.g., Goodchilds *et al.*, 1988; O'Connor, 1992; Patton and Mannison, 1995) indicate that many adolescents endorse rape-supportive attitudes. That is, they state that forced sexual intercourse is acceptable under certain circumstances; for example, if the male spends a lot of money on the female, if she is stoned or drunk, and if she has had intercourse with other males. The meaning of coercive attitudes and behaviours may vary for different individuals. In a sample of adolescents with behaviour problems (Chase *et al.*, 1998), males' aggression towards dating partners (and its justification) were part of a generalized pattern of dating aggression; in contrast, females' physical aggression was generally partner-specific.

In discussing adolescent sexuality it is important not to overstate the prevalence of problem behaviours. In a review of Australian studies of sexual norms and behaviours, for example, Collins (1993) highlighted the complexity of the messages about sexuality that impinge upon adolescents. According to Collins, Australian adolescents are more sexually conservative than might be assumed from media reports. Although there has clearly been an increased acceptance of premarital sexual intercourse, studies of sexual attitudes and behaviours indicate that most adolescents do not condone promiscuity. Adolescents of all ages form committed, caring relationships, and high levels of sexual intimacy are usually accompanied by high levels of affectional intimacy.

Conflict and jealousy

Sexuality is not the only area in which young people are likely to strike conflict in their romantic relationships. As couple relationships develop, many issues of disagreement may arise. Some of these issues will stem from partners' differing backgrounds, and involve differences in personality, attitudes and values. In addition, negotiation of the couple relationship may be hampered by disagreements about how much time should be given to the relationship, and how much commitment is expected. Such disagreements reflect the ongoing tension between needs for connection and needs for autonomy (the 'Me–We Pull'; Baxter, 1990). In fact, this dilemma has been seen as the central 'contradiction' in relating: too much autonomy can lead to distancing between the partners, but too much connection can stifle individuality.

Related to these issues of commitment and expectations, jealousy sometimes becomes a problem. Jealousy has been defined as 'an aversive emotional reaction evoked by a relationship involving one's current or former partner and a third person' (Buunk and Bringle, 1987, p. 124). Jealousy is a response to a perceived threat to the relationship, and is more likely to arise when one partner is highly emotionally dependent. Feelings of jealousy can be quite overwhelming, and because of their intensity, can cause serious arguments between partners (Buunk and Bringle, 1987). Ironically, jealous behaviour may bring about the very outcome that the jealous partner fears most – the loss of the relationship.

It is important to note that responses to jealousy and other conflict issues vary widely in terms of outcome. For example, refusing to discuss an issue limits the possibility of that issue being resolved, and may create resentment in the aggrieved partner. Dominating, and acting coercively, are also likely to be destructive; these behaviours may lead to the person 'getting their way' in the short term, but may undermine or even destroy the relationship in the long term. In contrast, being open and honest about conflict issues gives each person a chance to express their feelings and opinions, and is more likely to lead to a satisfactory resolution of the issues at hand.

Linking experiences in family and romantic relationships

As we have already seen, some adolescent dating relationships are supportive and affectionate, whereas others are coercive or manipulative. This observation raises important questions about the origin of difficulties in romantic relationships. A large body of research suggests that individuals who experience poor relationships with their parents and between their parents tend to develop romantic relationships that are less happy and less stable. This phenomenon is known as 'intergenerational transmission' of relationship difficulties. Although there is substantial support for the concept of intergenerational transmission (e.g., Feldman, 1997; Harvey, Curry and Bray, 1991), the mechanisms underlying this pattern are quite complex (Amato, 1996; Caspi and Elder, 1988). For example, both social learning and attachment principles can be used to explain how children translate the messages transmitted by parents into interpersonal behaviours used in peer interactions.

With regard to social learning, theorists have argued that parents act as role models for the relationship behaviour that children enact with peers. Parents who consistently engage in aggression or avoidance provide powerful models of these negative behaviours; further, they may fail to provide models for the supportive and affectionate behaviours that are vital to maintaining relationships. Cross-sectional studies provide indirect evidence of modelling of family conflict patterns. For example, Martin (1990) assessed links between marital conflict, parent–adolescent conflict, and conflict between the adolescent offspring and their romantic partners. Marital conflict was related to aggressive and avoidant patterns of parent–adolescent conflict, and these patterns were similar to those used in conflict with romantic partners. Social learning processes are not confined to the direct effects of modelling; rather, parents also transmit ways of thinking about close relationships, which have indirect effects on the bonds that their children form later in life. Hence, conflicted parental relationships may contribute to offspring's dysfunctional thinking about relationships.

According to the attachment perspective, parents who have experienced disruptions in their own childhood attachment bonds tend to have difficulty in establishing stable romantic bonds, and in providing a secure base for their children (Benoit and Parker, 1994; Weiss, 1991). In this way, attachment insecurity may be transmitted across generations. (This represents another indirect effect of one generation on another.) Consistent with these claims, adolescents with weaker attachment to their parents are prone to a range of adjustment difficulties.

Rice (1990) conducted a meta-analysis of 30 studies investigating the link between attachment in adolescence and adjustment difficulties, published between 1975 and 1990. Supporting the argument that the offspring of insecure parents are prone to relationship difficulties, the meta-analysis showed a reliable association of secure attachment with measures of emotional and social adjustment. By contrast, attachment to parents was not linked with measures of academic adjustment. Almost all of the studies analysed by Rice assessed attachment using a single index of quality of attachment to parents. As we discuss in the next section, researchers have also begun to study individual differences in attachment to romantic partners.

Conceptualizing romantic bonds as attachments

In Chapter 2 we discussed the work of Bowlby, Ainsworth and others, on the attachment bonds that form between young children and their caregivers. Although Bowlby focused on childhood attachment, he regarded the attachment system as playing a crucial role in social and emotional development across the lifespan. Similarly, Ainsworth (1989) and Weiss (1986, 1991) have argued that the key functions of attachment behaviour (proximity seeking, separation protest, secure base, and safe haven) apply to some relationships involving adolescent or adult partners. Indeed, this argument is central to Hazan and Zeifman's (1994) studies investigating the transfer of attachment functions from parents to peers.

A key tenet of attachment theory is that early interactions with parents lead to the formation of 'mental models' of attachment, which reflect children's perceptions of their own self-worth and their expectations about the responsiveness of others. These mental models are carried forward into later relationships, where they guide emotional, cognitive and behavioural responses to relationship events (Collins and Read, 1994).

If mental models influence responses to relationship events, and if peers come to serve as attachment figures in adolescence, it would not be surprising if individual differences in attachment style could be observed in adolescent and adult relationships, as well as in relationships between infants and their caregivers. This perspective on romantic relationships was first tested by Hazan and Shaver (1987). These researchers reported two studies of romantic love, one using a broad sample (ranging in age from 14 to 82), the other using a sample of undergraduates. Although these samples were not restricted to adolescents, it is important to discuss them at this point, as they laid the foundation for studies into individual differences in romantic attachment style.

To assess attachment style, Hazan and Shaver used a simple three-paragraph measure designed to capture the features of the major attachment styles (secure, avoidant, anxious-ambivalent), which they extrapolated from studies of infant attachment. Participants were asked to choose the paragraph that best described their feelings in close relationships, and to complete questionnaires assessing aspects of relationships in childhood and beyond. The three groups defined by this measure of attachment style differed in their reports of early family relations, beliefs about love relationships, and love experiences (see Table 3.5 for a summary of results).

Hazan and Shaver's studies have generated a huge amount of research into romantic attachment. One reason for this interest probably lies in the intuitive appeal and simplicity of the attachment typology. However, the attachment perspective does offer some important advantages over previous approaches to the study of love and romance. It is grounded in theory, in contrast to many earlier studies that focused on specific forms of love. The attachment perspective is also integrative, in several senses: it is developmental in nature (that is, it links romantic love with early social experiences); it explains both healthy and unhealthy forms of love; and it encompasses related concepts such as grief and loneliness.

Romantic attachment: further evidence

Hazan and Shaver's studies were soon followed by reports from other researchers, involving replications and extensions of their work. Most of this work has been conducted with samples of late adolescents (especially first-year college students). However, for ease of presentation, these studies of romantic attachment in dating relationships will be included here; the issue of attachment in marriage is taken up in Chapter 4 (in relation to newly-weds), and in Chapter 5 (in relation to mature marriage).

TABLE 3.5 *Characteristics of the three major attachment groups*

	Secure	Avoidant	Anxious-ambivalent
Major themes of the paragraph being endorsed	Ease and comfort with closeness and interdependence; lack of anxiety about close relationships	Discomfort with closeness; distrust; difficulty in depending on others	Desire for extreme closeness; anxieties about being unloved and being abandoned
Perceptions of early family relationships	Relationships with parents and between parents described as affectionate and caring	Mothers described as cold and rejecting	Fathers described as unfair
Mental models of self, others and romantic love	Easy to know; few self-doubts; liked by others; others well-intentioned; love seen as lasting	Love seen as not lasting; love loses its intensity; rare to find someone you can love	Many self-doubts; misunderstood; frequently fall in love; real love seen as rare; others less willing to commit
Characteristics of own experiences of romantic love	Happy; trusting; friendly; acceptance of partner	Fear of closeness; low acceptance of partner	Obsession; jealousy; strong sexual attraction; emotional highs and lows; desire for union

The implications of attachment style for the quality of romantic relationships in late adolescence have been studied by Simpson (1990), Collins and Read (1990), and Feeney and Noller (1990), among others. These studies have consistently linked secure attachment with higher levels of trust, commitment and relationship satisfaction, and with more open communication. Avoidant attachment has been related to low levels of interdependence and trust, and anxious-ambivalent attachment has been related to jealousy and to low levels of trust and satisfaction.

Another early study of romantic attachment investigated the salience of attachment-related issues for young dating couples (Feeney and Noller, 1991). These researchers noted that previous studies in this area had relied mainly on questionnaire measures of attachment style. These measures are prone to the problem of experimenter demand; attachment-related issues may not feature in young people's relationship thinking, unless primed by researchers' questions. Feeney and Noller (1991) addressed this problem by asking first-year students to give open-ended accounts of their current dating relationships. Most respondents spontaneously talked about attachment-related issues such as closeness and affection, often discussing the issues at length. Further, the content of their accounts was related to Hazan and Shaver's (1987) measure of attachment style, which was completed two weeks later. Secure respondents tended to seek a balance between autonomy and interdependence in their relationships. Avoidant individuals tried to maintain interpersonal distance, sometimes accusing partners of being 'clingy', 'pressuring', or 'wanting to be joined at the hip'. In contrast, anxious-ambivalent individuals showed signs of falling in love very readily ('I seemed to know him immediately'), and overdependence ('If we spend more than a day apart, I go haywire'). See Table 3.6 for additional extracts from members of the different attachment groups.

A more recent study (Cooper, Shaver and Collins, 1998) extended research on romantic attachment styles to a large North American community sample of adolescents aged between 13 and 19 years. This study explored the relations between attachment styles, emotional regulation and adjustment. Both secure and avoidant adolescents reported fewer risky behaviours (educational underachievement,

TABLE 3.6 *Extracts from open-ended reports of romantic relationships supplied by subjects from the three attachment groups*

Secure We're really good friends, and we sort of knew each other for a long time before we started going out – and we like the same sort of things. Another thing which I like a lot is that he gets on well with all my close friends. We can always talk things over. Like if we're having any fights, we usually resolve them by talking it over – he's a very reasonable person. I can just be my own person, so it's good, because it's not a possessive relationship. I think that we trust each other a lot.

Avoidant My partner is my best friend, and that's the way I think of him. He's as special to me as any of my other friends. His expectations in life don't include marriage, or any long-term commitment to any female, which is fine with me, because that's not what my expectations are as well. I find that he doesn't want to be overly intimate, and he doesn't expect too much commitment – which is good . . . We're very close – it's a kind of a comfort, but sometimes it's a worry – that a person can be that close to you, and be in such control of your life.

Anxious-ambivalent So I went in there . . . and he was sitting on the bench, and I took one look, and I actually melted. He was the best-looking thing I'd ever seen, and that was the first thing that struck me about him. So we went out and we had lunch in the park . . . so we just sort of sat there – and in silence – but it wasn't awkward . . . like, you know, when you meet strangers and you can't think of anything to say, it's usually awkward. It wasn't like that. We just sat there, and it was incredible – like we'd known each other for a real long time, and we'd only met for about ten seconds, so that was – straightaway my first feelings for him started coming out.

Source: From Feeney and Noller, 1991. Copyright © 1991. Reprinted by permission of Sage Publications, Inc.

delinquency, substance use and sexual activity) than anxious-ambivalent adolescents. However, the secure and avoidant groups differed in terms of psychological symptoms and self-concept, with the secure group showing better adjustment. Anxious-ambivalent adolescents showed the worst adjustment (marked by poor self-concept, and high levels of symptoms and risky behaviours). The high incidence of problem behaviours among members of this group was explained, in part, by their levels of depression and hostility. Although the effects of attachment style generally held up across age, gender and racial group, some results highlighted the need to consider the combined effects of these variables. For example, anxious-ambivalent females showed especially high levels of depression, anxiety and sexual activity.

Other studies have suggested new ways of conceptualizing and measuring romantic attachment styles. For example, Bartholomew (1990) and Bartholomew and Horowitz (1991) proposed a four-group attachment typology, based on Bowlby's concept of working models of self and others. The attachment styles described in this typology are secure, preoccupied (cf. anxious-ambivalent), dismissing avoidant (characterized by a devaluation and down-playing of close relationships), and fearful avoidant (marked by distrust and fear of rejection). Another important development involves identifying the major dimensions underlying attachment styles: comfort with closeness and anxiety over relationships (Feeney and Noller, 1996). Regardless of the measures used, studies of romantic attachment point to the importance of attachment styles as predictors of relationship behaviour and other aspects of adjustment.

Summary and Conclusions

Adolescence is a time when young people being to loosen their ties to their families, and to focus much more on the peer group. During this period they begin in same-sex cliques, move to mixed-sex crowds, and finally end up as groups of couples in late adolescence. Part of this process involves the gradual transfer of attachment functions from parents to peers, a process that usually culminates in the establishment of long-term romantic relationships. In these relationships, the romantic partner would normally be relied on to meet needs for comfort and security.

Adolescents tend to experience emotional highs and lows, and are generally much more emotional about everyday experiences than their parents are. They also report experiencing a lot of social discomfort, and are likely to demand high levels of privacy. The time they spend alone, however, seems to have recuperative value, and may provide an important balance to the pressures of adapting to the peer group.

The family, however, remains an important influence, and adolescents seem to need 'the secure base' of a constructive and healthy relationship with their parents. Positive family relationships, which provide appropriate monitoring and consistent enforcement of rules, minimize the possibility of adolescents becoming involved in antisocial activities or substance abuse. Conversely, high levels of parent–child conflict have been linked with high levels of these problem behaviours. Thus, adolescence can be a difficult time for both parents and offspring. However, the successful negotiation of this stage equips the young person for dealing with the many tasks of adulthood.

4

Early Adulthood

Becoming an Adult

Before we discuss the relationship experiences and challenges of young adults it is important to think about the nature of the transition to 'adulthood'. What does it mean to become an adult? This question is not easy to answer, because the transition to adulthood tends to be seen differently by different cultures and at different points in time.

In two recent studies of young people (aged between 18 and 28 years) in the United States, Arnett (1997) found that the most commonly endorsed criteria for being an 'adult' focused on aspects of individualism. For example, young people in these samples emphasized the importance of adults taking responsibility for the consequences of their actions, deciding on their own beliefs and values, and establishing a more equality-based relationship with their parents. Specific role transitions, such as entering the workforce, getting married, and becoming parents, were generally seen as less important markers of adulthood. However, as we have already noted, perceptions of adulthood depend in part on the culture being studied; even within a particular country, the importance of individualism during the transition to adulthood may depend on racial and ethnic group (Oyserman, Gant and Ager, 1995).

Moreover, the increasing emphasis on individualism in early adulthood does not negate the importance of close relationships. Adults' self-definition is relational in nature (Gergen, 1991). In other words, young adults define themselves as individuals, in large part, by assessing how they relate to others (including their parents). In this way, relationship issues are an integral part of the transition to adulthood. Indeed, in Arnett's (1997) studies, more than half of the sample considered that essential aspects of adulthood included the ability to run a household and ensure the safety of family; one-third of the sample considered 'making lifelong commitments to others' as an essential aspect.

In comparison to previous generations, those undergoing the transition to adulthood in recent times face more extended periods of education and higher levels of unemployment (these trends apply in many countries; see also Chapter 3). Related to these trends, there has been an increase in the proportion of young adults who still live with their parents (Cordon, 1997). Given these demographic patterns, it is important to consider the nature and impact of young adults' parental relationships.

The Importance of Relationships with Parents

As we mentioned earlier in this chapter, young adults generally strive to establish more equal relationships with their parents. It could be argued that this striving for equality might be made more difficult by the increasing period of financial dependence on parents. However, a recent study of French youth suggests that the extended stay of young adults within the family setting is not generally associated with problematic parent–child relationships; young women, in particular, usually succeed in maintaining (or even improving) their relationships with their parents (Galland, 1997).

The continuing importance of young adults' parental relationships is supported by other research studies. For example, a large-scale longitudinal study of families in the United States (Thornton, Orbuch and Axinn, 1995) involved researchers interviewing parents and their children during the offspring's late adolescence (at age 18) and early adulthood (at age 23). Parents and offspring tended to see their relationships somewhat differently; for example, mothers reported more enjoyment of joint activities than their offspring did. Nevertheless, both generations generally saw parent–child relationships (especially relationships with mothers) as positive and supportive. There was strong continuity in the quality of individual relationships across the course of the study; in other words, young people with positive parental relationships in the teenage years tended to have positive relationships later. However, the overall quality of parent–child relationships improved substantially as the children passed through the transition to adulthood, with respondents reporting increased respect, enjoyment, understanding and affection.

Similarly, another large-scale longitudinal survey of American parents across their children's transition to adulthood supports the presence of both stability and change in parent–child relationships (Aquilino, 1997). Emotional closeness and level of conflict were fairly stable over this period, suggesting that past relationship patterns tend to persist as the offspring become adults. However, as we would expect, other aspects of family relationships changed as the offspring adopted adult roles. For example, as the children left home to live independently, there tended to be a decrease in conflict and power issues with parents, but also a decrease in shared leisure time.

The importance of parent–child relationships in young adulthood is highlighted by research linking experiences in these relationships with the offspring's long-term adjustment. In a 20-year follow-up of a sample recruited during early adulthood (aged 16 to 26), those young adults whose relationships with parents were high in feelings of closeness and understanding showed higher self-esteem at the later time (Roberts and Bengtson, 1996). This finding suggests that relationships with parents play an important role in fostering a sense of self-worth, which, in turn, is likely to be associated with positive attitudes and behaviours in a wide range of relationship contexts.

Sibling Relationships

Other family relationships are also important in the lives of young adults. In an analysis of the developmental tasks involved in sibling relationships, Goetting (1986) argued that siblings provide emotional support and companionship over the entire lifespan. Consistent with this claim, most adult siblings, despite their reduced physical proximity, continue to communicate with each other and to share visits and recreational activities (Cicirelli, 1995).

Changes in patterns of sibling involvement across the life cycle are rather contentious (see Chapter 6 for a discussion of sibling relationships in old age). In the absence of longitudinal research on the sibling bond across the adult age range, conclusions have to be based on cross-sectional and retrospective studies (Cicirelli, 1995). The most consistent finding from these studies is that the frequency of contact between siblings decreases in early adulthood (Cicirelli, 1995). This change is likely to result from factors such as geographic mobility, and individuals' increasing involvement with paid employment and household responsibilities.

There is less consensus concerning changes in the emotional tone of sibling relationships. With regard to negative emotion, self-report studies generally show a decrease in sibling rivalry and competitiveness in early adulthood. However, studies using clinical interviews and projective techniques suggest that many adults continue to feel sibling rivalry, and that attempts to repair rivalrous sibling relationships are often not made until later adulthood (Ross and Milgram, 1982). The experience of positive emotion in sibling relationships is also poorly understood. Although some studies have suggested that feelings of closeness and affection towards siblings decrease in early adulthood, others have reported that such feelings increase, or remain relatively stable (Cicirelli, 1995).

These mixed findings concerning emotional experience probably reflect two factors. First, different researchers have used different measures and samples, making it difficult to compare results. Second, the emotional tone of sibling relationships is affected by individual life events (Connidis, 1992). For example, the marriage of one sibling tends to be linked with reports of changes in the sibling relationship. These changes can be either positive or negative, depending on such variables as family members' acceptance of the sibling's spouse. Having children is also linked with changes in the sibling relationship. These changes typically include reports of more positive feelings between siblings, but also decreased contact; again, the reduced contact seems to reflect the increasing responsibilities and demands of adult life.

Understanding differences in sibling relationships

Young adults' sibling relationships are affected not only by individual life events but also by gender, and by racial and ethnic factors. In terms of gender, most studies do not find strong gender differences in adults' overall feelings of closeness to siblings. However, young men and women may experience and express closeness to their siblings in different ways (Floyd, 1995). For example, women in Floyd's study were more likely than men to regard talking to their siblings about personal issues as an indicator of closeness; men were more likely to associate closeness with talking about sexual issues. In cross-sex sibling relationships, women considered doing favours for each other and 'hanging out' together as more important indicators of closeness than did men.

Racial and ethnic differences in adult sibling relationships have been reported by researchers such as Riedmann and White (1996), who conducted a large-scale interview study of African, Hispanic, Asian and Anglo American groups. (This study was not restricted to young adults, but cohabiting and newly married people were oversampled.) The survey did not suggest that one racial or ethnic group had stronger sibling bonds, overall, than any other. However, the groups differed on some dimensions: African-American and Hispanic adults were more likely than other groups to live with their siblings; Asian-Americans showed a high willingness to call on their siblings, despite physical distance; and Anglo-Americans reported high levels of actual social support from siblings.

Researchers have also tried to establish whether adult sibling relationships can be classified into a small number of discrete types. A recent study focusing on younger adults (Stewart, Verbrugge and Beilfuss, 1998) identified four types of sibling dyads, defined primarily by differences on measures of warmth (similarity, intimacy, affection, admiration, support, acceptance, knowledge and contact). These groups were labelled Caretaker (high on all measures of warmth), Buddy (high on warmth, but not as high as Caretakers on emotional support, admiration or affection), Casual (low on all measures of warmth), and Loyal or Unresolved (moderate on most measures of warmth, but high on intimacy, acceptance and knowledge). Group status was related to reports of rivalry (specifically, maternal favouritism): perceptions that one's sibling was favoured were related to Casual status for older siblings and to Caretaker status for younger siblings. These findings are subject to the same limitations as all typologies, in that they describe individual differences in very simple terms. However, they support other research in showing the importance of warmth and rivalry as dimensions of sibling relationships, and the effects of perceived parental favouritism on these variables.

Do siblings serve as attachment figures for young adults?

Recent interest in adult attachment theory has prompted researchers to ask whether the sibling relationships of young adults can be conceptualized as attachment

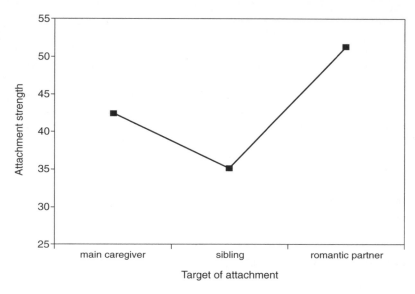

FIGURE 4.1 Strength of attachment to siblings and other targets

relationships (Cicirelli, 1985, 1995; Hazan and Shaver, 1994). As we have already seen, sibling relationships serve a number of developmental functions (including emotional support) across the lifespan. Hence, it is plausible that bonds between adult siblings may qualify as attachments.

Two recent questionnaire studies of young adult samples support this suggestion. In a study of Australian university students, Feeney and Humphreys (1996) found that many participants rated their siblings as important figures in terms of providing closeness, comfort and security, although they generally rated parents and romantic partners even more highly (see Figure 4.1). This finding suggests that adult siblings can serve the functions of proximity seeking, safe haven and secure base, which have been identified as the key functions of attachment relationships (see Chapters 2 and 3). A study of Canadian university students (Trinke and Bartholomew, 1997) supported these findings. In terms of overall strength of attachment, siblings ranked above best friends, but behind partners and parents. Expert judges who examined the response patterns classed 58 per cent of participants as being 'attached' to at least one sibling; for 8 per cent of participants a sibling was the primary attachment figure. In short, it seems that siblings can be important sources of comfort and security for young adults. The strength of sibling attachments may depend on the quality of attachments to parents and romantic partners, but this question requires further research.

Living Together

Despite the continuing importance of parental and sibling relationships, romantic partners clearly become central in the lives of young adults. Using an interview technique, Hazan and Zeifman (1994) showed that adolescents gradually came to rely on friends and romantic partners, rather than parents, to fulfil their attachment needs (that is, needs for closeness, comfort and security; see Chapter 3). In addition, adults with relatively long-term romantic partners generally relied on their partners to fulfil their attachment needs, whereas other adults reported turning either to friends or parents (or to romantic partners if they had them). Similarly, Fraley and Davis (1997) found that the extent to which romantic partners were used as attachment figures increased with the length of the relationship, and that partners in relationships of two years' duration and longer generally served as primary attachment figures.

Cohabitation: a new stage of the life cycle

Although romantic partners are extremely important at this stage of the life cycle, young adults often choose to live with their partners, rather than (or prior to) getting married. In fact, Cate and Lloyd (1992, p. 30) described cohabitation as 'a new stage of the courtship system'. Consistent with this claim, recent data from several western countries (Australia, Britain and the United States) show that more than 50 per cent of those who marry have lived with their partner prior to the marriage; this pattern represents a dramatic change from only 30 years ago, when the corresponding figures ranged from 10–20 per cent (de Vaus, 1997a; Newman and Smith, 1997).

Cohabitation is particularly common among younger adults. For example, recent Australian data show that almost three-quarters of very young couples who live together (those with one or both partners aged under 20 years) are cohabiting, rather than married; in contrast, only one in ten couples with partners aged in their early thirties are cohabiting (de Vaus, 1997a). Similarly, in Britain the peak age for cohabiting is from 20 to 24 years for women, and from 25 to 29 years for men (Newman and Smith, 1997). These cross-sectional data may reflect a cohort effect (i.e., couples born more recently may be more accepting of cohabitation), or a developmental effect (couples may tend to move from cohabitation into marriage as they become older), or both. There is certainly a growing acceptance of cohabitation, although most people see cohabitation as a postponement of marriage, rather than an ongoing alternative to it (Cunningham and Antill, 1994; de Vaus, 1997a).

Unmarried cohabitation exists in a number of different forms or types, which vary in their structure and purpose. Sarantakos (1992) has distinguished between three main types of cohabitation. The one most relevant to young adults is 'trial cohabitation', which is mainly preferred by young people, and is seen as a prelude

TABLE 4.1 *Sample statements used to assess attitudes towards cohabitation*

- It is all right for a couple to live together without intending to get married.
- It is a good idea for a couple who intend to get married to live together first.
- The law should treat de facto couples the same as married couples.
- It is all right to have children without being married.
- Trial marriage is an appropriate preparation for a lifelong relationship.

to marriage. Other types identified by Sarantakos are liberal cohabitation (preferred by well-established persons who hold a strong anti-marriage ideology), and de facto relationships (entered into primarily for economic reasons).

Why is cohabitation relatively popular among young adults? A number of surveys of attitudes towards cohabitation have been conducted (e.g., Evans, 1991; see Table 4.1 for examples of the types of questions asked in these studies). Results of the surveys suggest that there is a widespread belief that cohabitation before marriage is beneficial for couples. This finding seems to reflect a number of more specific beliefs: for example, that living together results in a more egalitarian relationship, and that it erodes unrealistic illusions about the partner (and hence assists in the process of mate selection). There appear to be some gender differences in beliefs about cohabitation, however, with men being more likely than women to emphasize the advantages of retaining independence and limiting commitment (Glezer, 1991). These gender differences in beliefs may cause problems for some cohabiting couples, especially if women are unaware of their tendency to hold more romantic and dependent attitudes.

Quality of cohabiting relationships

Are cohabiting relationships really more egalitarian than marriages? There is mixed support for this belief. Cunningham and Antill (1994) reported a study of young adults' relationship status, which combined retrospective and prospective methods. In the retrospective component, couples who had cohabited before marriage differed in several ways from those who had not: for example, the former reported more permissive sexual attitudes and less traditional division of labour. In the prospective component, those who continued to cohabit also differed from those who went on to marry: the former reported less equal interest in sex, lower levels of love for their partner, and less traditional division of labour. Although these results suggest that couples who cohabit may strive particularly hard at establishing equitable patterns of household work, a series of studies by Sarantakos (1991) did not find greater egalitarianism in cohabiting than in marital relationships.

It is also important to note that the long-term outcomes of cohabiting relationships are not necessarily positive. In particular, given that most young adults who live together plan to marry at some point in their lives, the possible effect of prior cohabitation on marital success is an important issue. Studies show that cohabiting before marriage is associated with a substantially higher probability of divorce. This finding is robust, being reported across samples from several western countries (Bumpass, Sweet and Cherlin, 1991; DeMaris and Rao, 1992; Glezer, 1992; Lilliard, Brien and Waite, 1995).

The reasons behind this effect are likely to be complex. In fact, it is not clear whether the effect is causal, or whether it reflects selection factors. For example, those who do *not* cohabit before marriage may come from particular religious and ethnic backgrounds which also discourage marital breakdown. Conversely, those who do cohabit may have less commitment to the partner, may make less effort to maintain their relationships, or may adapt less readily to the role expectations of traditional marriage. Alternatively, or in addition, some couples who have been living together may marry in an attempt to save a relationship that is already showing signs of distress. Finally, many couples enter into cohabiting relationships quite quickly, and such rapid involvement may signal a 'needy' approach to relationships and a lack of sound decision-making. For example, one study has shown that one-fifth of those in cohabiting relationships had been in those relationships for three months or less before moving in together (Glezer, 1991).

Researchers have also been interested in the long-term psychological adjustment of those involved in cohabiting relationships. Horowitz and White (1998), for example, reported on a large sample of young unmarried adults in the United States who were first sampled between the ages of 18 and 24, and surveyed again seven years later. At the later time, the researchers compared the mental health of three groups: those who were married, those who were cohabiting, and those who had remained single. The groups did not differ in levels of depression, but cohabitation was associated with more problems with alcohol, even when initial level of adjustment was statistically controlled. Together, the various findings discussed in this section tend to challenge the assumption that premarital cohabitation is an unequivocally positive factor in individual and relationship development.

Marriage

Given that contemporary young adults are more likely to be involved in cohabiting relationships than in the past, it is not surprising that they are tending to marry at a later age. Again, this trend has been observed in several western countries, as shown by Table 4.2. Most of the figures for 1997 represent a delay of about four years in median age at first marriage, in comparison with data from just two decades earlier.

Studies of courtship patterns, however, show marked differences in couples' pathways to marriage. For example, Cate and Lloyd (1992) describe three major pathways, defined in terms of couples' retrospective reports of their 'chance of marriage' at each month throughout their courtship. These patterns were labelled 'prolonged' (marked by a slow, up-and-down progression), 'accelerated' (moving quickly to a high degree of commitment) and 'intermediate' (moving relatively

TABLE 4.2 *Median age at first marriage in 1997 and 1977, in three western countries*

	Men		Women	
	1997	*1977*	*1997*	*1977*
Australia	27.8	23.8	25.9	21.4
England and Wales	28.6	23.8	26.7	21.5
United States	26.8	24.0	25.0	21.6

slowly in the early stages, then showing a moderate increase in commitment). These different courtship patterns were linked to diverse factors such as age at meeting, parents' attitudes towards the relationship, and the degree of conflict and ambivalence within the relationship.

Similar findings have emerged from a recent survey of perceptions of readiness for marriage in a large sample of young adults (Holman and Li, 1997). Respondents in this study were asked to rate how ready they felt they were for marriage (not necessarily marriage to any specific partner) in terms of emotional, sexual, financial, and overall feelings. This combined measure of readiness was related to demographic characteristics (education, income and age), approval of the relationship from significant others, the quality of couple communication, and the extent of couple agreement. Satisfaction with relationships in the family of origin did not have a direct effect on readiness for marriage, but predicted readiness indirectly through such variables as approval of significant others and quality of couple communication. Again, these results show the continuing influence of family-of-origin experiences on adults' relationship attitudes and behaviours. This influence probably reflects multiple mechanisms, including observational learning, and the effects of the expectations that are embodied in working models of attachment.

The concept of 'readiness for marriage' implies a growing sense of commitment to the relationship. In fact, it could be argued that commitment is a central distinction between cohabiting relationships and marriages. Several researchers have developed theoretical models of commitment processes. For example, Rusbult and Buunk (1993) analyse commitment processes in close relationships in terms of the investment model. In this model, they argue that commitment becomes stronger not only because of increasing satisfaction but also because alternatives to the relationship are seen as less attractive, and important resources (including time, energy and money) have been invested in that relationship. As well as increasing the probability that partners will stay together through hard times (Kelley, 1983), commitment promotes behaviours that are important to the growth and maintenance of the relationship (e.g., dealing with conflicts as they arise; spending time together).

Predicting satisfaction in early marriage

Despite their explicit commitment to their relationships, young couples are not immune to the problems of marital distress. Current figures from several western countries (Australia, Great Britain and the United States) indicate that marriages are much more likely to break down during the first ten years than during any other period (de Vaus, 1997b; Newman and Smith, 1997). Furthermore, these surveys show that the rate of early separation is higher for more recent marriages, and for those in which the partners married as teenagers. Hence, a substantial number of couples face marital dissolution in their twenties or early thirties. (Separation and divorce are discussed in more detail in Chapter 5.) The importance of individual differences in marital satisfaction is also highlighted by longitudinal data which show that young adults' marital happiness predicts their later sense of general well-being (Ruvolo, 1998).

What factors best explain the differing levels of marital happiness which exist even in the earliest years of marriage? Not surprisingly, this question has been a major focus of studies of young married couples. The most consistent finding to emerge from these studies is the important role of couple communication and understanding.

For example, longitudinal studies of newly-wed couples in the United States have linked marital satisfaction to perceived similarity and understanding of partner (Acitelli, Douvan and Veroff, 1993, 1997), and to problem-solving behaviour (Cohan and Bradbury, 1997). In the study by Acitelli *et al.* (1997), the researchers found that, over time, satisfaction was predicted more strongly by perceptions of constructive acts and less strongly by perceptions of destructive acts. It seems that, as couples come to face the inevitable instances of conflict and disagreement in their relationship, positive acts become very important as a buffer against feelings of negativity. The importance of both positive and negative aspects of communication is supported by Cohan and Bradbury's study, in which wives' marital adjustment was predicted by both positive verbal behaviours and expressions of anger. These results also highlight the key role of emotional expressiveness in marriage.

Similarly, a two-year study of young Australian married couples (Feeney, Noller and Callan, 1994; Noller *et al.*, 1994) has linked marital satisfaction with a range of communication behaviours. Communication patterns were linked with both concurrent and later marital satisfaction, although the predictors of later satisfaction were somewhat different for husbands and wives. For wives, later satisfaction was predicted by less negativity and disengagement during conflict, and by diary-based reports of constructive and satisfying day-to-day communication; for husbands, later satisfaction was predicted by high self-disclosure and low conflict in day-to-day communication.

An interesting finding emerging from these studies concerns the relative stability of communication measures across the early years of marriage. Acitelli *et al.* (1997) found that spouses' perceptions of each other were quite stable over the three-year period of their study. Similarly, Noller *et al.* (1994) found that communication patterns in response to conflict were relatively stable over the first two years of marriage. These results suggest that many marital problems have their roots in destructive behaviours that are present at the time of marriage. The importance of ongoing problems is also highlighted by the fact that many conflicts which appear to involve specific topics are actually driven by underlying issues of power and control. Power differences between partners tend to make conflicts more difficult to resolve, and are also linked to marital unhappiness (Cahn, 1990).

Another way of understanding marital conflict is provided by the dialectical perspective, which argues that personal relationships are marked by the presence of opposing relational forces, pertaining to desired levels of closeness, openness and novelty (Baxter and Montgomery, 1996). In other words, personal relationships require both connection and autonomy, both openness and closedness, both novelty and predictability. Partners are likely to differ in terms of their preferred balance on these dimensions, but this balance can also fluctuate over time, as individuals mature and their relationships develop. Particularly in a close relationship like marriage, it is important for couples to work out ways to manage these contra-dictions. Noller, Feeney and Blakeley-Smith (2000) had spouses report on the extent of difference between them and their partners on these three contradictions, and found that greater differences were related to lower levels of relationship satisfaction.

Attachment styles are also important in explaining differences in marital happiness, as shown by recent research (see Chapter 3 for a discussion of attachment styles and dating relationships, and Chapter 5 for a discussion of attachment in mature marriage). For example, the two-year study by Feeney, Noller and Callan (1994) included scales measuring comfort with closeness and anxiety over relationships (the major dimensions of adult attachment). Secure attachment was linked to concurrent satisfaction for both husbands and wives, and there were significant longitudinal effects for husbands: husbands' insecurity predicted later marital dissatisfaction, but dissatisfaction also predicted later insecurity. The latter finding is important, because it supports attachment theorists' claims that relationship experiences (in this case, negative experiences) can lead to a revision of working models.

Another study linking secure attachment with marital satisfaction (across all stages of the marital life cycle) showed interactive effects of partners' attachment styles, for young couples only (Feeney, 1994). Among these couples the negative effects of wives' relationship anxiety were particularly marked when husbands were low in comfort with closeness (that is, not comfortable with high levels of intimacy and mutual dependence). This finding suggests that in young couples, relationship dynamics involving both partners' patterns of security and insecurity are quite important. Specifically, it seems that the needs of young wives who are highly dependent and anxious about their relationships are not likely to be met adequately by husbands who are uncomfortable with intimacy.

The studies we have discussed so far point to the importance of communication patterns and attachment security in the relationships of young married couples. Recent data further suggest that these two sets of variables can be integrated in a broad model of marital satisfaction. Communication variables may mediate the effect of attachment security on relationship happiness; that is, secure individuals may report more satisfying relationships because they communicate more openly and directly (Feeney, 1994, 1999a; Feeney, Noller and Roberts, 1998). This type of finding is summarized in Figure 4.2.

Predicting young couples' marital satisfaction is not a simple task, however, as indicated by at least two findings. First, it appears that *initial* levels of satisfaction and *changes* in satisfaction may be explained by different factors. In their four-year study of newly-wed couples, for example, Karney and Bradbury (1997) found that neuroticism was associated with lower levels of initial satisfaction, but behaviour in marital interaction (especially negativity) was associated with changes in satisfaction.

The second complicating factor is the need to consider differences due to gender and ethnicity. In the study just mentioned, Karney and Bradbury found that the effects of negativity on changes in satisfaction depended on gender: husbands' negativity had detrimental effects on wives' satisfaction, but wives' negativity had positive effects on both their own and their spouses' satisfaction. Perhaps, for wives only, behaviours such as blame and criticism are seen as reflecting commitment and a willingness to work on difficult issues. Similarly, using the same sample reported by Acitelli *et al.* (1997; discussed earlier), Henderson-King and Veroff (1994) noted that some relations between sexual satisfaction and marital well-being depended on gender and race. For example, in the first year of marriage, white husbands were the only group for whom sexual satisfaction was linked with marital happiness, and the only group for whom sexual satisfaction was *not* linked with feelings of competence in the marriage. Such differences are likely to reflect differences in socialization (e.g., the extent to which particular groups are socialized to think of sex in terms of self-interest or in terms of mutuality).

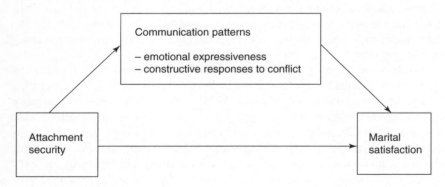

FIGURE 4.2 Relations among attachment security, communication patterns and marital satisfaction

Transition to Parenthood

The transition to parenthood is a very important developmental phase in the lives of many young adults. In fact, this transition has been described as one of the most precipitous changes that takes place in most people's lives (Rossi, 1968). The role of parent is demanding; further, this role is acquired abruptly, and most people have relatively little preparation for it (Miller and Sollie, 1980; Rossi, 1968; Terry, 1991a). It is not surprising, then, that first-time parenthood has been the focus of a great deal of research. Early theorists suggested that the transition to parenthood is experienced as a crisis (Hill, 1949). More recent research has tended to see the transition in less negative terms, however, as a specific developmental phase marked by significant personal, familial and social change (Levy-Shiff, 1994).

With the arrival of a new baby, many additional family tasks are created. Parents have to deal with physical demands, such as loss of sleep; emotional demands, such as uncertainty about one's competence as a parent; marital strains, including changes to the couple's sexual relationship; and lifestyle changes, such as financial burden (Miller and Sollie, 1980). In addition, the experience of providing childcare itself may be quite stressful (Terry, 1991b). It is also important to recognize that many first-time mothers are not married; in some western countries, approximately one-third of live births are to unmarried mothers. Although some of these mothers are in cohabiting relationships, others experience the transition to parenthood without significant support from the baby's father. Because the majority of babies continue to be born to mothers in established couple relationships, however, we focus in this section on how both mothers and fathers cope with the tasks of new parenthood.

Methodological issues

Before we discuss the changes that couples face at this time, it is important to consider the methods that researchers have used to study these issues. Research in this area has become more sophisticated over time, allowing for stronger inferences to be made about the changes that occur during the transition to parenthood and the reasons why they occur. The major methodological issues are summarized in Table 4.3, and discussed in more detail below.

Sampling. Some early studies of new parenthood were based on clinical samples (e.g., Benedek, 1959). These samples were often small and atypical, consisting of individuals presenting with emotional problems. Another issue is that samples recruited solely from medical settings may be biased towards higher socioeconomic levels. This issue is important, because the extent of distress reported during new parenthood seems to depend on socioeconomic level, with somewhat more stress being reported by middle-class respondents than by blue-collar respondents (Grossman, 1988).

Research design. Earlier studies were mainly cross-sectional and retrospective, often carried out years after the babies were born. Longitudinal designs are needed

TABLE 4.3 *Methodological issues in studying the transition to parenthood*

Sampling
Sample bias may result from recruiting:
- clinical samples
- samples from medical settings

Research design
Rigorous research requires:
- longitudinal designs to track changes as they occur
- objective interpretation of data
- inclusion of a comparison group of childless couples

Comprehensiveness of the research
It is important for researchers to:
- include both men and women
- focus on experiential aspects of parents' lives
- combine methods of data collection
- extend studies at least till the end of the child's first year

---

to track changes as they occur. The move away from clinical methods has also resulted in more objective interpretation of data. Perhaps the most crucial design issue, however, concerns the use of a comparison (or 'control') group of childless couples. Inclusion of such groups has become common only in recent years. Without a comparison group, it is impossible to tell whether any observed changes are a function of parenthood, or of time in the couple relationship more generally.

Comprehensiveness of the research. Until recently, few studies have included both men and women, and few have focused in any detail on experiential aspects of parents' lives. It is also useful for researchers to combine methods of data collection so that one method can compensate for the weaknesses of another, and so that differences across methods can be assessed. For example, there is some evidence that new parents report higher levels of distress when they are being interviewed than when they respond to mailed questionnaires (Grossman, 1988). Finally, studies should ideally extend at least till the end of the first year of the child's life. Many factors affecting parents' adjustment (e.g, loss of sleep) may start to stabilize around this time. (Also see Chapter 2 for details on how the infant's development over the first year of life is likely to contribute to changes in the quality of the parent–child relationship.)

How do couple relationships change in response to parenthood?

Given the multiple demands of the transition to parenthood, it is not surprising that many studies have shown changes in couples' interaction patterns at this time. The following descriptions of observed changes are based on several studies (e.g.,

Belsky and Pensky, 1988; Cowan and Cowan, 1992; Huston and Vangelisti, 1995; Levy-Shiff, 1994; Ruble *et al.*, 1988; Sanchez and Thomson, 1997).

The most consistent finding from these studies concerns the more traditional division of labour among new parents. Both small-scale and large survey studies show that parenthood tends to crystallize a gender-based division of labour. Men's patterns of paid and unpaid work show little change, although some studies suggest that men may increase their hours of paid work at this time (Bittman, 1991). However, women's routines change markedly: women typically cease or curtail paid work, and become more involved with instrumental activities around the house. Further, on average, women report doing much more of the housework and childcare than they had expected. This increasingly traditional division of labour is usually not planned. Rather, it results from a complex of factors, including couples' attempts to apply their skills as efficiently as possible to the various demands on their time and energy, and women's tendency to adapt to partners' preferences for task allocation (Johnson and Huston, 1998).

There is also evidence that companionate activities decrease with the arrival of the first child. Not surprisingly, given the demands of childcare and the gender-based division of labour noted above, most couples report that leisure activities become less frequent. Similarly, many couples report that they spend less time conversing, and that the presence of the new baby tends to inhibit spontaneity and to hamper their sexual relationship. At the same time, it is important to recognize that positive exchanges between partners continue at a reasonable rate; for example, in Huston and Vangelisti's (1995) study, couples going through the transition to parenthood expressed affection towards each other at similar levels as those who were childless. There has also been debate about changes in levels of conflict. Some studies have reported that conflict increases with the arrival of the baby (e.g., Belsky and Pensky, 1988; Levy-Shiff, 1994), whereas others have found no significant change (Huston and Vangelisti, 1995).

In terms of overall relationship quality, most studies show a decline in reported relationship satisfaction. This decline is generally more marked for women than for men. However, Cowan (1988a) has argued that this apparent gender difference depends on when measures are taken; men may be slower to experience the impact of becoming a parent than women, in terms of the timing of the drop in satisfaction. Of course, this different rate of change may, in itself, create distance and conflict for some couples.

To sum up these findings, the transition to parenthood is clearly a difficult time for many couples, with the multiple stressors resulting in changes in several aspects of the couple relationship. However, the changes are modest in size, and are probably best seen as simply accentuating changes that occur in couple bonds over time (Belsky and Pensky, 1988). Like any major transition, first-time parenthood involves both positive and negative aspects; it has the potential to bring disequilibrium and distress, but also to stimulate new coping skills (Cowan, 1988). Parenthood may actually enhance some relationships.

What predicts adjustment to new parenthood?

Given that new parenthood can have such diverse effects on couples, we turn now to consider the variables that predict adjustment to the transition. Belsky and Pensky (1988) note that three sets of variables are relevant: factors of the infant, of the parents, and of the couple relationship.

Important factors of the infant include health and temperament. Clearly, not all babies are alike, and 'difficult' babies place greater demands on parents. The effects of infant difficulty appear to depend, however, on other factors. For example, adjustment to a difficult baby is generally poorer if the mother tends to be badly organized or easily overwhelmed by demands, and if the father values parenthood less highly (Levy-Shiff, 1994). More extreme conditions of the infant, such as prematurity and handicap, are associated with high levels of parental stress, not only because of the demands for extra care but also because of the uncontrollability and unpredictability of the situation, and the violated expectations of a normal birth (Parke and Beitel, 1988).

Factors of the parents that predict adjustment include expectations and personality traits. Discrepancies between expectations of parenthood and actual experiences (e.g., spending more time on baby-related tasks and less time going out than expected) tend to be associated with poorer outcomes (Grossman, 1988). In terms of personality variables, Levy-Shiff (1994) reported that decreases in marital satisfaction were smaller for men who viewed themselves as nurturing and caring, and for women who were low in autonomy and high in impulse control and ability to organize.

Despite these factors of infants and parents, the couple relationship plays a particularly central role in predicting adjustment to parenthood. Better adjustment has been linked to cohesive and satisfying couple bonds (Belsky and Pensky, 1988), and Grossman (1988) has argued that the couple relationship is especially important to women's sense of comfort and confidence in the transition. In fact, studies with comparison groups show that level of adaptation at the beginning of the study explains more of the variation in adaptation than does the fact of having a child (Osofsky and Culp, 1993).

More specifically, how couples deal with the allocation of childcare and other household tasks has emerged as a strong predictor of adaptation to parenthood. For example, Levy-Shiff (1994) reported that low paternal involvement, especially in childcare, was the strongest predictor of change in satisfaction for both sexes. Again, partners' expectations are crucial: violated expectations for the sharing of responsibilities predict lower satisfaction (Hackel and Ruble, 1992), whereas the perception that one's spouse is contributing fairly has actually been associated with an increase in females' satisfaction (Terry, McHugh and Noller, 1991). Finally, Osofsky and Culp (1989) suggest that adjustment to new fatherhood is influenced by the *process* of decision-making around the division of tasks, as much as by the division of tasks *per se*.

Given the central role of the couple relationship, an important development in studying the transition to parenthood has been the application of adult attachment theory. Feeney *et al.* (1998) reported results from an ongoing study, in which the first phase involved measures of attachment, caregiving, sexuality and marital satisfaction being completed by a group of couples in the second trimester of pregnancy, and by a comparison group of childless couples. As expected, secure participants (in both groups) gave more favourable evaluations of their caregiving, sexuality and satisfaction. Although the two groups of couples showed similar scores on all measured variables, attachment was more strongly linked with caregiving styles for those who were expecting a child. That is, insecure persons' tendency towards less responsive caregiving was more pronounced in the unfamiliar and challenging situation. Similarly, Mikulincer and Florian (1998) applied attachment theory to the study of new parenthood, comparing a group of women who had become mothers some months earlier with a group who had no children. Motherhood was associated with higher levels of psychological distress only for those who were insecurely attached to the partner. Hence, a secure couple bond seems to buffer the potentially negative effects of new parenthood.

Importantly, the benefits of a secure couple bond at this point in the life cycle are likely to extend to all members of the developing family. Among young adult samples, secure individuals report greater confidence in their ability to relate to young children, less endorsement of harsh disciplinary practices, and less tendency to be easily aggravated by children (Rholes, Simpson and Blakely, 1995; Rholes *et al.*, 1997). Observational studies of mothers of infants and young children have also linked secure attachment with more supportive parenting behaviour in a laboratory teaching task (Rholes *et al.*, 1995). These findings support the suggestion that secure adults are better able to provide a secure base for their offspring (Weiss, 1991).

Adult Friendships

In addition to the family and couple relationships which we have discussed so far, young adults form and maintain relationships of a voluntary nature, with friends. Like sibling relationships, friendships serve important functions across the lifespan. Among all age groups, friends provide us with affection and companionship, advice and understanding. More specifically, research suggests that the experience of friendship is defined by a large number of dimensions, which fall into three broad categories: affective (expressions of intimacy and affection), communal (assistance and involvement in shared activities), and sociable (provision of recreation and amusement). These functions generally apply across the lifespan, although they may be shaped to some extent by developmental tasks (de Vries, 1996).

Young adults, like people in other age groups, tend to form friendships with those who are similar to themselves in terms of sex, age, race, education, income, occupational status and marital status (Fischer, 1982). This tendency for homogeneity in friendships can be understood, in part, by the contexts in which friendships are formed. For example, in early adulthood, the entrance into paid employment provides a new context for friendship formation – the workplace – and this context tends to draw together people of similar education and occupational status.

As we can see from the example of workplace friendship, each period in the lifespan is somewhat unique with regard to the opportunities for meeting friends and for maintaining friendships. Different stages of the life cycle are also characterized by differences in the attitudes and skills associated with friendships (Adams and Blieszner, 1996). Although researchers have recognized this point, they have generally studied friendship patterns in terms of wide age bands, particularly among adults, with very little research focusing specifically on the friendships of young adults. Further, the available research has been described as studies of 'college student' friendships, rather than 'young adult' friendships (Blieszner and Adams, 1992), reflecting the narrow samples used to study this topic. The limited research conducted on young adults' friendships has looked at four main issues: the extent and depth of friendships, perceptions and understandings of friendship, gender differences, and behavioural processes in friendships (for example, communication and support-giving).

Extent and depth of friendships

In Chapter 3 we saw that adolescence is marked by an increase in the importance of the peer group, and by a tendency to draw away from parental authority. Further, young adults' involvement with pursuits such as education, career development and mate selection tend to focus them on people and things outside of the family (Marcia, 1980). However, with marriage, or the establishment of other committed love relationships, there is usually an increase in involvement with family, and an accompanying decrease in the role of friends. These changes intensify with the transition to parenthood (de Vries, 1996).

The decreasing role of friends at this point in the life cycle is evidenced by decreases in the reported number of friends, the amount of contact with friends, and the intimacy of friendships. These changes are thought to reflect several factors. First, modern conceptions of the ideal marriage often include the spouse being considered as 'best friend'. Second, members of the partner's family provide the individual with new kin relations, thus adding to their social network in important ways. Third, the family of origin tends to be reconceptualized more positively as the individual becomes a parent. Fourth, new family responsibilities and constraints reduce the amount of time available for social and leisure activities (de Vries, 1996). In summary, the tendency for the role of friends to diminish at this time reflects the importance of new demands, together with changing perceptions of self and family (Auhagen, 1996; de Vries, 1996).

Understandings of friendship

There have been relatively few studies of young adults' understanding of friendship. However, an interesting example of work in this area is a series of studies assessing lay people's beliefs about relational satisfaction with best friends, conducted with a range of student samples (Cole and Bradac, 1996). Participants in the first sample were asked to identify the qualities and characteristics that a best friend should possess in order to create a satisfying relationship. Those in the later samples were asked to judge the similarity of the resulting characteristics, and the causal relations among them.

Characteristics of friends that were seen as important to satisfying relationships included being approachable, having good communication skills, being socially popular, enriching one's life, being open-minded, being emotionally balanced, and 'caring about me'. Some of these characteristics were seen as immediate, or primary, sources of satisfaction (e.g., being approachable). Others were seen as more distal; that is, as points of origin (e.g., 'caring about me'), or as mediating variables in a causal chain (e.g., having good communication skills). In other words, factors such as 'caring about me' were seen as resulting in good communication, which, in turn, resulted in greater approachability. This type of causal chain suggests that young adults have well-developed perceptions of the factors that create satisfying friendships. In Cole and Bradac's studies, young men and women generally placed a similar value on the various causes of friendship. However, gender differences exist in other aspects of young adults' friendships.

Gender differences

We have already noted that young adults tend to form friendships with those of the same sex. Moreover, men's and women's friendships differ in important ways. For example, women tend to emphasize the importance of caring, interdependence and expressiveness; in other words, emotional concerns loom large in their friendships. In contrast, men's friendships often revolve around specific activities or roles (such as work or sport), and appear to be less emotionally intimate (Parker and de Vries, 1993; Winstead, 1986). As we discuss in the following section, gender differences in intimacy and expressiveness are reflected in behavioural processes such as communication and support-giving between friends.

There has been some debate, however, over the extent of gender differences in friends' social and emotional behaviour (e.g., Duck and Wright, 1993). The tendency for greater emotional expression among female friends may be more marked in young adults than in older samples, reflecting the greater disparity in men's and women's lifestyles in early adulthood (Johnson and Troll, 1994). It has also been suggested that differences between men's and women's friendships may be less evident in those relationships which are very close, and which have developed over a long period of time (Wright, 1982).

Behavioural processes

As we noted earlier, important behavioural processes in friendships include communication and support. Recent research into young adults' friendships has assessed the functions of such under-studied communication features as babytalk and gossip. For example, Bombar and Littig (1996) studied babytalk in close relationships, in a student sample consisting mostly of young adults. Half the sample reported having used babytalk in interacting with friends (although friends were less likely than romantic partners to be the target of this form of speech). Men and women were equally likely to report engaging in babytalk to friends of the opposite sex; women, however, were more likely than men to use babytalk to same-sex friends, perhaps because of women's emphasis on intimacy and emotional bonding. Similarly, it has been argued that gossip may play an important role in some female friendships. Leaper and Holliday (1995) studied the amount of gossip in conversations between pairs of young adult friends. Again, there were no gender differences in mixed-sex pairs. Female pairs were the most likely to engage in gossip of a critical nature, and most likely to respond encouragingly to a friend's gossip. Leaper and Holliday suggest that women's less powerful social position may cause them to rely on gossip to establish solidarity and compete for status.

Support processes between same-sex friends have been studied in a sample ranging in age from pre-adolescence to young adulthood (Denton and Zarbatany, 1996). In each friendship pair, one individual (the 'subject') was chosen at random to talk to the friend about a negative event they had experienced. Compared with younger people, adult friends were less likely to try to divert attention away from the negative event. Adults were also more likely to validate subjects' attempts to reduce their own responsibility for the event, and to feel better when friends helped them to evade responsibility. These age differences suggest that adults may be more willing or more able to help friends make sense of their problems in a way that is psychologically comfortable. Males in all age groups used more diversion than females, consistent with their tendency to be less comfortable with emotional and intimate topics.

Another study of support processes in young adults' friendships highlights the role of ethnicity. Samter *et al.* (1997) compared Euro-American, Afro-American, and Asian-American men and women in terms of their perceptions of the importance of emotional support in same-sex friendship and the effectiveness of various comforting strategies. The strongest differences in these variables were between Euro-American and Afro-American women. The former placed more emphasis on the capacity of same-sex friends to provide emotional support, and on the importance of discussing and legitimizing feelings (rather than solving problems). Such differences in perceptions may impact on relationships between members of different ethnic groups, potentially contributing to difficulty in maintaining close friendships (Samter *et al.*, 1997).

Social Support

The range of relationships that we have considered in this chapter (family relationships, couple relationships and friendships) all serve to provide young adults with various forms of support. Social support can also be provided by other types of relationships, such as those formed with neighbours and work colleagues. Social support is a complex phenomenon, and has been described as a meta-construct; that is, one that subsumes a number of related constructs (Vaux, 1988). Reflecting this complexity, social support has been defined and measured in many different ways. Winemiller and colleagues (1993) provided an integrative view of available measures of social support, describing them in terms of such factors as the type of social support measured, the category of social support, and the source of social support. These factors are summarized in Table 4.4.

How does social support affect young adults?

There have been two major hypotheses concerning the beneficial effects of social support: stress-buffering and direct effects. The stress-buffering hypothesis states that social support limits, or buffers, the effect of stressful life circumstances. In other words, social support helps people when they face conditions of high stress. In contrast, the direct-effect hypothesis asserts that social support has a beneficial influence, whether individuals are experiencing stressful circumstances or not. The

TABLE 4.4 *Measuring social support*

Measures vary in terms of their focus on:

Type of support
- Perceived (subjective perception of support provided or received)
- Behaviourally referenced (frequency of supportive behaviours)
- Network orientation (willingness to utilize support)
- Provided (support given *by* the individual)
- Network structure (size, density, proximity, etc.)

Category of support
- Social companionship (recreational time with others)
- Esteem (emotional or expressive support)
- Instrumental (provision of resources or services)
- Informational (information, advice and referral)
- Global (broad or unspecified)

Source of support
- Family
- Friend
- Spouse
- Service provider
- Group member
- Work-related
- Neighbour

relative support for these hypotheses has been mixed, perhaps because of the variety of different measures of social support. Cohen and Wills (1985) suggested that individuals' perceptions of being supported by others have a stress-buffering effect, whereas the actual extent of social contact with others has a direct effect. However, the effects of social support may be more complex than this, with the same measure of social support sometimes having a stress-buffering effect on one outcome variable and a direct effect on another (Hobfoll, 1996).

The effects of social support are also complex because, in order for social support to be helpful in coping with a given stressful event, the type of support has to be appropriate to the situation. That is, different types of support may be beneficial in different circumstances. This concept has been called 'social support fit'. For example, in a longitudinal study of low-income pregnant women, Collins *et al.* (1993) found that physical health outcomes were predicted better by task and material support than by emotional (confiding) support. This finding may reflect the women's need for help with strenuous activities during this time. In contrast, in a study of recently separated mothers living with their young sons, confiding support predicted more effective parenting practices (DeGarmo and Forgatch, 1997). The relevance of emotional support to these mothers can be understood in terms of the difficult personal and parenting issues that they were likely to be facing.

Individual differences in social support

What factors influence the amount of social support that different people give and receive? Gender is one relevant variable, with women generally providing and receiving more social support than men do (Hobfoll, 1996). However, a study of newly acquainted dyads suggests that support-giving and support-seeking may be influenced by the gender composition of the dyad, rather than by the gender of the support-provider or recipient alone (Mickelson *et al.*, 1995). Specifically, these researchers found that opposite-sex support providers offered more emotional support than same-sex providers, whereas same-sex providers listened more than opposite-sex providers.

Personality variables are also important in the social support process. For example, a longitudinal study which followed young people from late adolescence to early adulthood has shown reciprocal relations between perceptions of social support and the personality variables of self-esteem and gregariousness (Newcomb and Keefe, 1997). That is, adolescents who were more gregarious and higher in self-esteem tended to perceive their adult relationships as more supportive, but adolescents who perceived their relationships as supportive also tended to score highly as adults on measures of self-esteem and gregariousness. The latter finding was consistent across the various phases of the study, and underlines the beneficial effects of supportive relationships.

Characteristics of the individual facing the stressful event are also relevant to the concept of social support 'fit', which we discussed in the previous section.

That is, the effective support of an individual may require not only a 'fit' between the support and the coping requirements, but also that the individual has the skills required to form and maintain supportive relationships, and the personality and willingness to exercise these skills (Sarason, Pierce and Sarason, 1990).

A number of researchers (e.g., Bartholomew, Cobb and Poole, 1997; Coble, Gantt and Mallinckrodt, 1996) have argued that attachment theory offers a useful approach to these issues, with individual differences in attachment style being likely to influence various aspects of the support process. That is, security of attachment is likely to impact on individuals' appraisals of stressful events, their help-seeking behaviour, and both enacted and perceived support. A growing number of studies support these links. For example, young adults who are securely attached are more likely to seek social support when facing stressful events, and less likely to resist supportive behaviours from others (Feeney, 1998; Simpson, Rholes and Nelligan, 1992).

Recent studies of adult attachment have also helped to clarify the distinction between 'attachment' relationships and 'supportive' relationships. In the question-naire study mentioned earlier in this chapter, Trinke and Bartholomew (1997) asked young adults to list the significant people in their lives (people to whom they felt strong emotional ties), and to rate the extent to which they met various attachment needs. On average, participants listed ten significant people, but response patterns suggested that only half of these met the criteria for attachment relationships: romantic partners were rated the most highly in terms of overall strength of attach-ment, followed by mothers, fathers, siblings and best friends. Participants in this study also completed a measure of perceived social support, which required them to report on the number of supportive relationships available to them in different contexts. The number of attachment figures was only moderately correlated with the number of sources of social support, suggesting that attachment and social support are reasonably independent constructs. That is, attachment relationships are an important aspect of social support, but other relationships can also be supportive.

Before we leave the topic of social support, it is important to note that, as lay people are usually well aware, relationships can be the source of negative, as well as positive, feelings. Rook and Pietromonaco (1987) propose that negative social exchanges fall into three broad types. The first type is ineffective or excessive help; this category includes grudging assistance, insensitive comments and unsound advice. The second type is unwanted or unpleasant social contact; examples include criticism, rejection, invasion of privacy and non-reciprocated affection. The final type is negative regulation; this term refers to interactions that promote deviant or unhealthy behaviour (for example, applauding dangerous behaviour, or modelling ineffective self-care). These three types of exchanges, sometimes referred to as social strains, appear to be just as important as positive exchanges in predicting psychological adjustment (Holahan, Moos and Bonin, 1997; Rook, 1990).

Summary and Conclusions

In summary, a number of key themes emerge from the study of young adults' relationships. Family relationships are important to young adults in terms of the affection and companionship that they provide, and in terms of the relationship attitudes and behaviours that are learned from observing and interacting with family members. Attachment relationships (especially couple bonds) play a central role in the lives of young adults, but other types of relationships also provide social support. There are important individual differences in young adults' relationship experiences: relationship processes and outcomes may be affected by gender and ethnicity, and by personal characteristics such as attachment style. Finally, it is important to recognize that young adults' relationships are shaped quite markedly by the life circumstances and transitions that occur at this time; marriage and parenthood affect not only the individuals in the new family unit, but also existing bonds with parents, siblings and friends.

5

Relationships in Middle Age

Defining Middle Age

Middle age can be defined in many ways; for example, chronologically (as the age period from approximately 35 to 55 years), biologically (as the latter decades of reproductively mature adulthood), or in relationship terms as the time when children grow up and leave the family home (Krause and Haverkamp, 1996). Middle age also tends to be a time when one's parents are old and needing care and attention.

A central theme in the awareness of midlife seems to be the finiteness of the time left to live (Neugarten, 1968; Notman, 1979). As they watch their parents age, or even die, middle-aged people become more conscious of their own mortality and of the limited amount of time people spend on earth. Kovacs (1992) claims that people at midlife 'sense that a period of preparation has come to an end and that the moments have arrived to create (or recreate) that which will be the central project or projects giving definition to the meaning of their existences' (p. 105). Further, O'Neil and Egan (1992) see the tasks of midlife as 'reconciling past failures, facing future fears and developing new life structures' (p. 107). This is similar to Erikson's concept of generativity which he views as building upon successful earlier accomplishments, such as the development of identity (see Chapter 3). For Erikson, the generativity crisis involves a striving to contribute creatively to the nurturance and well-being of future generations in a manner that will endure even after the end of the mature adult's finite lifespan.

The dividing line between middle age and old age is no longer clear, however. Middle age tends to overlap to some extent with the concept of the 'young-old', who are usually seen as aged from 65 to 75 years, provided that health remains reasonably sound over this period. Similarly, age 65 and retirement are no longer clear divisions, given that some people take early retirement, perhaps as early as 55, and some keep working into old age (Neugarten and Neugarten, 1987).

Gender and Middle Age

Lock (1998) discusses the gendered nature of perceptions of middle age. She claims that, for women, there is a strong emphasis on gynaecological issues – on barrenness, oestrogen deficiency, and symptoms of menopause. In a comparison of Japan and western countries, she shows that the situation is different in Japan, where there is more focus on changes to the autonomic nervous system during midlife. She claims that, in Japan, menopause is seen more as a process, rather than a single event (as it tends to be seen in America), and is more directly tied in with the overall ageing process. In addition, menopause is not understood as a bad thing, or a disease-like condition, in Japan.

Similarly, Notman (1979) argues against the emphasis on menopause as a critical event for women at midlife, on the grounds that many of the symptoms attributed to stages of the menopause are more likely to be related to the stresses of midlife, including personal, family and societal pressures. For many women, according to Notman, the end of the childbearing years can bring about greater autonomy and new possibilities for skill development and new interests. For women who have focused their lives totally on their children, however, the departure of those children from the family home may produce a sense of uselessness and feelings of depression.

For men, on the other hand, there tends to be still a strong emphasis on achievement and career at midlife, with a reassessment at this time of both past achievements and likely achievements in the future. There is little focus on men's physiology at midlife, despite the fact that physiological changes may include sexual problems (such as impotence), weight gain, loss of strength and vitality, and loss of hair.

According to O'Neil and Egan (1992), midlife is also a time when men and women are likely to reanalyse and question the gender roles they have adopted, and re-evaluate their conceptions of masculinity and femininity. Changes in assumptions about gender roles, the value placed on these roles, and concept of self, are all likely to be considered at this time of life. Such reanalysis can be stimulated by events such as divorce, death of the partner, children leaving home, career changes, or loss of stamina associated with signs of ageing. According to these authors, successful negotiation of these issues can produce a less restrictive and stereotypic way of dealing with issues of sex and gender, together with a more satisfying concept of self.

Marital Relationships in Middle Age

In the USA, and in other western countries like England and Australia, marriage tends to be the primary relationship choice for older couples. Cohabiting tends to be unusual in older age groups, with fewer than 1 per cent of middle-aged couples being in cohabiting relationships. This trend may change over time, however, given the growing popularity of cohabitation among the young (see Chapter 4).

During midlife, many persons take on substantial responsibilities in work, parenting, family care and community leadership, and this period of life can be a very busy one. Wives are likely to become more self-confident and assertive, and husbands are likely to become more dependent on the marriage and more accommodating in the marital relationship (Huyck and Gutmann, 1992).

Marital satisfaction

Early studies tended to show a curvilinear relationship between stage of the life cycle and marital satisfaction, with the lowest satisfaction being reported during the childrearing years, and higher satisfaction in early and late marriage (e.g., Lerner and Spanier, 1978). More recent analyses have involved longitudinal data, larger and more representative samples, and efforts to control for selective attrition through divorce. These studies suggest that no single pattern of satisfaction is associated with age or with phase of the family life cycle. In fact, Weishaus and Field (1988) found that the curvilinear pattern was only one of several different patterns discovered in their small sample of older couples.

Husbands typically report higher marital satisfaction than wives (Rollins, 1989), with qualitative studies revealing a tendency for husbands to be willing to idealize the situation and deny existing tensions. Wives, on the other hand, are likely to show a greater willingness to recognize problems and to press for changes, particularly once the children have left home.

In the Berkeley Longitudinal Study of Marriages (Skolnick, 1981), highly satisfactory marriages were compared with marriages low in satisfaction. The researchers found that highly satisfactory marriages tended to be characterized by strong affective commitment to the spouse, a tendency to confront rather than avoid conflict, and a realistic approach to relationships. (Spouses in these relationships did not expect perfection.) Low satisfaction marriages, on the other hand, tended to be characterized either by conflict avoidance, or by serious conflicts which tended to result in hostility and tension.

As we noted in the chapter on early marriage, the dialectical contradictions discussed by Baxter (autonomy–connectedness, openness–closedness, and novelty–predictability) are central to close personal relationships like marriage (Baxter, 1990; Baxter and Montgomery, 1996). As well as finding that the extent of difference on these contradictions was predictive of marital satisfaction, we also found evidence for systematic patterns of change over time (Noller *et al.*, in press). Overall, moves for change tended to be in the direction of more autonomy, more openness, and more predictability. These moves reflect couples' changing needs and circumstances. For example, some couples reported a move towards greater autonomy for wives whose children were becoming less dependent on them. In addition, factors such as time constraints, limited financial resources and greater familiarity with one another were seen as mitigating against high levels of novelty and spontaneity in these more established relationships.

Other issues likely to affect marital satisfaction at this midlife stage include changes in the original implicit contract between partners, unfulfilled goals, sexual problems, fertility problems for those who have not had children, issues related to remarriage, and problems caused by physical disability (Nadelson, Polonsky and Matthews, 1981). Changes in the original implicit contract often centre around gender issues, such as the division of household work, or the more deep-seated gender issue of who was to be strong and who was to be dependent. Physical disability or retrenchment from work may result in the woman, who was 'supposed' to be the more dependent one, becoming the provider for the needs of the family. A wife's physical disability, on the other hand, may mean that the husband has to assume many of her housekeeping tasks, with him being the carer and her being the cared for.

Those who have not achieved the professional success or wealth they craved, and those who have not had children, may have to face their unfulfilled goals at this stage of their relationship. Couples whose goals for their children have not been achieved may also have to deal with disappointments about the lack of achievement or unsatisfactory lifestyles of their offspring. Such issues can, of course, cause problems in the couple relationship, especially if partners tend to blame each other for the unsatisfactory outcomes.

It is interesting to note that the majority of older people rate their marriages as happy or very happy. We need to keep in mind, however, that a 'survival' effect occurs here. Those who have divorced over the years (around 40 per cent of all those who married) are no longer included in the samples. On the other hand, longer marriages may be more immune to divorce because the partners have survived the periods of greatest risk. In addition, these marriages are likely to benefit from marital partners' growing investment in children, property and each other, over time (Mattessich and Hill, 1987).

Marriage styles

According to Huyck (1995), qualitative studies in particular provide evidence for a diversity of marriage patterns in later life, and a basic continuity in marriage styles over long periods of time. In other words, marriages can take a range of different forms, but those forms tend to be fairly stable. For example, Huyck notes that several styles of midlife marriages have been identified, according to partners' focus. Some couples tend to focus on the marital relationship and on building closeness and satisfaction with the spouse; others focus on general family relationships, such as those with adult children and grandchildren; and yet others tend to be focused outside the family and invested in a wide range of outside activities.

Marriage and mental illness

Salokangas, Mattila and Joukamaa (1988) studied pre-retirement adults (with a mean age of 62) in terms of the impact of social support on the likelihood of mental illness. They found that there was less psychiatric disturbance and fewer depressive symptoms in those who were living in a close marital relationship with an empathic spouse. Those who were living in an emotionally distant relationship with an unempathic spouse tended to present with the highest levels of psychiatric symptoms. These researchers argued that being in a positive marital relationship seemed to provide a shield against depression, whereas being in a negative marital relationship tended to make individuals more vulnerable to depression.

It also seems clear that neuroticism (generalized anxiety and negative emotionality) in at least one partner has a negative impact on marital relationships. Kelly and Conley (1987) reported data from a major longitudinal study of marriage that spanned the period from engagement to old age, a total of 45 years. One of the variables that best discriminated between the divorced, the unhappily married and the happily married was the neuroticism level of both spouses (rated by friends during young adulthood), with the happily married having lower levels of neuroticism. Low impulse control (or high impulsiveness) in the husband was also a strong predictor of early divorce.

Marriage and sex

Huyck (1995) reports that interest in sex tends to be relatively stable across the life cycle, with the overall finding that men tend to be more interested in sex than women. In addition, there is evidence that individual differences tend to be maintained across the life cycle; continuity is less clear for women, however, because a woman's level of sexual interest and activity tends to be closely related to the interests of her partner. Being satisfied with the sexual relationship is strongly associated with relationship satisfaction for both partners (Blumstein and Schwartz, 1983; Field and Weishaus, 1992). Sexual activity tends to decline faster than sexual interest, and any decline in activity tends to be gradual, unless there are serious health problems such as diabetes (which can cause erection problems; George and Weiler, 1981). Arthritis, prostrate enlargement and side effects of medication can all have an impact on both desire and responsiveness in midlife couples (Huyck, 1995).

Garza and Dressel (1983) surveyed married persons in the USA about their level of sexual activity. They found that 53 per cent of those over 60 and 44 per cent of those over 65 had had sexual intercourse with their spouse during the previous month. One problem with these data is that 34 per cent of the sample refused to answer this question, and we have no way of knowing whether that group was still sexually active or not. These researchers also found that sexual activity generally stops when the husband loses interest or capability; both husbands and wives agreed that this was the case.

Equity and marriage

According to equity theory, marriages are more satisfying when there is equity – that is, when each partner receives as much from the relationship as they contribute (Feeney, Peterson and Noller, 1994; Hatfield, Utne and Traupmann, 1979). Those who are underbenefited (receiving less than they contribute) tend to feel less satisfied and to experience anger and resentment; those who are overbenefited tend to experience less satisfaction because of a sense of guilt about the level of benefit derived from the relationship (Traupmann and Hatfield, 1983). Table 5.1 shows the level of women's contentment as a function of the equity of the marital relationship. The data cover dating relationships through to those of 60-year-olds and show that those in equitable relationships tended to be more contented than those in relationships where they were underbenefited or overbenefited.

In the marital relationship, when one spouse feels underbenefited (and therefore the partner may well feel overbenefited), doubts may be raised about the partner's ability to perform effectively in a particular social role, with negative implications for the relationship. Traupmann and Hatfield (1983) studied equity in marital relationships across the lifespan, using middle-aged and elderly respondents who reported retrospectively on the patterns of equity in marriage. They found that women tended to report having felt overbenefited in the early years of marriage and underbenefited in the middle years, and generally seemed to experience their relationships as equitable by the time they reached late middle age. However, when Feeney, Peterson and Noller (1994) surveyed couples at different stages of the marital life cycle, wives' perceptions of equity were lower than those of their husbands during the childrearing years, fairly similar during the launching stage (when children were leaving home), and lower than those of their husbands again

TABLE 5.1 *Women's contentment as a function of equity of the marital relationship for different age groups*

	How equitable is the relationship?			
Period	*Overbenefited*	*Equitably treated*	*Underbenefited*	*F*
Dating	1.63	2.03	1.14	5.22*
Newly-wed	0.46	2.08	0.26	39.42†
30s	0.30	1.89	–0.06	30.34†
40s	1.08	1.60	–0.28	17.38†
50s	1.48	1.84	–0.52	24.43†
60s	2.00	2.10	–0.08	19.42†

Note: The higher the number, the greater the level of contentment the women report experiencing. For age groups above 60, only small numbers of subjects were available and results were nonsignificant.

* $p < 0.01$; † $p < 0.001$.

Source: Adapted from Traupmann and Hatfield, 1983

during the empty-nest phase. Together, these findings suggest that perceptions of equity during midlife may vary, depending on factors such as the composition of the household.

Midlife marital disruption

Hiedemann, Suhomlinova and O'Rand (1998) used a hazards framework to estimate the effects of women's economic independence, couples' economic status, and family life course factors on the risk of middle-age separation or divorce. This framework focuses on the risk factors that predict a negative outcome (in this case, marital disruption). They found that both economic independence and economic status influenced the risk of midlife marital disruption. Moving into the empty-nest phase also influenced the risk of marital disruption, but this effect tended to depend on the duration of the marriage.

More specifically, the risk of marital disruption was positively related to the wife's economic independence, with her current employment status being highly statistically related to that risk. In fact, working women were around 80 per cent more likely to separate or divorce than women who did not work. When the researchers controlled for education and work experience, an increase in the wife's employment or wages appeared to increase the probability of marital disruption. Martin and Bumpass (1989) also found evidence that women's economic independence tends to influence wives to leave unsatisfactory marriages.

These findings go against general trends which show that greater educational attainment (generally correlated with economic independence) significantly reduces the possibility of marital disruption. These latter findings have usually been explained by the tendency for well-educated couples to marry later, and to have more choices about their lifestyle and generally better life prospects. These better-educated couples are also more likely to own their own homes (which reduces the risks of marital disruption) and may see themselves as having more to lose from divorce.

In trying to reconcile all these findings, it is important to keep in mind that women have become more concerned about autonomy and independence over the last several decades, and today's working women with independent means may be more ready to break up their marriages than was true for previous generations. Hiedemann *et al.* (1998) argue that women's growing economic independence is arguably the principal factor in the increase in separation and divorce across the life cycle. It is interesting to note that South and Spitze (1986) also found that education and home ownership affected the likelihood of separation or divorce in marriages of over ten years. Again in that study, higher levels of education tended to increase disruption, and home ownership tended to decrease the likelihood of disruption in marriages from 3–20 years' duration.

Data from an American longitudinal survey of mature women (conducted from 1967–89) found fewer divorces in the middle-aged group than among younger couples. By the late 1970s, divorce rates of women aged 45–49 were approximately 25 per cent as high as those of women aged 25–29, but divorce tended to rise among the older age groups during the 1980s.

The empty-nest phase

It is important to keep in mind that findings about the empty-nest phase of the family life cycle tend to be mixed. Some studies show increased marital well-being associated with the empty nest (Menaghan, 1983). In a Chicago sample, for instance, significant increases in marital well-being were reported by couples who had reached the empty-nest stage. It is possible that the lower levels of parental responsibility of this stage may remove some of the pressures, and give the couple more time to enjoy each other. This phase contrasts with the heavy responsibility of the children's adolescent years, that tends to increase the risk of marital dissatisfaction and divorce (Heaton, 1990; Raschke, 1987). McLanahan and Sorensen (1985) also found evidence of positive experiences during the empty-nest phase, with participants in marriages that had survived the demands of childrearing reporting that this phase was accompanied by a sense of euphoria.

McGrath (1992) notes that there are three possible issues related to the empty nest that can affect women at midlife. One is that the nest that was once full is now empty, another is that the nest that should be empty is still full, and the third relates to those who have not been able to have children and who need to come to terms with the fact that the possibility of a nest is now past. McGrath cites research findings indicating that, for many women, the empty nest is seen as providing a new sense of freedom and the opportunity for new activities. Other women, as we have already noted, are likely to be overcome by a sense of purposelessness and depression.

Remarriage in midlife

The few available studies of remarriage indicate that later life remarriages are more likely to be successful when partners are in good health, have adequate incomes, have had a successful first marriage, and have friends and relatives who support the new marriage (Bengtson, Rosenthal and Burton, 1990). Men are substantially more likely to remarry following divorce or widowhood than are women, and divorced people are more likely to remarry than are widowed people (Brubaker, 1985).

Parenting in Midlife

Although many parents go through the empty-nest phase in midlife, some still have children living in the family home. Whether the children are living in the family home or not, they are likely to have some impact on their parents' relationship, as the parents seek to keep in contact with their children and provide them with support as needed.

In Huyck's (1995) discussion of the effects of children on the couple relationship, she highlights four important themes. First, having children and grandchildren can be part of a generalized enjoyment of family life, particularly as the parents now have less direct responsibility for providing for their children's needs and for offering training and discipline.

Second, for those couples whose marital relationship is not very rewarding, relationships with children can provide an alternative source of gratification. Children can continue to give their parents a point of contact, and interesting things to do and to talk about. This trend may be more evident for working-class women, some of whom may avoid dealing with issues in their marriage by putting their energy into doing things for their children and grandchildren (Farrell and Rosenberg, 1981).

The third issue raised by Huyck (1995) is somewhat antithetical to the second issue. She argues that responsibilities for children may distract from an otherwise satisfying marital relationship, with childrearing responsibilities reducing the time available for companionship and intimacy. The increased opportunities for companionship available when children leave home may be one reason for the increased marital satisfaction reported by some couples at this time.

The fourth issue concerns the fact that responsibility for dependent children may be a major influence on the extent of gender differentiation in the marriage (Gutmann, 1987). Certainly, there is evidence for sex roles becoming more traditional when children arrive. Huyck (1995) argues that, as children become more independent, each parent can 'reclaim repressed aspects of the self' (p. 192); repressed, that is, because of the parental imperative. This proposition is supported by the research of Huyck and Gutmann (1992), who found that wives who no longer had children living at home were more assertive in marriage, compared to those who still had children in the home.

Attachment in Relationships between Adult Children and their Parents

Relationships between parents and children continue to be important throughout life (Krause and Haverkamp, 1996). The majority of parents and children will spend 50 years in contact with one another, and many grandparents will know their grandchildren for 20 years or more (Hagestad, 1985). New problems can develop in the relationship between elderly parents and their adult children around the time when those adult children reach middle age. Mancini and Blieszner (1989) have argued that the concept of attachment can be fruitfully applied to understanding and dealing with conflict between adult children and elderly parents, given that the quality of parent–child relationships at this stage is likely to be affected by the quality of the relationships established earlier. After all, an assumption of attachment theory is that the parent–child bond continues throughout life and is influenced by internal working models that develop during childhood and adolescence.

The majority of adult children report feeling close or very close to their elderly parents, and only a very small percentage report being 'not at all close' (Cicirelli, 1981). Parents continue to provide emotional and instrumental support to adult children (Spitze and Logan, 1991), and there are generally high levels of support between middle-aged daughters and their elderly mothers (Walker and Thompson, 1983).

The quality of the parent–child relationship has implications for the well-being of middle-aged sons and daughters. There is evidence that their well-being is correlated with how close they feel to their mothers, and that this effect is particularly strong for those adult daughters who have not been mothers themselves (Baruch and Barnett, 1983). The better the relationship middle-aged children have with their parents, the less anxiety and depression they are likely to experience (Barnett *et al.*, 1991).

Stressors unique to relationships between adult children and older parents include changes in the parents' lives such as ill health and widowhood. In addition, the divorce of parents may adversely affect the attitudes and behaviour of adult children.

Parent–child relationships are also affected by the life stage of each member of the dyad. According to Erikson (1950), the central psychological crises of middle age are intimacy versus isolation, and generativity versus stagnation. At this stage, adult children may also be challenged by biological changes related to growing older, as well as being pressured by the demands of family, and concerns about financial obligations (both for the present and the future). Some have described the middle-aged as 'the sandwich generation: caught between growing children and aging parents' (Zal, 1992). This stage is also frequently referred to as the 'middle-aged squeeze', for similar reasons.

The older parents also have their share of challenges, including retirement, decreased health and the death of the spouse. Family ties are likely to become particularly important at this stage of life, with consequent expectations on adult children of more frequent interaction. Where obligations conflict, and expectations are different or unrealistic, there is likely to be conflict between the parent and adult child. A mismatch in developmental needs is also likely to bring conflict (Walsh, 1982). Adult children may withdraw to avoid problems associated with this stage, or, alternatively, they may try to take over the parent's life, not allowing them to make decisions that they are quite capable of making.

Caring for elderly parents

Caregiving may also become important at this time, especially when a parent has already been widowed, or when both parents are elderly and frail. Middle-aged children may even need to arrange more permanent care, such as that provided in hostels or nursing homes. A sense of attachment to the parent has both direct and indirect effects on the commitment to provide care (Cicirelli, 1983); reasons for caregiving tend to be based on making sure that the parents' needs are met, and on love for the parent, rather than on feelings of duty (Cicirelli, 1986).

As we have already noted, there is a substantial degree of continuity between an adult child's early experiences with their parents, and their current relationships with them (Pearson *et al.*, 1993). Whitbeck, Simons and Conger (1991) found that adults who recalled their parents as rejecting in childhood were less likely to report close relationships with those parents when they were old.

Consistent with these findings, Norris and Forbes (1987) identified factors which can reduce the chances of a successful caregiving experience for the frail elderly and their adult child carers. They argued that when the relationship is overly close or cohesive, and has not fully developed into a healthy and balanced attachment bond, the adult child is likely to be impaired in their ability to meet the parents' needs. These adult children can feel guilty or depressed, or they may even become physically ill themselves. These symptoms are particularly likely to emerge in a situation involving markedly unequal power, with the elderly mother or father dominating the adult child.

Dykstra (1993) found that relationships with adult children had high support potential for elderly parents, but the willingness of adult children to provide support depended on the availability of alternative sources of care (such as a spouse or a cohabiting partner). She also found that where a partner was available to the parent, relationships with adult children were less important in terms of dealing with loneliness.

Stein and her colleagues (Stein, 1992; Stein *et al.*, 1998) explored the importance of felt obligation to elderly parents. They found that the extent of felt obligation was affected by the gender of the adult child, with women feeling more obliged to help parents and other family members than men. Their results also highlighted the importance of the type of relationship; more obligation was experienced to one's own parents than to parents-in-law, and more obligation was experienced by those adults with only one parent still alive than by those adults with two living parents. In addition, Ganong and his colleagues (Ganong *et al.*, 1998) have shown that individuals feel less obligation towards step-parents than towards biological parents, particularly when the step-parent was 'acquired' later in life.

Cicirelli (1983) explored the factors which predicted strain in adult children who were the primary caregivers for parents, and found a relationship between the level of dependency of the parent and the strain experienced by caregivers. Many adult children reported feeling physically worn out, emotionally exhausted, frustrated, impatient and irritated. Their frustration tended to come from being tied down in terms of their daily schedules, and, consequently, having to give up social activities that were important to them. Middle-aged adults caring for an elderly parent routinely report stress-related symptoms such as anxiety, depression and fatigue (King, 1993; Parks and Pilisuk, 1991). Most adult children are ill-prepared for making decisions related to the ageing and eventual death of their parents, and for coping with the accompanying emotional stress.

Daughters tend to be the primary carers for elderly mothers, especially for widowed mothers; daughters-in-law may fill the breach, if no daughter is available (Brody, 1985). The care provided may include medically related care, such as giving medication or helping with exercises; personal care, such as assisting with toileting or showering; household tasks, such as cleaning and laundry; shopping for basic necessities, such as food and clothing; and providing transportation to shops or medical appointments. It is important to keep in mind that age of marriage and parenthood vary widely, and that, as Brody notes, the timing of marriages and parenthood of both generations influences the availability of care.

If the parent is needing care when the adult daughter is heavily involved in caring for her own children, for example, she will be less free to provide extensive care for the mother. The situation is further complicated by the fact that women may have a number of caring roles (Brody, 1985). A woman could be providing care for her father who is in a nursing home, her mother who is still living at home, an elderly maiden aunt who has no one else to provide care, as well as for her husband and children. Working daughters are more likely to be expected to adjust work schedules because of caring responsibilities than are working sons, and even those daughters who adjust work schedules, or even give up work completely, report that they often feel guilty about not doing enough for their elderly parents.

According to Starrels *et al.* (1997), there is clear consensus about the negative effects of the older person's cognitive impairment on caregiver stress, but little consensus about the effects of physical impairment on caregiver stress. Overall, studies seem to show little relation between the declining physical health of the care recipient and the caregiver's stress or burden (e.g., Barber, 1989; Miller, 1990a, 1990b), although there is some evidence for increases in caregiver distress when the older person's physical impairment is very severe. Caregiver distress may be greater in this situation because of the seriousness of the illness, or because of the physical stress involved when a patient requires constant care and help with all aspects of living.

With regard to cognitive impairment, the effects on caregiver stress are much clearer. Adult children caring for cognitively impaired parents tend to report higher levels of emotional, physical and financial strain than do those who care for parents with physical impairment only, at least when the caregivers are also trying to hold down jobs (Brody, 1990). In their study of a large sample of employed sons and daughters caring for parents, Starrels and her colleagues (1997) found that the direct effect of impairment on caregiver stress was stronger for cognitive than for physical impairment. In addition, they found that the amount of caregiving required and the need to take time off from work also had indirect effects on caregiver stress.

Parental death in middle age

The importance of the parent–child bond is further highlighted when we look at the reactions of adult children to the death of their parents (Cicirelli, 1991), reactions that are affected by past experiences in the relationship in line with attachment theory. For example, Gutmann (1991) found evidence that the death of a parent has implications for conflict in the marriages of middle-aged offspring. She argues from psychodynamic principles that, following the parent's death, the bereaved partner can project his or her negative relationship with the parent on to the spouse. Similarly, in the case of the over-idealized parent, the partner may be blamed for not being able to replace the parent and ease the partner's grief.

Taylor and Norris (1993) carried out a study of middle-aged women's experiences of their mother's death. The deaths seemed to have more long-lasting effects in cases where attachments had been disrupted by parental abuse. Almost half of the women with avoidant or ambivalent attachment styles reported instances of abuse during their childhood, whereas only 10 per cent of the women with secure attachment relations reported having experienced abuse. Taylor and Norris argue that the poor models of attachment that the insecure women had to contend with, as well as the difficulties they experienced in the parent–child relationship, seemed to cause these women problems in their other significant relationships, even after the mother's death.

Friendships in Midlife

The majority of middle-aged people have friends and these friendships can serve a range of functions, including 'providing affection and enjoyment, understanding and social support, companionship and counsel' (Adams and Blieszner, 1996). Friendships that fulfil these functions are likely to make an important contribution to the health and well-being of those involved (Hobfoll and Stokes, 1988).

Adams and Blieszner (1996) claim that there is more variability in friendship patterns at midlife than at any other period of life. Because middle age is also a time when there tend to be high levels of responsibility in family and work lives, keeping in contact with friends can be particularly difficult. On the other hand, many friendships are initiated through other family members or through contact at work. In addition, many middle-aged people become concerned about the welfare of future generations, and may become involved in various types of voluntary work to improve the physical and social environment. These pursuits can provide new opportunities for relationships with people of like mind, but the time taken up by such activities may leave little time for actual social activity.

According to Adams and Blieszner (1996), friendship patterns in middle age are affected by the personality dispositions of the individuals (e.g., extraversion, agreeableness) and by the individual's position in the social structure (e.g., age, gender, race or class), as well as by the context in which they live (e.g., alone or with other family members). The activities the person tends to engage in are also important, along with the regularity with which those activities occur, and the extent to which they provide opportunities for social relationships. As Adams and Blieszner (1996) note, 'It is the process of living from day to day that shapes friendship patterns' (p. 342). An individual's personal maturity and development also have an impact on friendship patterns.

Summary

Midlife can be a time of heavy responsibilities for both men and women in work and family areas. People are generally at the peak of their careers, with heavy demands and significant levels of responsibility. Family responsibilities can be high, especially for women, who may be launching children and also caring for elderly parents – hence the term 'sandwich generation' which has been applied to middle-aged women. Middle age can also be a time when people become more conscious of the finiteness of life, and of unfulfilled goals, and more aware of the physical and psychological symptoms of ageing. It can be a time for reassessment, and for becoming involved in new and interesting activities.

Marriages that have survived through to middle age tend to be happy, although there can be a diversity of marriage styles at this time of life, depending on whether the focus of the couple is on their own relationship, on the family as a whole, or on outside activities. There is evidence that women tend to feel underbenefited in their marriages at this time in their lives, and the probability of divorce tends to be increased if women are financially independent and the children have left home.

People in midlife generally have to deal with the illness and death of parents, and may have to spend a considerable amount of time caring for parents. Although the majority of adult children report feeling close to their elderly parents, from an attachment theory perspective, it seems clear that relationships with elderly parents will depend on the quality of relationships developed earlier in life.

Friendships are also important in midlife, with these relationships providing affection and enjoyment, understanding and social support, companionship and counsel. Friendship patterns at this stage of life tend to be affected by personality factors, the individual's position in the social structure, the context in which they live, and the activities in which they engage.

6

Personal Relationships and the Elderly

Defining Old Age

There is great variability in terms of the age when people experience physical, psychological, or social limitations because of advancing age. One way to define old age would be as the time when poor health creates a major limitation on activity. In a 1981 US survey, half of all people aged 75 to 84 reported no such health limitations, and even in the over-85 group, one-third reported no limitations due to health, and another third reported only minor limitations. The other third, however, were unable to carry out any of their everyday activities (cited in Neugarten and Neugarten, 1987).

Demographic changes such as the increase in life expectancy have led to larger numbers of elderly people present in western societies. These changes provide a challenge for us to change the way that we deal with the elderly, who are often not well integrated into our families and our societies (Vanzetti and Duck, 1996, p. 497). As these authors point out, as far as marriage is concerned, ''til death us do part' may mean 50, 60, or even more years. The parent–child relationship is also likely to extend for 65, 70, or even more years, with adult (and sometimes elderly, themselves) children being called upon to provide care for a parent. The sibling relationship is likely to continue for 80 or more years. And who knows how these demographic trends will shape society in the future?

Of course, there are countervailing trends such as later marriage, later parenting and more frequent divorce, that will also have an impact on the length of our close relationships. There is evidence of gender differences in these trends, with women tending to live longer than men (about eight years or so), to have longer widowhoods, and to be less likely than widowed men to remarry, especially if they are over 50 years of age (Grambs, 1989).

Pessimistic Views of Later Life

Few of the images of old age offered by our culture involve healthy later-life adjustment within a family context (McGoldrick, Heiman and Carter, 1993; Walsh,

1982). According to McGoldrick *et al.* (1993), myths about the elderly tend to focus on institutional care, and to assume either lack of family or little relationship with family members. In fact, many elderly people do not live alone or in institutions, but rather live with family members. In addition, contact with family members tends to be fairly frequent, with most elderly people living within relatively easy access of at least one of their children (Walsh, 1982).

Not only are there pessimistic views in the media and the culture about the family ties of elderly people, there are also negative views of the elderly people themselves. The elderly are often portrayed as sick, senile or feeble (McGoldrick *et al.*, 1993), when, in actuality, large numbers of them make an important contribution to our society and to the well-being of others through voluntary work in churches, hospitals and other agencies. However, many of the roles in which elderly people engage are devalued by our society. Asian societies are more likely to value their elderly people and to see them as sources of wisdom.

Importance of Relationships in Later Life

Hansson and Carpenter (1994) argue that, because of the declines in personal and social functioning that can accompany old age, personal relationships and the support of family and friends are critical. They also note, however, that families and support networks need to adapt to the changing needs of the elderly person. Maintaining positive and supportive relationships can be critical for the mental and physical well-being of the elderly person, with lack of support likely to lead to loneliness, depression and poor health outcomes (Silverstein and Bengtson, 1991).

Ambivalent Relations between Family Members and Elderly People

Evidence concerning the positive effects of contact with family on the morale of elderly people is mixed (Mares, 1995). Elderly parents tend to have larger networks of friends than childless adults, to be more integrated into their neighbourhoods, and to be more likely to own their own homes (Rempel, 1985). On the other hand, childless adults tend to be in better health than their counterparts who are parents. There is also evidence that where relationships between elderly parents and their adult children are close, recently widowed parents cope better with the death of the spouse than do those who have weaker social networks (Silverstein and Bengtson, 1991).

Luescher and Pillemer (1998) propose a new way of looking at intergenerational relationships. They claim that, rather than thinking about these relationships in terms of solidarity or conflict, what really characterizes these relationships is intergenerational ambivalence. The three aspects of ambivalence that they discuss are dependence versus autonomy, conflicting norms, and solidarity.

With regard to dependence, these theorists argue that ambivalence between the two poles of autonomy and dependence characterizes many intergenerational relationships in modern western societies. They see this ambivalence as involving the desire of elderly parents and their adult children for support and help from family members, together with the desire of the children to be independent of their parents. Of course, those parents who live to a 'grand old age' are likely to become dependent on their children, but these parents are also likely to resent intrusions on their autonomy by those same children. In this situation, well-intentioned and not so well-intentioned offers of help from daughters are likely to be seen by some mothers as attempts to control (Cohler and Grunebaum, 1981). Barrera and Baca (1990) found that such reactions were more common when there was continuing conflict in the parent–adult child relationship.

With regard to conflicting norms, George (1986) discusses the conflict between the reciprocity norm and the solidarity norm with regard to relations between elderly people and other members of their families. The reciprocity norm requires a relationship in which each person gives help to the other, whereas the solidarity norm requires that help be given when needed, without any consideration of receiving something in return. George argues that the ambivalence resulting from these conflicting norms is likely to be experienced by both parent and adult child, with the caregiver experiencing distress at the disruption of the more reciprocal relationship of the past, and the care-receiver feeling guilty and helpless about their inability to reciprocate the help provided.

Ambivalence over solidarity is illustrated by the mutual dependence often seen to characterize parent–child relationships in which the elderly parent is abused (Wolf and Pillemer, 1989). Although the disabled parent in such relationships is generally highly dependent on the adult child, the adult child may also be highly dependent on the parent in terms of such needs as housing and financial assistance (Pillemer, 1985, 1993). Pillemer has claimed that many of these adult children have had problems in separating from their parents, and have experienced feelings of powerlessness and helplessness which seem to be linked to the abusive way they related to their parent. We will return to this issue of elder abuse later in this chapter.

Transitions in Later Life

There are a number of transitions related to later life. These include retirement from work, becoming a grandparent, loss of spouse and other loved ones, and changes in accommodation because of needs for care. We will look at the changes brought about by retirement in this section, and examine the other transitions in later sections of this chapter.

Retirement

Retirement has implications not only for the individual who is giving up work after so many years but also for other family members. From the perspective of the individual, retirement is likely to involve giving up status and power, although the extent of this loss depends on the kind of work they have been involved in, and the level at which they have worked (McGoldrick *et al.*, 1993). Even those who have experienced little in the way of status or power may have defined themselves primarily or totally in terms of their work, and may experience a sense of meaninglessness about their lives (McGoldrick *et al.*, 1993). Those who have had considerable status and power may have great difficulty giving up this power, especially in contexts such as family businesses.

Because many of our nonfamily relationships are developed in the work context, retirement can also mean the loss of friends and acquaintances, and of opportunities for social interaction. Unless the retired person seeks new social contacts through becoming involved in recreational or service activities, they may become isolated. Where possible, taking the opportunity to become more involved with children and grandchildren can enhance the availability of ongoing close relationships.

Retirement can put pressures on the marital relationship as husbands and wives, who have generally spent their working lives in different spheres, now have to develop new ways of living together, with much more frequent contact. There is evidence that these new arrangements affect women's perceptions of the marital relationship more than they affect the perceptions of men (Lee, 1988).

There are several reasons for these differing effects. First, there tends to be unequal division of labour in the home, with the lowest levels of relationship satisfaction being reported by wives who are still working when husbands have retired (Rexroat and Shehan, 1987). These wives may expect that household chores will be taken over by the retired husband; further, they may be disappointed when they find that they are still taking major responsibility for these tasks, given that husbands and wives tend to maintain patterns established earlier in their relationship (Brubaker, 1990).

Second, even if (or perhaps especially if) the wife is not working full time, there may be extra demands on her time for companionship, and for preparing meals, etc. (Keating and Cole, 1980; Ward, 1993). In Keating and Cole's sample of retired teachers, the division of household tasks was no more egalitarian than it had been pre-retirement, and there were more demands on the wives' time. If wives find that they have less autonomy than previously in terms of deciding how they use their time, they are likely to feel dissatisfied.

Financial pressures are also very real for the retired couple, since they generally have to learn to live on less money than they have had in the past. Working out how the more limited resources are to be spent, and coming to an equitable arrangement, can be difficult. Those who have to live on government pensions may need to make drastic changes to spending patterns. On the other hand, the incomes of self-funded retirees are subject to a number of factors beyond their control, such as interest rates. Those who have worked out the funds needed for retirement 20 years ahead may find those funds inadequate when economic circumstances change.

Dealing with Change

Elderly people experience age-related declines in a number of areas, and there is considerable variability in the age at which such declines occur. Changes can occur in physiological capacity, cognitive capacity, economic status and social stress (Hansson and Carpenter, 1994).

Because of the changes referred to above, elderly people generally experience changes in accommodation needs in later life (Hansson and Carpenter, 1994), and these living arrangements and the degree to which elderly people are integrated into families can be quite diverse. In the USA, 67 per cent of those aged 65 and over live with at least one family member, usually a spouse (Hansson and Carpenter, 1994). An American survey has also shown that 80 per cent of elderly adults have living children, and that two-thirds of those children live within half an hour of the parent/s, and have regular contact with them either through visits or telephone calls. Because older adults can vary widely in terms of health or illness, economic security or poverty, and their levels of coping skills, family members need to be available to provide help and support when it is needed.

There is evidence that attitudes to co-residence with elderly parents have changed, with adult children now feeling less obligation to have their frail elderly parents living with them (Goldscheider and Lawton, 1998). It is interesting to note that those adult children whose grandparents had lived in the family when they were children experienced a stronger sense of obligation to parents. Other researchers have shown that women are likely to feel more obligated to care for parents than are men, and that those with only one living parent feel more obliged to provide care than those with two living parents: presumably, in this latter case, the spouse is seen as able to provide care (Stein *et al.*, 1998). However, Ganong and his colleagues (Ganong *et al.*, 1998) found no sex differences in willingness to care for elderly parents. They also showed that obligations tended to be stronger to biological parents than to step-parents, unless the relationship with the step-parent was perceived as very close.

Marriage Relationships in Later Life

The relationship between spouses in older marriages depends, at least to some extent, on the historical context of the marriage (Mares, 1995). Mares argues that when the relationships of those who were married in the 1920s and 1930s are compared with those who were married in the 1960s and 1970s, and those married more recently, a number of differences emerge. For example, in the earlier marriages there is less emphasis on communication and shared activities (Caplow *et al.*, 1982), and the likelihood of divorce is lower. In more recent years, on the other hand, there has been decreased emphasis on marriage as a normative lifestyle for women (Faver, 1984), higher divorce rates, and more emphasis on egalitarian decision-making (Holahan, 1984).

A typology of older marital relationships

Weishaus and Field (1988) developed a typology of couples in long-term marriages, on the basis of data collected from a small group of 17 couples (see Table 6.1). They found four different types of couples and labelled them curvilinear (seven couples), stable-positive (five couples), stable-neutral (three couples) and stable-negative (two couples). Curvilinear was the most common pattern, with these couples reporting that their marriages started out with high levels of positive affect, but that there was a drop in satisfaction somewhere in the middle years, followed by an increase in later years. This pattern is commonly reported, with the drop in satisfaction generally related to having children in the home (Lerner and Spanier, 1978).

The five stable-positive couples reported a close vital relationship throughout marriage, although not without some ups and downs. Despite problems, their love and respect for each other was sustained at a high level. The stable-neutral relationships involved less investment in the relationship on the part of the spouses; there

TABLE 6.1 *Types of couples in long-term marriages*

Couple type	Frequency and characteristics
Stable-positive	Five marriages out of 17. Close vital relationship sustained by a strong affective component. Some ups and downs but spouses spoke highly of one another and of the relationship.
Stable-neutral	Three marriages out of 17. Marriage was not their major emotional investment. Little passion and little conflict, and spouses generally got on fairly well together.
Stable-negative	Two marriages out of 17. Stable marriages but with negative affect throughout the relationship. Hostility not overt but little sign of positive affect.
Curvilinear	Most common pattern. Seven out of 17 couples reported this pattern. High levels of affect and satisfaction early in the marriage, a decrease in the middle years and an increase in later years after the children left home.
Continuous decline	Not present in the sample. Some may have terminated earlier, and some may have shown the curvilinear pattern, with an increase later in the marriage.
Continuous increase	None of the couples showed this pattern. It may be more common in arranged marriages.

Source: Noller and Fitzpatrick, 1993. Copyright © 1993 by Allyn & Bacon. Reprinted by permission.

was little passion but also little conflict, with the spouses tending to get along fairly well together. The stable-negative couples reported negative affect as being present throughout the relationship. They also reported that the conflict was less overt in later years.

Weishaus and Field (1988) found that none of their couples fitted the two other possible patterns: continuous decline in satisfaction or continuous increase. They suggested that those who had experienced continuous decline would probably have divorced long before, whereas continuous increase might be more likely in the case of arranged marriages.

Relationship satisfaction in later life marriages

Pearson (1996) reports that long-term marriages tend to involve increased companionship, less sharing of information, idiosyncratic ways of communicating with each other that are more implicit and less explicit, and a less analytic and more noncommittal style (Zietlow and Sillars, 1988). According to Swenson and his colleagues (Swenson, Eskew and Kohlhepp, 1981), relationship satisfaction is generally reasonably high in long-term marriages, but the relationships tend to be more disengaged, with lower levels of disclosure and higher levels of unexpressed feelings. Others have described the typical marriage of 'later years' as disengaged but congenial (Mares, 1995), as involving more deference than earlier marriages (Zietlow and Van Lear, 1991), and as involving fewer gender differences in the use of control.

Nevertheless, there is evidence that later in life women are more responsive to the needs of their spouses than are men (Quirouette and Gold, 1992). These researchers see this pattern as related to the years of family caregiving on the part of wives that have made them attentive to the needs of others, even though they may not have received a similar level of attentiveness in return. Marital satisfaction seems to correlate with spousal attributes such as intimacy, trust, interpersonal sensitivity, altruism and being able to take the perspective of another (Davis and Carpenter, 1987). Given that these attributes are generally associated more with women, and that these researchers found no correlation between marital satisfaction and scores on these attributes, it again seems likely that women will tend to have lower satisfaction.

Loss of Spouse

Almost inevitably one spouse is left on their own in old age because of the death of the partner. The primary needs of widows and widowers, of course, is to accept the loss of the spouse and to carry on with their lives. Adjustment difficulties are almost inevitable, as the individual first deals with the grief and then learns to deal with the tasks that were previously carried out by the partner. Anticipating death (e.g., following a long illness) does not seem to reduce adjustment difficulties (Hill, Thompson and Gallagher, 1988). Losing the partner is likely to mean losing the most intimate relationship, and the daily lives of widows and widowers are likely to change dramatically. Men are likely to have to do household tasks generally done by their wives, and women may have to learn to manage financial tasks like banking, paying bills, keeping records and completing tax returns. Of course, not all households operate with strict gender differentiation of roles, and not all differentiation follows the same pattern. While some younger widows remarry, remarriage is generally more likely for men than for women (Grambs, 1989). Thus it is more likely that widows will have to learn to manage on their own.

Other important tasks for the recently widowed include finding new activities and interests, and rebuilding the support network (Lamme, Dykstra and Broese Van Groenou, 1996). The loss of the partner generally means losing relationships that were part of the lifestyle of the married couple, and personal relationships need to be reorganized to provide for adequate support (both tangible and emotional). Lamme and her colleagues studied a group of people who had been widowed within the last ten years. They found that only 27 per cent of the widows in their sample reported new members in their social networks. To qualify as new network members, these relationships had to be important to the widow (in their top 12 social ties) and involve regular contact (at least monthly). These relationships often formed with neighbours. Those who were regular church attenders were less likely than others to form new relationships, contrary to what was expected. Lamme and her colleagues argue that church attenders may already have strong support networks, or may compensate for their loss, at least to some extent, through their relationship with God.

Relationships with Adult Children

As we noted earlier, increasing life expectancy generally means that the parent–child relationship is longer (Kaufman and Uhlenberg, 1998). Given that people are generally becoming parents at a later age, however, this trend may not continue. Contact between the parent and the adult child tends to be frequent (Shanas, 1980), although there are effects for gender of child on frequency of contact.

As Spitze and Logan (1990) show, having at least one daughter is important for three kinds of support: phoning, visiting and providing tangible help. Tangible help may include cleaning, shopping or taking the parent to medical appointments. Other variables affecting the frequency and type of contact include geographic proximity and the level of affect in the parent–adult child relationship (Bengtson and Roberts, 1991). Relationships with adult children have a relatively high support potential, although the extent to which that potential is utilized will depend on need (Dykstra, 1993). Dykstra found that formerly married parents received more support from their children than did those currently married or cohabiting. Those with a resident partner may have less need, or children may be less willing to provide help when there is a resident partner who can be expected to provide support.

It is important not to think of elderly parent–adult child relationships as one-way, with the adult children providing all the support. As noted earlier, elderly parents may also provide support for their adult children, including accommodation and financial support. Adult children who are married with children of their own tend to be seen as more successfully socialized, and are therefore seen in a more favourable light by their parents. On the other hand, when it comes to providing direct support, parents are likely to respond to the level of need of the individual adult child (Aldous, 1987). In general, those who are single or divorced are seen as more needy, perhaps because they often do not have an intimate other to provide support. Adult children can also have an impact on the well-being of the parents. For example, Pillemer and Suitor (1991) found that those whose children had problems, and those who were in conflict with their children, were more likely to be depressed.

Sibling Relationships in Later Life

Sibling ties tend to be strong throughout life (Mares, 1995). There is often frequent contact between siblings (Scott, 1983), although contact varies with stage of the life cycle (Goetting, 1986) (see also Chapter 4). Those busy raising their own children are likely to have less contact with siblings during that period, but may see them more frequently once childrearing responsibilities decline. There are a number of factors that are seen as predictors of sibling contact, including how close the siblings live to each other (Lee, Mancini and Maxwell, 1990), the size of the family of origin, the presence of other close relationships (Connidis, 1989), sex and ethnicity (Gold, 1989).

According to Connidis (1989), the larger the family, the lower the percentage of siblings who are considered as good friends, but also the higher the probability that at least one sibling will be seen as a close friend. Where one sibling is single, there tends to be more contact than between married pairs, suggesting that sibling relationships may be seen by adults as compensatory, in the sense that there is more contact between siblings when one of them does not have an intimate partner (Connidis, 1989).

Sex of sibling affects the level of contact between siblings, with sisters tending to have more contact with one another in later life than brothers or brother–sister dyads (Gold, 1989). Gold found that brothers reported higher resentment and lower acceptance of siblings than was true for sisters. Ethnicity also has an effect on contact between siblings, with African-Americans having more contact with each other than Anglo-Americans, and Italian-Americans having more contact than white Protestant families or Italian-Americans who married Non-italians.

Roles elderly siblings perform for one another

Elderly siblings perform a number of roles for one another. One of the more important ones is in terms of having someone to reminiscence with about their common experiences, and from whom to receive validation of their perceptions of family life (Cicirelli, 1980; Goetting, 1986). Although siblings might provide material aid for one another, their contribution in this regard is generally not as significant as that of children (Kivett, 1985a; Scott, 1983). Of course, single siblings who do not have children to support them, and those whose children live a long distance away, may need more help from their siblings. Stoller (1985) found that aid that could not be reciprocated led to lower morale in the elderly person, although there may be gender effects, with sisters tending to see such situations less negatively (Brubaker, 1990). Overall, siblings seem to have little or no effects on each other's well-being in later life, although sometimes the effects can be mildly negative (Essex and Nam, 1987).

Grandparenting

A number of changes in society have implications for the grandparent role (Hagestad, 1988). The longer life expectancy could mean that there will be more great-grandparents, and great-great-grandparents. Because of the reduction in the length of childbearing years, there is less likely to be overlap between active parenting (that is, older couples with dependent children still living in the family home) and grandparenting. A countervailing effect, however, is the tendency for couples to marry later and to have their children in their thirties and forties.

Increases in divorce and remarriage (Mares, 1995) have meant that more elderly people have step-grandchildren. The changes in remarriage patterns have also increased the possibility of loss of contact with grandchildren, who may even move to a different country when, for example, a former daughter-in-law remarries. The older the step-grandchild when a parent remarries, the less involvement step-grandparents are likely to have with those children (Cherlin and Furstenberg, 1986). Overall, the relationship with step-grandparents is seen as less important by step-grandchildren than their relationship with their biological grandparents, and the quality of the relationship with grandparents depends on whether those grandparents have a biological link with the parent with whom the child spends most time (Johnson and Bahrer, 1987). When a couple divorces, the woman's parents generally drop the former husband from their social network, whereas the man's parents maintain contact with the former wife, as well as expanding their network to include the new wife as well (Cherlin and Furstenberg, 1986; Matthews and Sprey, 1984).

Roles of grandparents

The majority of grandparents find comfort, satisfaction and pleasure in the grand-parenting role, although about one-third acknowledge some negative aspects, such as conflict with parents over how the children are being raised (Neugarten and Weinstein, 1964). These researchers developed a typology of grandparents, according to their approach to the grandparenting role and the activities they engaged in with their grandchildren (see Table 6.2).

'Formal' grandparents tended to see their role as providing special treats for their grandchildren. Although they would babysit occasionally, they maintained clear lines between being parents and being grandparents. The group of grand-parents labelled as 'fun-seekers' tended to be involved with their grandchildren to have fun, and to enjoy interactions with them. These grandparents tended to see authority as irrelevant to their relationships with their grandchildren. Another group of grandparents were labelled as 'distant figures' because contact occurred only (or primarily) on holidays and ritual occasions, such as birthdays or weddings. A further category of grandparent was labelled 'reservoir of family wisdom'. This group consisted predominantly of grandfathers, who were seen as authoritative older figures who provided advice when it was needed.

Some grandparents take on the role of surrogate parent, and do many of the tasks normally carried out by parents. Those who take on this role are a relatively small group, consisting mostly of grandmothers. In 1991, 3.3 million in the USA lived with a grandparent (Jendrek, 1993), and in 28 per cent of those cases no parent was present in the home. There is some evidence that children raised by grand-parents do not fare as well in terms of emotional, social and educational outcomes as children raised by parents, but this effect may stem from the factors leading to

TABLE 6.2 *A typology of grandparents*

Type of grandparent	Role	Activities with grandchild
Formal	Providing special treats for grandchildren	Occasional babysitting, special gifts and outings, few parenting tasks
Fun-seeker	Having fun and enjoying interactions with grandchildren	Outings, reading stories, playing games, etc.
Distant figure	Contact primarily on holidays and ritual occasions	Attendance at ritual occasions such as weddings, birthdays and Christmas
Reservoir of family wisdom	Provide advice when needed – mostly grandfathers	Little involvement in fun activities or special treats – available for advice

Source: Neugarten and Weinstein, 1964

the grandparent taking on the role (such as illness, death or incarceration of the parent), rather than the way in which the grandparents carry out the parenting tasks (Amato, 1993).

A later typology of grandparents focused on the meaning or significance of the grandparenting role to grandparents (Kivnick, 1983). Some grandparents saw the grandparenting role as central to who they were as people, whereas others saw themselves as a valued resource person who could provide help, such as childcare, when needed. Other grandparents focused on the importance of continuing the family line, or on opportunities to relive aspects of their own lives through their grandchildren. A further group emphasized that grandparents could be indulgent with their grandchildren in ways that they were not able to be with their own children.

More recently, Peterson (1999) studied a sample of 146 Australian grandfathers and grandmothers, aged 41 to 88 years, using some of the same measures as had

TABLE 6.3 *The 'best thing' about grandparenthood according to Australian grandfathers and grandmothers*

		Grandfathers mentioning		Grandmothers mentioning	
Category of reason	*Example*	*N*	*%*	*N*	*%*
Contemplation of development	Watching them grow up	13	28	36	36
Shared activity and companionship	Just being with them	6	14	28	28
Shared love and affection	Loving them and feeling special because they love you	9	20	18	18
Freedom from responsibility	You can give them back at the end of the day	7	15	17	17
Family and/or biological renewal	They make me feel young again	6	13	12	12
Pride (personal and vicarious)	Watching their success in their careers	7	15	10	10
Own usefulness	You feel they really need you	5	11	9	9
Teaching/conveying wisdom and experience	I can tell them my philosophy of life based on my experiences	4	9	7	7
Ritual family events	Christmas with the whole family	4	9	7	7

Note: Percentages may total more than 100 per cent, as respondents could give more than one reason.

been employed in the USA by Neugarten and Weinstein (1964), several decades earlier. The results confirmed the findings, cited above, that a majority of contemporary grandparents find the role to be satisfying and enjoyable. Indeed, fewer than 10 per cent of these grandparents reported being disappointed or dissatisfied with this role. Further, approximately 10 per cent claimed that none of their other roles in life (including parent and spouse) afforded them more satisfaction than grandparenting. Some of the specific aspects of the grandparent–grandchild relationship that provided high levels of satisfaction are shown in Table 6.3.

Variables Affecting the Grandparent–Grandchild Relationship

The grandparent–grandchild relationship depends, at least to some extent, on the ages of the grandchild and of the grandparent. Kahana and Kahana (1970) found that young children discussed their grandparents in egocentric terms ('What they do for me'), whereas 8- and 9-year-olds focused more on the mutuality in the relationship. Children in the 11 to 12 age group were the least likely to express preferences for particular grandparents, although they still preferred indulgent grandparents who gave them lots of treats.

According to Neugarten and Weinstein (1964), older grandparents tended to have more formal relationships with their grandchildren, whereas younger grandparents were more likely to have distant or fun-seeking relationships with their grandchildren. It is possible that the role played by the grandparent is dictated by age of child more than by the age of the grandparent, with grandparents becoming more formal as grandchildren move into adolescence.

The gender of the grandparent also seems to affect the type of role played in grandchildren's lives. Children in the study by Kahana and Kahana (1970), mentioned earlier, generally tended to express preferences for maternal grandmothers. There is also evidence that grandmothers and grandfathers take rather different perspectives on grandparenting (Crawford, 1981). Grandmothers attempt to influence grandchildren in interpersonal as well as instrumental contexts (Hagestad, 1985), and tend to be more satisfied with grandparenting (Thomas, 1986a), especially when they see themselves as responsible for providing help. Grandfathers tend to see the grandparenting role as less important than their voluntary work at the church, or their participation in leisure activities such as golf or bowls (Kivett, 1985a, 1985b).

Proximity is also seen as an important factor affecting relationships between grandparents and grandchildren. According to an American study, geographic distance accounts for over 60 per cent of the variance in frequency of contact between grandparents and their grandchildren (Cherlin and Furstenberg, 1986). College students' reports of their relationships with their grandparents could be predicted by the frequency of interactions during childhood, with grandparents who were in contact more than three times per year seen as being 'close' (Matthews and Sprey, 1984).

As might be expected from a systems perspective, the relationship between grand-parents and parents provides the emotional context for grandparent–grandchild interaction (Whitbeck, Hoyt and Huck, 1993). Grandparents who reported emotionally close relationships with their daughters saw their grandchildren about twice as often as those who did not have close relationships with their daughters. The grandmother's relationship with her own mother-in-law can also be an important predictor of the frequency of contact with grandchildren (Matthews and Sprey, 1984). If, as a young mother, she had difficult relationships with her mother-in-law she is less willing to become involved with her son's wife and family.

Doka and Mertz (1988) interviewed a sample of great-grandparents. These older people generally had favourable reactions to being a great-grandparent, reporting that they saw reaching this milestone as a mark of longevity. Having a great-grandchild provided a sense of personal and familial renewal and a diversion from their daily lives, with new things to do and places to go, at least for those well enough to go on outings. Most, however, maintained a fairly remote style of great-grandparenting, characterized by limited and ritualistic contact. This situation may occur because older people find visits with great-grandchildren too tiring (Wentowski, 1985).

Friendships in Later Life

Because of women's skill in developing support relationships they tend to have larger and more diverse friendship networks than men, as well as more trusted confidants. These larger networks should make it more likely that appropriate support will be available, despite the inevitable loss of network members that occurs with age (Hobfoll, 1988).

According to Hansson and Carpenter (1994), relationships with friends become more important than family relationships in old age. Arling (1976), for example, found that relationships with friends were more strongly related to morale than were relationships with family members. Once the elderly person needs care, family members again become more important. At that stage, care is usually undertaken, first by a spouse and then by adult children, with the possibility of formal support from agencies when the care becomes too onerous for family members.

An interesting illustration of the importance that friends can assume in old age comes from the work of Meyerhoff (1980), who described the experiences of a group of elderly Jewish émigrés in America whose adult children and grandchildren had completely assimilated into the local culture, losing their ties to their religion, language and culture. For these elderly citizens, peer relationships came to be extremely important, providing a safe haven in an alien world. The friends spent time together each day, sharing their common background and supporting each other.

Of course, with age, the friendship network tends to diminish as peers die or move into nursing homes. Those who remain living independently have a smaller and smaller network of friends, and it is important that they can adapt to their new circumstances. Of course, the death of friends of one's own age raises the issue of mortality for all of us. Finding new friends may be important at this stage. Because of the expectation that friends should be in the same age group, however, new friendships are also likely to be vulnerable, and the death of friends becomes a relatively common occurrence.

Relational competence seems to be particularly important to maintaining and initiating relationships in old age. Hansson and Carpenter (Hansson, 1986; Hansson and Carpenter, 1986, 1994) have explored the ways in which shyness, and consequent loneliness, impacts on the networks of elderly persons. For example, lonely older widows were less likely to have discussed their situation with other older widows. They also had greater difficulty in making new friends because of their lack of social skills, saw their neighbourhoods as less safe and predictable, and had less knowledge about the social services available to them.

In similar vein, general communication skills (such as being able to initiate new contacts, and being assertive) tend to be related to more satisfaction with relationships. Carpenter (1993) found that assertive, outgoing elderly people had more friendships that were close and supportive, and felt less lonely and anxious. Those with high levels of relational competence are likely to have more friends and also be better able to cope with the social transitions required of elderly people (widowhood, moving to new neighbourhoods, making new friends). They are also better able to deal with stressful situations, with consequent positive effects on health and well-being.

As Matthews (1996) points out, social skills are not the only factor likely to affect the relationships of the elderly. Lack of mobility, problems with vision and hearing, and frailty are all likely to have an impact. Becoming frail, dependent and housebound increases the possibility of losing friends or reducing contact with friends. In addition, as relationships become less reciprocal, with one partner requiring more attention because of frailty or illness, friendships can be expected to fade away, even when there is goodwill between the partners (Allan, 1989).

The friendship networks of elderly people are far from static. Adams (1986) studied the friendship networks of elderly people over a three-year period, and found that some of those networks had expanded during that time. In fact, because of moving into retirement communities, or moving from larger family homes into smaller accommodation, elderly persons may have to make new friends at several points after retirement.

Based on life history interviews with 63 elderly people, Matthews (1996) discusses three friendship styles characteristic of the elderly: acquisitive, discerning and independent. Those with an acquisitive style continue to make and 'collect' friends throughout their lives. Some people interviewed were still in contact with friends acquired early in life (e.g., at school or college). Those with a discerning style tend to have few friends, but are highly committed to each of them. These people also draw a clear distinction between friends and acquaintances. Finally, those with an independent style interact socially through joint activities, but tend not to have close friends. They are rather private people who are unwilling to accept the obligations that go along with friendship.

Disengagement theory emphasizes the tendency for older adults to relinquish important relationships, perhaps because of problems with both physical and psychological energy. This behaviour may also be a response to social losses such as widowhood, with its consequent period of grief, or perhaps because of social forces such as ageism which can make life more difficult for the elderly person to be a full member of society. There are also likely to be effects of individual differences: some elderly people may be quite happy about having fewer social contacts and obligations as they age (Larson, Zuzanek and Mannell, 1985), whereas others may choose to spend their time only with those with whom they have the most rewarding relationships (Norris and Tindale, 1994). There are likely to be cultural effects as well on how elderly people spend their time and with whom they spend it.

There is evidence that older people become increasingly selective in their choices about social partners (Frederickson and Carstensen, 1990) as well as less tolerant in their appraisals of others. It seems that they prefer to invest time and energy in relationships perceived as having positive outcomes, and to divest themselves of relationships that are, or have been, problematic. Experience may make them wiser in choosing friends, and they may develop a 'well-tested working model for potential attachments that helps screen, organize and analyse relevant social information' (Pratt and Norris, 1994). Of course, it is possible that this selectivity could lead to missed opportunities for companionship and support in later life (Norris and Tindale, 1994). On the positive side, this selectivity may save them time and energy, as well as potential hurt.

Illness and the Elderly

Hansson and Carpenter (1994) note that the increased longevity of elderly people does not necessarily mean that they will be in good health throughout later life. In fact, a large percentage of them are likely to have chronic health conditions such as arthritis (more than 50 per cent of those aged 75 and older), hypertension (34 per cent of those aged 75 or older) or a heart condition (32 per cent of those aged 75 or older). They are also likely to have various kinds of functional limitations, leading to problems with walking (23 per cent aged over 75 and 40 per cent aged over 85), bathing (28 per cent over 85), preparing meals (26 per cent over 85) and shopping (37 per cent over 85).

According to Rolland (1993) the effects of illness involve three interacting factors: the nature of the illness, the characteristics of the individual and the stage of the family life cycle. The elderly are prone to progressive diseases such as arthritis, Alzheimer's disease, Parkinson's disease and senile dementia (Suitor and Pillemer, 1992). They are also prone to such chronic diseases as asthma, emphysema and angina, and to sudden onset diseases such as heart attack and stroke. These sudden onset diseases may be fatal, or they may leave an elderly person (and even the not so elderly) with disabilities, such as difficulties in moving or speaking.

Another problem for the elderly is the possible loss of basic faculties, through loss of hearing or sight. These disabilities can severely limit the amount of social interaction the elderly person engages in, as well as the activities in which they can be involved. Someone with hearing loss is likely to have problems conversing with others, even when they have a hearing aid. The problem is likely to be particularly severe when they are interacting in groups (such as large family groups), and they are also likely to have difficulty using the telephone. In addition, they will have only limited success in listening to the radio and watching television, and may become isolated from what is happening in the world. Loss of sight makes it difficult for otherwise mobile people to be independent. It may also cause problems with social activities, as well as making reading or watching television impossible.

Care of the Elderly

Many elderly people reach a stage where they are unable to look after themselves. Depending on the level of infirmity, they may need help only with heavy cleaning and shopping, or they may need help with basic tasks such as bathing, dressing and food preparation. Those with only mild levels of infirmity may be able to stay in their own homes with help from family members and/or community agencies. These agencies can provide help with cleaning, with bathing and dressing, or with prepared meals.

Care needed by the elderly can be categorized into three types: physical, organizational and emotional (Nolan, Grant and Keady, 1996). Physical care includes performing such tasks as housework, home maintenance, shopping and transportation; organizational care includes making the appropriate links between the elderly person and the formal services; and emotional work involves providing companionship for the elderly person and cheering them up.

In a Canadian survey of what is considered appropriate care for the elderly, the consensus seemed to be that elder care should enhance the independence of the elderly person (Harlton, Keating and Fast, 1998). Respondents emphasized the need for elderly people to maintain control of their affairs and to remain in their own homes for as long as possible, with services provided for them reflecting their needs.

Generally, there are three alternative possibilities for caring for an elderly person who can no longer care for themselves: spousal care, care provided by an adult child (generally when there is no spouse available to care), and institutional care. Hansson and Carpenter (1994) note that families are generally willing and able to assume caregiving responsibilities and to make the necessary changes to enable family members to cope. Of course, there may be excessive burdens on members of the family who live close by, who do not work outside the home, or who have a home large enough to accommodate the elderly person (Brody, 1985; Stephens and Clark, 1996).

In general, wives are more likely than husbands to be the caregiver to an elderly spouse (Stephens and Clark, 1996), given that they tend to be younger and to live longer. In addition, women have generally been socialized to take on caring roles when necessary. Nevertheless, when husbands are available they tend to give as much care as wives (Brubaker, 1990). In addition, husbands and wives are equally likely to quit their paid jobs in order to care for spouses.

Spousal caregivers tend to experience higher levels of emotional, physical and financial strain than do other family caregivers, perhaps because caregiving violates the reciprocity norm that is central to marriage, particularly modern marriage. In addition, these spouses are likely to be old themselves. Wives tend to find caretaking more stressful than husbands, at least initially (Zarit, Todd and Zarit, 1986), and report more depression and more intense feelings of burden. There are several possible reasons why husbands may find caregiving less stressful than wives. It may be because they get more help from other relatives than do wives, or it may be that husbands and wives approach caregiving in quite different ways. Men may be able to approach caregiving in a more task-oriented and detached way, while women may have difficulty distancing themselves emotionally from the caregiving tasks and the implications for them, and for their marital relationship (Zarit et al., 1986).

Caregiver burden (Clark and Stephens, 1996) and caregiver resentment (Thompson, Medvene and Freedman, 1995) have both been studied as problems for those families caring for elderly family members. Thompson et al. (1995) found that resentment about caregiving was higher when the caregiver felt underbenefited in the relationship, was more exchange oriented (expected reciprocity), and thought that the partner was not putting in enough effort to improve their own health.

Edwards and Noller (1998) conducted a study of community-residing spousal dyads, half of which involved wives caring for husbands, with the other half involving husbands caring for wives. These researchers were interested in the communication between the spouses, and the implications of that communication for the well-being of both caregivers and care-receivers. The type of communication used by the spouses was influenced by their gender, their earlier relationship with their spouse, and their level of well-being. Wives were more likely to use an overly directive communication style, particularly if they had had a great deal of autonomy in their earlier relationship with their spouse. Those carers who had a low level of life satisfaction tended to use a more patronizing tone in their interactions with their spouse. Those care-receivers who perceived the communication from their caregiving spouse as patronizing tended to report more negative affect and more conflict in the relationship. Overall, communication from carers which conveyed a lack of respect for the care-receiver had a negative effect on the well-being of the care-receiver.

Adult children tend to provide high levels of both instrumental and psychological assistance to their elderly parents (Dean et al., 1989). Families generally seem to organize themselves to provide the necessary care for their parents (Matthews and Rosner, 1988). The caregiving may be divided unevenly or equally, depending on the size of the family and the gender of the adult children. Matthews and Rosner found that family members who offered little assistance tended to be in large families, and in families involving sons. In general, daughters are more likely to be the carers for their elderly parent, even when they are in full-time employment, and elderly parents with at least one daughter are most likely to receive help from their children (Spitze and Logan, 1990). On the other hand, sons tend to be very much on the periphery when it comes to caring for elderly parents. If the sons are married, care may be provided by their wives if they have no sister available to do the caring.

Overdependency on the part of the parents can be a problem for adult children trying to provide help for their parents. Kahn (1975) suggested that care for the aged should be based on the principle of minimum care on the part of the carer and maximum independence on the part of the elderly person, to ensure that the older person does not become more and more dependent on the care that is provided. Caring for an elderly parent is also likely to have an impact on the offspring's family of procreation, since the amount of time spent on caring affects the amount of time available for the members of that family (Kleban *et al.*, 1989).

No matter how supportive family members are in caring for their elderly members, there may come a time when institutional care becomes the only viable alternative. Institutional care can be of several types. In hostel type care, meals and cleaning are provided, together with help with bathing, dressing and medications if needed. Nursing home care is more suitable for those who can no longer care for themselves, and who need help with functions such as eating and toileting. Those with severe cognitive problems (memory and orientation) are most likely to spend time in nursing homes, along with those who have severe physical disabilities.

Elder Abuse

As Hansson and Carpenter (1994) note, there is a high potential for caregiving relationships to involve feelings of frustration, resentment and helplessness, feelings which may lead to abuse of the elderly person. A study by Pillemer and Finkelhor (1988) in the United States suggested that around 3.2 per cent of the population of people over 65 had been abused by carers, with 2 per cent of the whole sample experiencing physical abuse and somewhat smaller percentages experiencing chronic verbal abuse or neglect. These figures represent a significant amount of suffering among elderly people, and are more likely to apply to those living with a spouse (Hansson and Carpenter, 1994). Abuse of the elderly is more likely to be perpetrated by the person with whom they are living, and most live either with a spouse or alone. Those most at risk of abuse are women (there are many more women than men in this group), those who are older or who have poorer health, those who create conflict in the family or have ongoing conflicts with the child who is caring for them. These latter factors underline the relevance of the quality of family relationships through the lifespan for parent–child relationships in old age.

Future Trends in Relationships of the Elderly

While it is always difficult to predict the future, it seems likely that life expectancy will continue to increase at similar rates as it has over the last couple of decades. Consequently, we are likely to have more and more elderly people needing care and attention in their eighties and nineties. Family members are likely to play an important part in this care, even though they may not be the primary carers. Even elderly people who are in institutional care need regular visits and assistance with shopping and with medical visits.

Those living with spouses or in the homes of adult children are also likely to need a lot of help as they move into their eighties and nineties. Given the later age at which many people are currently marrying and having children, and the large percentage of women in full-time careers, there may be fewer middle-aged women available to do the caring, and these women may be less willing to give up professional careers to care for ageing parents.

The high incidence of divorce in western culture may mean that there are fewer spousal carers available to care for elderly women, in particular. Given that divorced men who remarry are likely to marry younger women, these wives are likely to be healthier and more able-bodied when the husbands reach the point at which they need care. How many of these women will be available to care for ailing spouses, and willing to give up careers in midlife, is not clear. Perhaps these women will be willing and able to pay for professional care for their husbands, and we will see a rise in the availability of such services.

Grandparents will no doubt continue to play a range of different roles, depending on proximity to grandchildren, the age of those grandchildren, and the relationship between the grandparent and the parents of the grandchildren. The aspects of the grandparent role that are important to each grandparent are also likely to affect the level of involvement with grandchildren. Undoubtedly, some elderly persons will be highly involved in these relationships, whereas others will err on the side of formality.

Sibling relationships will probably also continue to be important, again depending on proximity and relationship quality. Sisters are likely to play a particularly important role for women without partners, whether the loss of partner stems from divorce or widowhood. Given families tend to be spread far and wide because of the need to gain access to employment; hence, friends may have to perform some of the functions often performed by siblings, such as providing companionship and material assistance where necessary.

The fact that siblings are highly likely to be living in different cities makes friends particularly important to the well-being of older people. The elderly person may prefer to continue living where their friends are, rather than make a major move to be with their siblings. In addition, given that families today are usually smaller than families of the past, there are likely to be fewer siblings to care for each other, and to care for ageing parents. More of the care traditionally provided by families may have to be provided by government agencies, who will need to put additional resources into these areas.

Summary

Because people are living longer, the elderly are becoming a more significant proportion of our society. Although there is a lot of variability in the age at which individuals develop major limitations in their activities, and in their ability to care for themselves, many need help from family and friends in their later years.

The quality of marital relationships in later life depends on the historical context of the marriage, and the history of the relationship. Relationship satisfaction is generally relatively high, but relationships are likely to be more disengaged but congenial. Dealing with the death of the partner is another aspect of old age, and both men and women have to make considerable adjustment and to learn new skills at this stage of life. They may also need to develop new interests and become involved in new activities to fill the vacuum created by the partner's death.

Relationships with family and friends are also very important at this stage of life, and these relationships can provide both companionship and support. Relationships with spouses, adult children, grandchildren, siblings and friends are all important to the well-being of elderly people. In the case of the very elderly, spouses and adult children may be called upon to provide care, depending on the cognitive and physical capacities of the elderly person. The relatively small proportion of elderly people requiring high-level care may need to receive this care in institutions.

7

Relationships Across the Lifespan
Key Themes And Concepts

In this chapter, our goal is to draw together the recurring themes highlighted in the introduction, and elaborated on in the various chapters of this book. These themes are central to relationship functioning across the lifespan, and include attachment, intimacy, communication, conflict, power and control, and cultural and subcultural issues. We also consider the changing face of family relationships, and the implications of these trends for future relationship patterns.

Attachment

The attachment relationship forms a cornerstone of infants' social, emotional and cognitive development. During the early months of life, infants display a preparedness for social engagement, but specific attachments to particular caregivers do not emerge reliably until about the age of 7 months. Thus relationships, as we have defined them, can be seen to develop their unique characteristics towards the end of the first year of life.

The infant's first close relationship is with the primary caregiver. Based on repeated interactions with that caregiver, the infant develops an attachment style that can be either secure or insecure. Unless there are major changes in family dynamics or life circumstances, there is likely to be substantial continuity between the quality of this early relationship and the child's relationship to that caregiver throughout the lifespan. For example, when middle-aged women reach the point where they need to provide care for an elderly parent, the quality of their prior relationship with that parent will affect the quality of caregiving. Where the parent and child have not resolved important attachment-related issues, the emotions and behaviours associated with the caregiving experience can be troublesome for both parties.

There is also growing support for the view that the quality of the attachment relationships formed between infants and their caregivers can have an enduring impact on the offspring's other relationships throughout life. As illustrated in Chapter 3, Hazan and Zeifman (1994) have charted the process by which attachment functions are gradually transferred from parents to peers through late childhood, adolescence and young adulthood. In particular, as stable romantic partnerships are formed in late adolescence and early adulthood, the romantic partner usually becomes the primary attachment figure.

Over the past decade much research on romantic attachment has focused on trying to identify discrete styles of attachment, analogous to those observed in infants. More recently, an important goal of attachment researchers has been to define the major dimensions underlying these attachment styles. In other words, individual differences in adult attachment have been increasingly conceptualized and assessed in terms of continuous dimensions, rather than discrete categories (Feeney, 1999b). This body of research suggests that individual differences in romantic attachment are important predictors of relationship functioning. For example, attachment measures are reliable predictors of satisfaction in early marriage, of vulnerability to divorce, and of relationships with one's own children as a parent.

Intimacy

Infants' and children's secure attachments to parents and other caregivers clearly show qualities of intimacy. These qualities of closeness, reciprocal affection and mutual support are likely to generalize to young children's early peer relationships. However, it may not be until middle childhood and early adolescence that genuine intimacy, in the sense of knowing and valuing a mutual friend as a unique person, is clearly evident.

As individuals move through the lifespan, intimacy in friendship retains an important role, especially when it comes to confiding, seeking advice, and giving and receiving social support. We have noted previously, however, that there is evidence for gender differences in intimacy, expressiveness and disclosure between friends. According to Reis (1998), for example, diary studies show that men's same-sex interactions are substantially less intimate than those of women. Further, women are more likely to self-disclose than men, and are more often the targets of disclosure from both sexes (Dindia and Allen, 1992).

Intimate relationships with romantic partners also provide emotional intimacy, together with sexual intimacy. Although not all sexual encounters are 'intimate', we have presented research suggesting that intimacy and caring are strong features of most adolescent sexual relationships. In addition, the development of intimate bonds in the form of cohabiting and marital relationships is a central dynamic in adult psychological development and adjustment. Erikson (1968) emphasized the importance of intimacy, contrasting intimacy and isolation as the alternative outcomes of adult development. Forming intimate bonds affects such key issues as who we live with, and the amount of social support we receive.

The sexual component of couple bonds tends to become somewhat less salient over time, but individual differences in couples' interest in sex are fairly stable across the life cycle. Satisfaction with the sexual relationship tends to be strongly related to overall relationship satisfaction for both partners, supporting the important role of this form of intimacy in pair bonds.

Despite the central role of friends and romantic partners in adolescence and adulthood, intimacy with parents and siblings continues to be important for many individuals. As adolescents strive to become emotionally independent of their parents, there can be fluctuations in levels of intimacy expressed in the relationship, with adolescents being very confiding at some points and very distant and protective of their privacy at others. The majority of adult children feel close or very close to their parents, however, and parents continue to experience intimacy with, and provide emotional support to, their adult children.

Communication

Communication is central to all relationships across the lifespan. Even before language skills develop, infants express needs and emotions to their caregivers, and obtain information from them, through the processes of mutual attention and social interaction. In this way, attachment and communication processes are closely intertwined, and the quality of the attachment relationship can be gauged by how effectively this early communication is achieved. As language develops, children engage in conversation, verbal negotiation and conflict resolution with their parents. Thus children learn to communicate their views, and to understand the views of others. These skills are also learned through interacting with siblings and other peers.

In adolescence, when the balance between family and peer relationships changes quite dramatically, the goals of communication depend more directly on the particular relationship involved. Communication with parents is critical to the renegotiation of the relationship to reflect the growing independence of the adolescent. At the same time, communication remains important to the development of healthy and constructive peer relationships. In these peer relationships, adolescents can take more risks in terms of disclosing their real feelings about a range of issues than they can with their parents, owing to the unequal power balance with parents, and the divergence in life experience across the generations. Further, communication skills play a crucial role in defining the nature of dating relationships, involving the negotiation of broad relational issues such as autonomy–connection needs, and more specific issues such as the extent of sexual activity.

It is also clear that communication patterns are powerful predictors of satisfaction in marriage. As we will discuss later in this chapter, strategies for resolving conflict play a particularly important role in this regard. However, other communication variables are also influential. Self-disclosure and emotional expressiveness, for example, promote shared understandings between partners. This process of ongoing mutual expression underpins the development of the couple relationship as a special bond, in which the partner plays a unique role as confidant and supporter. Decision-making is another important aspect of couple communication, which comes to the fore particularly at transition points, such as cohabitation, marriage and the transition to parenthood. At each of these points, partners need to respond to changing circumstances by renegotiating roles and tasks.

Similarly, as individuals become more involved in the diversity of adult roles, spousal communication must adapt to the demands on time and energy that go along with heavy responsibilities in the family, the workplace and the community. At this point in the life cycle, communication with parents continues to be important, but relationships with siblings and friends may become a less central or less regular focus for communication. The implications of spousal communication patterns may become especially evident in midlife marriage, when the children leave home and the couple need to rely on each other more for companionship and support.

Long-term marriages of the elderly tend to be very variable in quality, but communication patterns generally reflect couples' increased reliance on each other as companions, and their low levels of overt disagreement. Relationships are likely to be relatively congenial, but somewhat disengaged in terms of sharing information and confronting conflict. As at other phases of the life cycle, the more satisfying relationships tend to be those in which spouses are high in intimacy, trust, interpersonal sensitivity, altruism and perspective-taking.

Conflict

In Chapter 1 we noted that partners in personal relationships are, by definition, highly interdependent. Because interdependence involves each partner being affected by the attitudes and behaviours of the other, such relationships tend to be intensely emotional. It is this intensity of emotional involvement that creates the potential for conflict. In other words, we rarely get angry with people whose opinions do not matter to us, but can be deeply hurt by those to whom we are closest. Given that much of interpersonal communication centres on the need to resolve differences and disagreements, it is important to consider the varied processes involved in dealing with conflict, and their implications for relationships. These issues are important from early childhood through to old age.

In toddlerhood, conflict is played out in the context of parents socializing children to share, cooperate, be helpful, and take part in simple household tasks such as putting away toys and cleaning up after play. What the child learns about conflict and its resolution comes not only from direct interaction with parents but also from broader-based interaction involving other family members. For example, young children often observe conflict between their parents, and the mode of resolution of couple conflict has important implications for children's adjustment. Children are also likely to experience conflict and rivalry in interaction with their siblings, given that they are competing for their share of limited parental resources. Rivalry and jealousy tend to be more intense if the children perceive differential treatment from parents. The importance of the patterns of conflict children learn in their families is highlighted by sociometric studies that link peer popularity with ways of dealing with situations involving interpersonal aggression.

In adolescence, young people come to see their parents' rules and requirements as less legitimate and more arbitrary. Conflict between parents and adolescents increases as a result, and parents' responses to demands for increased autonomy are critical to the young person's psychological adjustment and their involvement in destructive or antisocial behaviours. For example, the ways in which important developmental tasks such as dating are handled affect both the frequency and intensity of conflict with parents. Dating relationships themselves can also be an arena for conflict and jealousy, and even for coercion and violence.

Conflict is not confined to dating partners, but is important at all stages of couple relationships, with issues such as autonomy–connection and openness–closedness providing a backdrop against which specific disagreements are played out. How conflict is dealt with, as much as the actual frequency of arguments, is a reliable predictor of marital satisfaction. It is not surprising that hostile and attacking responses to conflict tend to escalate the negativity, and hence lead to lower levels of satisfaction. However, disengaging from conflict appears to be equally destructive, because contentious issues are not resolved, and resentment is likely to build up. It is interesting to note that disengagement seems to be used more by elderly couples in long-term relationships. Perhaps these couples take the view that differences that have not been resolved by this late stage of their relationship are best either accepted or ignored.

It has been beyond the scope of this book to explore the complex topic of relationship dissolution, although this topic is clearly linked to that of conflict. Several researchers have provided useful discussions of relationship dissolution, describing the various approaches that individuals use to disengage from relationships, and the ways in which they present their 'stories' to other people (e.g., see Kayser, 1993; Weber, 1998).

Power and Control

As we have noted throughout this book, conflict between relationship partners often reflects underlying issues of power and control. This applies to all types of relationships and at all developmental stages. Given that close relationships involve high levels of interdependence and mutual impact it is not surprising that issues of power and control arise frequently.

From the earliest months of children's lives, parents are involved in the process of socializing and disciplining them. This process is strikingly apparent in the period known as 'the terrible twos', when toddler negativism is particularly at odds with parental attempts at control. However, this process of socialization continues throughout childhood and adolescence. Parenting style (or how parents try to exercise control) is also important, with considerable evidence showing that children who have authoritative parents are better adjusted and more competent than those with authoritarian or permissive parents.

Parents' attempts at controlling their offspring are also critical in adolescence, when young people are looking to establish more egalitarian relationships with their parents. While over-control and under-control are common reactions by parents to adolescents' demands for independence, both these reactions are detrimental to adolescent functioning. Over-control increases the risk of low self-esteem, depression and rebellion, and under-control tends to lead to increased involvement in problem behaviours.

Although marriage is generally regarded as a relationship between peers, issues of power and control also underlie many instances of marital conflict. For example, arguments over money may really be about who has the right to make decisions, whose desires are more important, and who is making the bigger contribution to the relationship. Similarly, other marital conflicts can mask underlying issues of power and control, making these conflicts difficult to resolve. In fact, such issues tend to resurface throughout the course of the relationship in response to changes in individual development, as well as to external events and pressures. Examples of events that are likely to affect the delicate balance of power include the transition to parenthood, promotions at work, the empty nest and retirement. Of course, an extreme example of the use of power and control is partner abuse, an issue we have not focused on in this volume. We recommend that interested readers consult a recent review by Christopher and Lloyd (2000).

With individuals' advancing age, power and control issues take on new meaning. Illness and infirmity, for example, can result in a person who was strong and independent becoming weak and dependent. Tasks once carried out without effort may need to be performed by others, and individuals who have been involved in a range of outside activities may find themselves confined to their homes. These changing patterns of dependence and independence can have major effects on relationships with spouses, siblings, adult children, and others who may adopt a caregiving role.

Cultural and Subcultural Issues

Cultural differences in relationship attitudes and behaviours can be studied in terms of differences between countries, or between different cultural groups within the same country. Most relationship research published in English language journals has been carried out in western countries, although some comparisons have been made across countries and across subcultural groups.

Attachment issues in childhood have been studied in several different countries, revealing some interesting differences. For example, Japanese babies, who are rarely left with babysitters, show relatively high rates of insecure attachment when observed using the Strange Situation procedure. Similarly, in Israel (where babies tend to have little contact with strangers), quite high rates of insecure attachment have been reported. These findings highlight the fact that the meaning of observed relational behaviours may depend on attitudes and practices that vary across cultures.

Cultural issues of relevance to relationships also arise at later stages of the life cycle. For example, Japanese and western cultures show very different attitudes towards menopausal women, with western cultures focusing on gynaecological issues (such as barrenness), and on other symptoms of 'ill health' within a disease model. In Japan, on the other hand, the emphasis is not on the reproductive system or on symptoms of disease, but on the stresses associated with the familial and societal pressures of midlife. It would seem that it could be more difficult for western women and their partners to focus on the potential positive changes that the end of childbearing can bring, with their attention being focused more strongly on the expectation of debilitating symptoms.

In terms of racial and ethnic differences within countries, considerable research has been conducted in the United States. African-American and Hispanic adolescents in urban areas tend to show high levels of early sexual activity, although both African-American and white adolescent females seem to feel pressured to engage in sexual activity in order to please male partners. Links between sexual satisfaction and relationship satisfaction have also been found to depend on ethnic group: sexual satisfaction has been linked with marital satisfaction for Anglo-American husbands, but with feelings of competence in the marriage for African-American husbands. These differences may reflect different emphases on the various meanings of sex, including sex as self-interest versus mutuality.

Not surprisingly, studies of other peer relationships (with both siblings and friends) show that these relationships are important to all ethnic groups. There seem to be some differences, however, in the behaviours and expectations that are associated with these relationships. For instance, although all ethnic groups report high levels of contact and joint activities with peers, Anglo-Americans are particularly likely to emphasize the importance of intimacy and emotional support.

Effects of One Relationship on Another

In writing about relationships, one fairly common approach has been to organize the findings in this complex area by relationship type (parent–child, sibling, etc.). However, an important point emerging throughout this book is that our understanding of any given relationship will be limited if we consider that relationship in isolation. Put another way, experiences in one relationship tend to have consequences for attitudes and behaviours in other relationships.

This issue has been recognized most clearly in relation to the formative role of the parent–child relationship. Positive parent–child relationships predict later self-esteem, together with positive attitudes and behaviours across various relationship contexts. These contexts include interactions with siblings and with friends, but in particular, as we noted earlier in this chapter, experiences in parent–child relationships are likely to have a profound effect on later couple relationships of the offspring. A basic tenet of adult attachment theory is that early interactions with parents produce 'mental models' of close relationships, which play an active role in shaping adult expectations and behaviour. Further, the quality and security of these later couple bonds predict spouses' adjustment to new parenthood, as well as having implications for the parenting of the new generation. This complex process is referred to as 'intergenerational transmission'.

The formative role of family-of-origin experiences is not restricted to the effects of the parent–child relationship. For example, the quality of the relationship *between* the parents has an effect on children's adjustment and on their relationships outside of the family. Frequent conflict between spouses has a negative impact on children, especially if the conflict interactions tend to be intense or hostile. These negative effects may arise from modelling, from stress created by the continual conflict, or from disruptions to the functioning of the parent–child relationship. For example, children who are highly stressed by their parents' marital conflict may rely on less mature behaviours, such as aggression and withdrawal, when dealing with their peers.

At the same time, it is important to recognize that children's attitudes and behaviours may impact, in turn, on parental attitudes and behaviours. For instance, as we noted earlier, adolescents' involvement in dating relationships tends to create conflict with parents over issues of autonomy and freedom. In this example, the new situation in which adolescents find themselves may shape the nature of interactions between parents and adolescents, and between the adolescents and their siblings. This example highlights the bi-directional nature of parent–child influence, together with the systemic nature of the family unit. Stafford and Bayer (1993) provide an interesting discussion of the patterns of mutual influence between parents and offspring.

Future Patterns in Family Relationships

One thing that is clear at the beginning of the new millennium is that patterns of family relationships are changing fairly rapidly. More people are staying single, and more couples are choosing not to have children. In addition, those who are having children are having them later in life, and families tend to be much smaller than in the past. Divorce rates have increased considerably over the last several decades, although there is some evidence that this trend is slowing. Further, most people who divorce go on to remarry, often resulting in step-families and blended families. Even the ways that people meet and relate are changing to some extent. We now hear stories about people who meet over the internet and may even change countries to be with someone they have met in this way. Email may also make it easier for people to have and maintain long-distance or commuting relationships.

Work patterns, particularly those of women, have also changed dramatically. Although work patterns of women with young children are quite variable, women's rates of participation in the paid labour force have clearly increased. This situation has created a huge demand for both formal and informal childcare. Whereas a lot of informal childcare has previously been provided by grandmothers and other members of the extended family, changing work patterns mean that these family members are less available to perform this task, at least until they retire from the workforce. In addition, given the frequent need for parents to relocate because of work demands, family members may live long distances from one another.

The changing demographic patterns that we have been describing have far-reaching implications, not only for the care of children but also for the care of the frail aged. People (especially women) are living longer than in the past, although the later years are not necessarily active and healthy. Midlife women, who have traditionally been the carers for their elderly parents, are likely to be at the peak of their careers, and much less available than in earlier times. Governments have been concerned for some time about the 'greying' of the population, and the resulting situation whereby fewer and fewer taxpayers will have to support more and more elderly people.

Because of the rapid change in family patterns, the generality of research findings in some areas of family relationships must be considered seriously. Researchers need to include the newer types of families, along with traditional families, in their research studies. It is important for researchers to address questions about the implications of these changing family patterns for the well-being of family members across the whole life cycle. What effects do parents' work patterns, and in particular long hours of formal childcare, have on the well-being of the offspring and on their later relationships? How are relationships between the generations affected by the recent trend for men and women to have children into their thirties and forties? Who will care for the frail aged when there are fewer offspring, and those offspring may live and work at great distances from their parents, or may still be working long hours into their sixties? The answers to such questions are clearly complex, but will be vital for future generations.

References

Acitelli, L. K., Douvan, E. and Veroff, J. (1993). Perceptions of conflict in the first year of marriage: How important are similarity and understanding? *Journal of Social and Personal Relationships*, **10**, 5–19.

Acitelli, L. K., Douvan, E. and Veroff, J. (1997). The changing influence of inter-personal perceptions on marital well-being among black and white couples. *Journal of Social and Personal Relationships*, **14**, 291–304.

Adams, R. G. (1986). Patterns of network change: A longitudinal study of friendships of elderly women. *The Gerontologist*, **27**, 222–227.

Adams, R. G. and Blieszner, R. (eds) (1989). *Older Adult Friendships*. Newbury Park, Calif.: Sage.

Adams, R. G. and Blieszner, R. (1996). Midlife friendship patterns. In N. Vanzetti and S. Duck (eds), *A Lifetime of Relationships* (pp. 336–363). Pacific Grove, Calif.: Brooks/Cole.

Ainsworth, M. D. S. (1967). *Infancy in Uganda*. Baltimore: Johns Hopkins University Press.

Ainsworth, M. D. S. (1973). The development of infant–mother attachment. In B. M. Cadwell and H. N. Ricciuti (eds), *Review of Child Development Research (Vol. 3), Child Development and Social Policy*. Chicago: University of Chicago Press.

Ainsworth, M. D. S. (1979). Infant–mother attachment. *American Psychologist*, **34** (10), 932–937.

Ainsworth, M. D. S. (1983). Patterns of infant–mother attachment as related to maternal care. In D. Magnusson and V. Allen (eds), *Human Development: An Interactional Perspective*. New York: Academic Press.

Ainsworth, M. D. S. (1989). Attachments beyond infancy. *American Psychologist*, **44**, 709–716.

Ainsworth, M. D. S. and Bell, S. (1969). Some contemporary patterns of mother–infant interaction in the feeding situation. In A. Ambrose (ed.), *Stimulation in Early Infancy* (pp. 133–170). New York: Academic Press.

Ainsworth, M., Blehar, M., Waters, E. and Wall, S. (1978). *Patterns of Attachment: A Psychological Study of the Strange Situation*. Hillsdale, NJ: Lawrence Erlbaum Associates.

Aldous, J. (1987). New views on the family life of the elderly and near elderly. *Journal of Marriage and the Family*, **49**, 227–234.

Allan, G. A. (1989). *Friendship: Developing a Sociological Perspective*. New York: Harvester Wheatsheaf.

Amato, P. (1993). Children's adjustment to parental divorce: Theories, hypotheses, empirical support. *Journal of Marriage and the Family*, **55**, 23–38.

Amato, P. R. (1996). Explaining the intergenerational transmission of divorce. *Journal of Marriage and the Family*, **58**, 628–640.

Aquilino, W. S. (1997). From adolescent to young adult: A prospective study of parent–child relations during the transition to adulthood. *Journal of Marriage and the Family*, **59**, 670–686.

Arling, G. (1976). The elderly widow and her family, neighbors and friends. *Journal of Marriage and the Family*, **38**, 757–768.

Armsden, G. C. and Greenberg, M. T. (1987). The inventory of parent and peer attachment: Individual differences and their relationship to psychological wellbeing in adolescence. *Journal of Youth and Adolescence*, **16**, 427–453.

Arnett, J. J. (1997). Young people's conception of the transition to adulthood. *Youth and Society*, **29**, 3–23.

Ary, D. V., Duncan, T. E., Duncan, S. C. and Hops, H. (1999). Adolescent problem behavior: The influence of parents and peers. *Behavior Research and Therapy*, **37**, 217–230.

Ary, D. V., Duncan, T. E., Biglan, A., Metzler, C. W., Noell, J. W. and Smolkowski, K. (in press). Development of adolescent problem behaviour. *Journal of Abnormal Child Psychology*.

Auhagen, A. E. (1996). Adult friendship. In A. E. Auhagen and M. von Salisch (eds), *The Diversity of Human Relationships* (pp. 229–247). New York: Cambridge University Press.

Axia, G. (1996). How to persuade Mum to buy a toy. *First Language*, **16**, 301–317.

Baltes, P., Reese, H. and Lipsitt, L. (1980). Life-span developmental psychology. *Annual Review of Psychology*, **31**, 65–110.

Barber, C. E. (1989). Burden and family care of the elderly. In S. J. Bahr and E. T. Peterson (eds), *Aging and the Family* (pp. 243–259). Lexington, Mass.: Lexington Books.

Barnett, R. C., Marshall, N. L. and Sayer, A. (1991). *Positive Spillover Effects from Job to Home: A Closer Look*. Wellesley College Working Paper no. 222, Wellesley, Mass.: Wellesley College Center for Research on Women.

Baron-Cohen, S. (1995). *Mindblindness*. London: Oxford University Press.

Barrera, M. and Baca, L. M. (1990). Recipient reactions to social support: Contributions of enacted support, conflicted support and network orientation. *Journal of Social and Personal Relationships*, **7**, 541–551.

Barrera, M., and Maurer, D. (1981). Recognition of mother's photographed face by the 3-month old infant. *Child Development*, **52**, 714–716.

Barrera, M., Jr. and Stice, E. (1998). Parent–adolescent conflict in the context of family support: Families with alcoholic and non-alcoholic fathers. *Journal of Family Psychology*, **12**, 195–208.

Bartholomew, K. (1990). Avoidance of intimacy: An attachment perspective. *Journal of Social and Personal Relationships*, **7**, 147–178.

Bartholomew, K. and Horowitz, L. M. (1991). Attachment styles among young adults: A test of a four-category model. *Journal of Personality and Social Psychology*, **61**, 226–244.

Bartholomew, K., Cobb, R. J. and Poole, J. A. (1997). Adult attachment patterns and social support processes. In G. R. Pierce, B. Lakey, I. G. Sarason and B. R. Sarason (eds), *Sourcebook of Social Support and Personality* (pp. 359–378). New York: Plenum Press.

Baruch, G. and Barnett, R. C. (1983). Adult daughters' relationships with their mothers. *Journal of Marriage and the Family*, **45**, 601–606.

Baumrind, D. (1971). Current pattern of parental authority. *Developmental Psychology Monographs*, **1**, 1–103.

Baumrind, D. (1975). The contributions of the family to the development of competence in children. *Schizophrenia Bulletin*, **14**, 12–37.

Baumrind, D. (1978). Parental disciplinary patterns and social competence in children. *Youth and Society*, **9** (3), 239–67.

Baumrind, D. (1991). To nurture nature. *Behavioral and Brain Sciences*, **14**, 386.

Baxter, L. A. (1990). Dialectical contradictions in relationship development. *Journal of Social and Personal Relationships*, **7**, 69–88.

Baxter, L. A. and Montgomery, B. A. (1996). *Relating: Dialogues and Dialectics*. New York: Guilford Press.

Belsky, J. and Pensky, E. (1988). Marital change across the transition to parenthood. *Marriage and Family Review*, **12**, 133–156.

Benedek, T. (1959). Parenthood as a developmental phase: A contribution to the libido theory. *Journal of the American Psychoanalytic Association*, **7**, 389–417.

Bengston, V. L. and Roberts, R. E. L. (1991). Intergenerational solidarity in aging families: An example of formal theory construction. *Journal of Marriage and the Family*, **53**, 856–870.

Bengston, V. L., Rosenthal, C. and Burton, L. (1990). Families and aging: Diversity and heterogeneity. In R. Binstock and L. George (eds), *Handbook of Aging and the Social Sciences*, 3rd edn (pp. 263–287). San Diego, Calif.: Academic Press.

Benoit, D. and Parker, K. (1994). Stability and transmission of attachment across three generations. *Child Development*, **65**, 1444–1456.

Berndt, T. (1979). Developmental changes in conformity to peers and parents. *Developmental Psychology*, **15**(6), 608–616.

Biglan, A., Duncan, T. E., Ary, D. V. and Smolkowski, K. (1995). Peer and parental influences on adolescent tobacco use. *Journal of Behavioral Medicine*, **18**, 315–330.

Bittman, M. (1991). *Juggling Time: How Australian Families Use Time*. Canberra, Australia: Office of the Status of Women, Department of the Prime Minister and Cabinet.

Blieszner, R. (1989). Developmental processes of friendship. In R. G. Adams and R. Blieszner (eds), *Older Adult Friendships* (p. 126). Newbury Park, Calif.: Sage.

Blieszner, R. and Adams, R. G. (1992). *Adult Friendship*. Newbury Park, Calif.: Sage.

Blumstein, P. and Schwartz, P. (1983). *American Couples: Money, Work and Sex*. New York: William Morrow.

Bombar, M. L. and Littig, L. W., Jr. (1996). Babytalk as a communication of intimate attachment: An initial study in adult romances and friendships. *Personal Relationships*, **3**, 137–158.

Bowlby, J. (1965). *Child Care and the Growth of Love*. Harmondsworth: Penguin Books.

Bowlby, J. (1969). *Attachment and Loss* (Vol. 1). London: Hogarth.

Bowlby, J. (1973). *Attachment and Loss* (Vol. 2). London: Hogarth.

Bowlby, J. (1977). The making and breaking of affectional bonds. *British Journal of Psychiatry*, **130**, 201–210.

Bowlby, J. (1980). *Attachment and Loss* (Vol. 3). London: Hogarth.

Boyer, C. B. (1990). Psychosocial, behavioral, and educational factors in preventing sexually transmitted diseases. *Adolescent Medicine: State of the Art Reviews*, **1**, 597–613.

Brazelton, T. B. (1984). *Neonatal Behavioral Assessment*. National Spastic Society Monographs, Clinics in Developmental Medicine no. 83 (pp. 1–123). London: Heinemann.

Brent, T. J. and Ladd, G. W. (1989). *Peer Relationships in Child Development*. New York: John Wiley & Sons.

Bretherton, I. (1992). The origins of attachment theory: John Bowlby and Mary Ainsworth. *Developmental Psychology*, **28**(5), 759–775.

Bretherton, I. and Waters, E. (1985). Growing points of attachment theory and research. *Monographs for the Society for Research in Child Development*, **50** (209), 1–211.

Brody, E. M. (1985). Parent care as a normative family stress. *Gerontologist*, **25**, 19–29.

Brody, E. M. (1990). *Women in the Middle: Their Parent Care Years*. New York: Springer Publishing Company.

Brody, G.H. (1998). Sibling relationship quality. *Annual Review of Psychology*, **49**, 1–24.

Brody, G., Stoneman, Z. and McCoy, J. (1994). Forecasting sibling relationships in early adolescence from child temperaments and family processes in middle childhood. *Child Development*, **65**(3), 771–784.

Brody, G. H., Flor, D. L., Hollett-Wright, N. and McCoy, J. K. (1998). Children's development of alcohol use norms: Contributions of parent and sibling norms, children's temperaments and parent–child discussions. *Journal of Family Psychology*, **12**, 209–219.

Brody, L., Copeland, A., Sutton, L., Richardson, D. and Guyer, M. (1998).

Mommy and daddy like you best: Perceived family favouritism in relation to affect, adjustment and family process. *Journal of Family Therapy*, **20**, 269–291.

Brown, J. R., Donelan-McCall, N. and Dunn, J. (1996). Why talk about mental states? The significance of children's conversations with friends, siblings and mothers. *Child Development*, **67**, 836–849.

Brubaker, T. H. (1985). *Later Life Families*. Beverly Hills, Calif.: Sage.

Brubaker, T. H. (1990). Families in later life: A burgeoning research area. *Journal of Marriage and the Family*, **52**, 959–981.

Bulcroft, K. and O'Connor, M. (1986). The importance of dating relationships on quality of life for older persons. *Family Relations: Journal of Applied Family and Child Studies*, **35**(3), 397–401.

Bumpass, L. L., Sweet, J. A. and Cherlin, A. (1991). The role of cohabitation in declining rates of marriage. *Journal of Marriage and the Family*, **53**, 913–927.

Burt, C. E., Cohen, L. H. and Bjorck, J. P. (1988). Perceived family environment as a moderator of young adolescents' life stress adjustment. *American Journal of Community Psychology*, **16**, 101–122.

Butterworth, G. (1994). Theory of mind and the facts of embodiment. In C. Lewis and P. Mitchell (eds) *Children's Early Understanding of Mind: Origins and Development* (pp. 115–132). Hove, UK: Lawrence Erlbaum Associates.

Butterworth, G. and Jarrett, N. L .M. (1991). What minds have in common is space. *British Journal of Developmental Psychology*, **9**, 55–72.

Buunk, B. and Bringle, R. G. (1987). Jealousy in love relationships. In D. Perlman and S. Duck, *Intimate Relationships: Development, Dynamics and Deterioration* (pp. 123–149). Newbury Park, Calif.: Sage.

Cahn, D. D. (1990). Intimates in conflict: A research review. In D. D. Cahn (ed.), *Intimates in Conflict: A Communication Perspective* (pp. 1–22). Hillsdale, N.J.: Lawrence Erlbaum Associates.

Caplow, T., Bahr, H. M., Chadwick, B. A., Hill, R. and Williamson, M. H. (1982). *Middletown Families: Fifty Years of Change and Continuity*. Minneapolis: University of Minnesota Press.

Carpenter, B. N. (1993). Relational competence. In D. Perlman and W. H. Jones (eds), *Advances in Personal Relationships* (Vol. 4, pp. 1–28). New York: Jessica Kingsley.

Caspi, A. and Elder, G., Jnr. (1988). Emergent family patterns: the intergenerational construction of problem behaviour and relationships. In R. A Hinde and J. Stevenson-Hinde (eds), *Relationships Within Families: Mutual Influences* (pp. 218–241). Oxford: Clarendon Press.

Cate, R. M. and Lloyd, S. A. (1992). *Courtship*. Newbury Park, Calif.: Sage.

Chao, R. K. (1994). Beyond parental control and authoritarian parenting style: Understanding Chinese parenting through the cultural notion of training. *Child Development*, **65**, 1111–1119.

Chase, K. A., Treboux, D., O'Leary, K. D. and Strassberg, Z. (1998). Specificity of dating aggression and its justification among high-risk adolescents. *Journal of Abnormal Child Psychology*, **26**, 467–473.

Cherlin, A. J. and Furstenberg, F. F. (1986). *The New American Grandparent: A Place in the Family, a Life Apart*. New York: Basic Books.

Christopher, F. S. (1996). Adolescent sexuality: Trying to explain the magic and the mystery. In N. Vanzetti and S. Duck (eds), *A Lifetime of Relationships* (pp. 213–242). Pacific Grove, Calif.: Brooks/Cole.

Christopher, F. S. and Cate, R. M. (1985). Premarital sexual pathways and relationship development. *Journal of Social and Personal Relationships*, **2**, 271–288.

Christopher, S. F. and Lloyd, S. A. (2000). Physical and sexual aggression in relationships. In C. Hendrick and S. S. Hendrick *et al.* (eds) *Close Relationships: A Sourcebook* (pp. 331–343). Thousand Oaks, CA: Sage.

Cicirelli, V. G. (1980). Sibling relationships in adulthood: A lifespan perspective. In L. W. Poon (ed.), *Aging in the 1980's* (pp. 455–462). Washington, DC: American Psychological Association.

Cicirelli, V. G. (1981). Kin relationships of childless and one-child elderly in relation to social services. *Journal of Gerontological Social Work*, **4**, 19–33.

Cicirelli, V. G. (1983). Adult children's attachment and helping behaviour to elderly parents: A path model. *Journal of Marriage and the Family*, **45**, 815–822.

Cicirelli, V. G. (1985). The role of siblings as family caregivers. In W. J. Sauer and R. T. Coward (eds), *Social Support Networks and the Care of the Elderly* (pp. 93–107). New York: Springer Publishing Company.

Cicirelli, V. G. (1986). The relationship of divorced adult children with their elderly parents. *Journal of Divorce*, **9**, 39–54.

Cicirelli, V. G. (1991). Attachment theory in old age: Protection on the attached figure. In K. Pillemer and K. McCartney (eds), *Parent–child Relations Throughout Life* (pp. 25–42). Hillsdale, N.J.: Lawrence Erlbaum Associates.

Cicirelli, V. G. (1995). *Sibling Relationships across the Life Span*. New York: Plenum Press.

Clark, S. and Stephens, M. (1996). Stroke patients' well-being as a function of caregiving spouses' helpful and unhelpful actions. *Personal Relationships*, **3**(2), 171–184.

Coble, H. M., Gantt, D. L. and Mallinckrodt, B. (1996). Attachment, social competency, and the capacity to use social support. In G. R. Pierce, B. R. Sarason and I. G. Sarason (eds), *Handbook of Social Support and the Family* (pp. 141–172). New York: Plenum Press.

Cohan, C. L. and Bradbury, T. N. (1997). Negative life events, marital interaction, and the longitudinal course of newlywed marriage. *Journal of Personality and Social Psychology*, **73**, 114–128.

Cohen, L. B., DeLoache, J. S. and Strauss, M. S. (1979). Infant Visual Perception. In J. D. Osofsky (ed.), *Handbook of Infant Development*. New York: John Wiley & Sons.

Cohen, S. and Wills, T. A. (1985). Stress, social support, and the buffering hypothesis. *Psychological Bulletin*, **98**, 310–357.

Cohler, B. J. and Grunebaum, H. (1981). *Mothers, Grandmothers, and Daughters. Personality and Childcare in Three-generation Families*. New York: John Wiley & Sons.

Coie, J. D. and Dodge, K. (1983). Continuities and changes in children's social status: A five-year longitudinal study. *Merrill-Palmer Quarterly*, **29**, 261–282.

Cole, T. and Bradac, J. J. (1996). A lay theory of relational satisfaction with best friends. *Journal of Social and Personal Relationships*, **13**, 57–83.

Collins, J. K. (1993). Approaches to adolescent sexuality: The Australian picture. *Australian Journal of Marriage and Family*, **14**, 126–136.

Collins, N. L. and Read, S. J. (1990). Adult attachment, working models, and relationship quality in dating couples. *Journal of Personality and Social Psychology*, **58**, 644–663.

Collins, N. L. and Read, S. J. (1994). Cognitive representations of attachment: The structure and function of working models. In K. Bartholomew and D. Perlman (eds), *Advances in Personal Relationships*. Vol. 5: *Attachment Processes in Adulthood* (pp. 53–90). London: Jessica Kingsley.

Collins, N. L., Dunkel-Schetter, C., Lobel, M. and Scrimshaw, S. C. M. (1993). Social support in pregnancy: Psychosocial correlates of birth outcomes and postpartum depression. *Journal of Personality and Social Psychology*, **65**, 1243–1258.

Collins, W. A. and Russell, G. (1991). Mother–child and father–child relationships in middle childhood and adolescence: A developmental analysis. *Developmental Review*, **11**, 99–136.

Connell, W. F., Stroobant, R. E., Sinclair, K. E., Connell, R. W. and Rogers, K. W. (1975). *Twelve to 20: Studies of City Youth*. Sydney: Hicks Smith.

Connidis, I. A. (1989). Siblings as friends in later life. *American Behavioral Scientist*, **33**, 81–93.

Connidis, I. A. (1992). Life transitions and the adult sibling tie: A qualitative study. *Journal of Marriage and the Family*, **54**, 972–982.

Cooper, M. L., Shaver, P. R. and Collins, N. L. (1998). Attachment styles, emotional regulation, and adjustment in adolescence. *Journal of Personality and Social Psychology*, **74**, 1380–1397.

Cordon, J. A. F. (1997). Youth residential independence and autonomy: A comparative study. *Journal of Family Issues*, **18**, 576–607.

Cowan, C. P. and Cowan, P. A. (1988). Who does what when partners become parents: Implications for men, women, and marriage. *Marriage and Family Review*, **12**(3–4), 105–131.

Cowan, C. P. and Cowan, P. A. (1992). *When Partners Become Parents: The Big Life Change for Couples*. New York: Basic Books.

Cowan, P. A. (1988a). Becoming a father: A time of change, an opportunity for development. In P. Bronstein and C. P. Cowan (eds), *Fatherhood Today: Men's Changing Role in the Family* (pp. 13–35). New York: John Wiley & Sons.

Cowan, P. A. (1988b). Developmental psychopathology: A nine-cell map of the territory. *New Directions for Child Development*, **39**, 5–29.

Crawford, M. (1981). Not disengaged: Grandparents in literature and reality, an empirical study in role satisfaction. *Sociological Review*, **29**, 499–519.

Cummings, E. M. and Davies, P. (1994). *Children and Marital Conflict: The Impact of Family Dispute and Resolution*. New York: Guilford Press.

Cunningham, J. D. and Antill, J. K. (1994). Cohabitation and marriage: Retrospective and predictive comparisons. *Journal of Social and Personal Relationships*, **11**, 77–93.

Davies, P. and Cummings, M. (1994). Marital conflict and child adjustment: An emotional security hypothesis. *Psychological Bulletin*, **116**(3), 387–411.

Davis, B. T., Hops, H., Alpert, A. and Sheeber, L. (1998). Child responses to family conflict and their effect on adjustment: A study of triadic relations. *Journal of Family Psychology*, **12**, 163–177.

Davis, V. K. and Carpenter, B. N. (1987). Relational competence and marital satisfaction. Paper presented at the annual meeting of the Southwestern Psychological Association, New Orleans, La.

Dean, A., Kolody, B., Wood, P. and Ensel, W. M. (1989). Measuring the communication of social support from adult children. *Journal of Gerontology: Social Sciences*, **44**, S71–S79.

DeCasper, A.J. and Spence, M. J. (1986). Prenatal maternal speech influences newborns' perception of speech sounds. *Infant Behavior and Development*, **9**, 133–150.

DeGarmo, D. S. and Forgatch, M. S. (1997). Confidant support and maternal distress: Predictors of parenting practices for divorced mothers. *Personal Relationships*, **4**, 305–317.

De Gaston, J. F., Weed, S. and Jensen, L. (1996). Understanding gender differences in adolescent sexuality. *Adolescence*, **31**, 217–231.

DeMaris, A. and Rao, K. V. (1992). Premarital cohabitation and subsequent marital stability in the United States: A reassessment. *Journal of Marriage and the Family*, **54**, 178–190.

Denton, K. and Zarbatany, L. (1996). Age differences in support processes in conversations between friends. *Child Development*, **67**, 1360–1373.

de Vaus, D. (1997a). Marriage. In D. de Vaus and I. Wolcott (eds), *Australian Family Profiles: Social and Demographic Patterns* (pp. 11–23). Melbourne, Australia: Australian Institute of Family Studies.

de Vaus, D. (1997b). Divorce. In D. de Vaus and I. Wolcott (eds), *Australian Family Profiles: Social and Demographic Patterns* (pp. 25–36). Melbourne, Australia: Australian Institute of Family Studies.

de Vries, B. (1996). The understanding of friendship: An adult life course perspective. In C. Magai and S. H. McFadden (eds), *Handbook of Emotion, Adult Development, and Aging* (pp. 249–268). San Diego, Calif.: Academic Press.

Dindia, K., and Allen, M. (1992). Sex differences in self-disclosure: A meta-analysis. *Psychological Bulletin*, **112**, 106–124.

Dodge, K. A. (1983). Behavioural antecedents of peer social status. *Child Development*, **54**, 1386–1399.

Doka, K. J. and Mertz, M. E. (1988). The meaning and significance of great-grandparenthood. *The Gerontologist*, **28**, 192–197.

Douvan, E. and Adelson, J. (1966). *The Adolescent Experience*. New York: John Wiley & Sons.

Dowdy, B. B. and Kliewer, W. (1998). Dating, parent–adolescent conflict, and behavioral autonomy. *Journal of Youth and Adolescence*, **27**, 473–492.

Duck, S. (1973). *Personal Relationships and Personal Constructs: A Study of Friendship Formation*. New York: John Wiley & Sons.

Duck, S. and Wright, P. H. (1993). Reexamining gender differences in same-gender friendships: A close look at two kinds of data. *Sex Roles*, **28**, 709–727.

Dunn, J. (1983). Sibling relationships in early childhood. *Child Development*, **54**, 747–811.

Dunn, J. (1993). *Young Children's Close Relationships: Beyond Attachment*. London: Sage.

Dunn, J. (1994). Changing minds and changing relationships. In C. Lewis and P. Mitchell (eds), *Children's Early Understanding of Mind: Origins and Development* (pp. 297–310). Hove, UK: Lawrence Erlbaum Associates.

Dunn, J. (1996). The Emanuel Miller Memorial Lecture 1995: Children's relationships: Bridging the divide between cognitive and social development. *Journal of Child Psychology and Psychiatry and Allied Disciplines*, **37**(5), 507–518.

Dunn, J. and Kendrick, C. (1982). *Siblings: Love, Envy and Understanding*. Cambridge, MA: Harvard University Press.

Dunn, J. and Munn, P. (1987). Development of justification in disputes with mother and sibling. *Developmental Psychology*, **23**, 791–798.

Dunn, J., Stocker, L. and Plomin, R. C. (1990). Sibling relationships: Links with child temperament, maternal behavior and family structure. *Annual Progress in Child Psychology and Psychiatry: 1990*, 242–260.

Dunphy, D. C. (1963). The social structure of urban adolescent peer groups. *Sociometry*, **26**, 230–246.

Dunphy, D. C. (1969). *Cliques, Crowds and Gangs*. Melbourne: Cheshire.

Dykstra, P. A. (1993). The differential availability of relationships and the provision and effectiveness of support to older adults. *Journal of Social and Personal Relationships*, **10**, 355–370.

Edwards, H. and Noller, P. (1998). Factors influencing caregiver–care receiver communication and its impact on the well-being of older care receivers. *Health Communication*, **10**(4), 317–341.

Ekstein, R. (1991). The psychology and psychotherapeutic treatment of borderline and psychotic conditions of childhood. In S. I. Greenspan and G. H. Pollock (eds), *The Course of Life*. Vol. III: *Middle and Late Childhood*. Madison, Wis.: International Universities Press.

Ellis-Schwabe, M. and Thornburg, H. D. (1986). Conflict areas between parents and their adolescents. *The Journal of Psychology*, **120**, 59–68.

Epstein, J. (1981). *The Quality of School Life*. Lexington, Mass.: Lexington Books.

Erikson, E. (1950). *Childhood and Society*. New York: W. W. Norton.

Erikson, E. (1968). *Identity: Youth and Crisis*. New York: W. W. Norton.

Essex, M. J. and Nam, S. (1987). Marital status and loneliness among older women: The differential importance of close family and friends. *Journal of Marriage and the Family*, **49**, 93–106.

Evans, M. (1991). Alternative to marriage. *National Social Survey Report*, **2**, 7–8.

Eyre, S. L., Read, N. W. and Millstein, S. G. (1997). Adolescent sexual strategies. *Journal of Adolescent Health*, **20**, 286–293.

Fantz, R. (1961). The origin of form perception. *Scientific American*, **204**(5), 66–72.

Farrell, M. P. and Rosenberg, S. D. (1981). *Men at Midlife*. Boston: Auburn House.

Faver, C. A. (1984). *Women in Transition: Career, Family, and Life Satisfaction in Three Cohorts*. New York: Praeger.

Feeney, J. A. (1994). Attachment style, communication patterns and satisfaction across the life cycle of marriage. *Personal Relationships*, **1**, 333–348.

Feeney, J. A. (1998). Adult attachment and relationship-centered anxiety: Responses to physical and emotional distancing. In J. A. Simpson and W. S. Rholes (eds), *Attachment Theory and Close Relationships* (pp. 189–218). New York: Guilford Press.

Feeney, J. A. (1999a). Adult attachment, emotional control and marital satisfaction. *Personal Relationships*, **6**, 169–185.

Feeney, J. A. (1999b). Adult romantic attachment and couple relationships. In J. Cassidy and P. R. Shaver (eds), *Handbook of Attachment: Theory, Research, and Clinical Applications* (pp. 355–377). New York: Guilford Press.

Feeney, J. A. and Humphreys, T. (1996). Parental, sibling and romantic relationships: Exploring the functions of attachment bonds. Paper presented at the 5th Australian Family Research Conference, Brisbane, Australia, November.

Feeney, J. A. and Noller, P. (1990). Attachment style as a predictor of adult romantic relationships. *Journal of Personality and Social Psychology*, **58**, 281–291.

Feeney, J. A. and Noller, P. (1991). Attachment style and verbal descriptions of romantic partners. *Journal of Social and Personal Relationships*, **8**, 187–215.

Feeney, J. A. and Noller, P. (1996). *Adult Attachment*. Thousand Oaks, Calif.: Sage.

Feeney, J. A., Noller, P. and Callan, V. J. (1994). Attachment style, communication and satisfaction in the early years of marriage. In K. Bartholomew and D. Perlman (eds), *Advances in Personal Relationships*. Vol. 5: *Attachment Processes in Adulthood* (pp. 269–308). London: Jessica Kingsley.

Feeney, J. A., Noller, P. and Roberts, N. (1998). Emotion, attachment, and satisfaction in close relationships. In P. A. Andersen and L. K. Guerrero (eds), *Handbook of Communication and Emotion: Research, Theory, Applications, and Contexts* (pp. 473–505). San Diego, Calif.: Academic Press.

Feeney, J. A., Peterson, C. and Noller, P. (1994). Equity and marital satisfaction over the family life cycle. *Personal Relationships*, **1**, 83–99.

Feeney, J. A., Ward, C., Noller, P. and Hohaus, L. (1998). Attachment, caregiving and sexuality in the transition to parenthood. Paper presented at the Society of Australasian Social Psychologists, Christchurch, New Zealand, April.

Fein, G. (1981). Pretend play in childhood: An integrative view. *Child Development*, **52**, 1095–1118.

Feldman, C. M. (1997). Childhood precursors of adult interpartner violence. *Clinical Psychology: Science and Practice*, **4**, 307–334.

Field, T. (1996). Attachment and separation in young children. *Annual Review of Psychology*, **47**, 541–561.

Field, T. and Weishaus, S. (1992). Marriage over half a century: A longitudinal study. In M. Bloom (ed.), *Changing Lives* (pp. 269–273). Columbia: University of South Carolina Press.

Fischer, C. S. (1982). *To Dwell Among Friends*. Chicago: University of Chicago Press.

Fisher, J. D. and Fisher, W. A. (1992). Changing AIDS-risk behavior. *Psychological Bulletin*, **111**, 455–474.

Fitting, M., Rabins, P., Lucas, M. J. and Eastham, J. (1986). Caring for dementia patients: A comparison of husbands and wives. *Gerontologist*, **26**, 248–252.

Flannery, D. J., Montemayor, R. and Eberly, M. B. (1994). The influence of parent negative emotional expression on adolescents' perceptions of their relationships with their parents. *Personal Relationships*, **1**, 259–274.

Floyd, K. (1995). Gender and closeness among friends and siblings. *Journal of Psychology*, **129**, 193–202.

Fraley, R. C. and Davis, K. E. (1997). Attachment formation and transfer in young adults' close friendships and romantic relationships. *Personal Relationships*, **4**, 131–144.

Frederickson, B. L. and Carstensen, L. L. (1990). Choosing social partners: How old age and anticipated endings make people more selective. *Psychology and Aging*, **5**, 335–347.

Galland, O. (1997). Leaving home and family relations in France. *Journal of Family Issues*, **18**, 645–670.

Ganong, L., Coleman, M., McDaniel, A. K. and Killian, T. (1998). Attitudes regarding obligations to assist an older parent or stepparent following later-life remarriage. *Journal of Marriage and the Family*, **60**, 595–610.

Garza, J. and Dressel, P. (1983). Sexuality and later life marriages. In T. Brubaker (ed.), *Family Relationships in Later Life* (pp. 91–108). Beverly Hills, Calif.: Sage.

George, L. K. (1986). Caregiver burden: Conflict between norms of reciprocity and solidarity. In K. Pillemer and R. Wolf (eds), *Elder Abuse: Conflict in the Family* (pp. 67–92). Dober, Mass.: Auburn House.

George, L. K. and Weiler, S. J. (1981). Sexuality in middle and late life: The effects of age, cohort, and gender. *Archives of General Psychiatry*, **38** (8), 919–923.

Gergen, K. J. (1991). *The Saturated Self: Dilemmas of Identity in Contemporary Life*. New York: Basic Books.

Glenn, N. (1981). Age, birth cohorts, and drinking: An illustration of the hazards of inferring effects from cohort data. *Journal of Gerontology*, **36**, 362–369.

Glezer, H. (1991). Cohabitation. *Family Matters*, **30**, 24–27.

Glezer, H. (1992). The importance of family background and early experiences on premarital cohabitation and marital dissolution. Paper presented at the International Conference on Family Formation and Dissolution: Perspectives from East and West, Taipei, Taiwan, Republic of China, May.

Goetting, A. (1986). The developmental tasks of siblingship over the life cycle. *Journal of Marriage and the Family*, **48**, 703–714.

Gold, D. T. (1989). Generational solidarity: Conceptual antecedents and consequences. *American Behavioral Scientist*, **33**, 19–32.

Goldscheider, F. K. and Lawton, L. (1998). Family experiences and the erosion of support for intergenerational coresidence. *Journal of Marriage and the Family*, **60**, 623–632.

Golomb, C. and Cornelius, C. B. (1977). Symbolic play and its cognitive significance. *Developmental Psychology*, **13** (3), 246–252.

Goodchilds, J. D., Zellman, G., Johnson, R. and Giarrusso, R. (1988). Adolescents and their perceptions of sexual interactions. In A. Burgess (ed.), *Rape and Sexual Assault* (pp. 245–270). New York: Garland Press.

Goodnow, J.J. and Bowes, J. M. (1994). *Men, Women and Household Work*. Melbourne: Oxford University Press.

Goodnow, J. J., Cashmore, J., Cotton, S. and Knight, R. (1984). Mothers' developmental timetables in two cultural groups. *International Journal of Psychology*, **19**, 193–205.

Goodwin, R. (1999). *Personal Relationships Across Cultures*. New York: Routledge.

Grambs, J. D. (1989). *Women over Forty: Visions and Realities* (rev. edn). New York: Springer Publishing Company.

Grossman, F. K. (1988). Strain in the transition to parenthood. *Marriage and Family Review*, **12**, 85–104.

Grotevant, H. D. and Cooper, C. R. (1986). Individuation in family relationships: A perspective on individual differences in the development of identity and role-taking skill in adolescence. *Human Development*, **29**, 82–100.

Grusec, J. E. and Goodnow, J. J. (1994). Impact of parental discipline methods on the child's internalization of values: A reconceptualization of current points of view. *Developmental Psychology*, **30** (1), 4–19.

Grych, J. H. and Fincham, F. D. (1990). Marital conflict and children's adjustment: A cognitive-contextual framework. *Psychological Bulletin*, **108**, 267–290.

Gutmann, D. L. (1987). *Reclaimed Powers: Toward a New Psychology of Men and Women in Later Life*. New York: Basic Books.

Gutmann, D. L. (1991). Patterns of psychological vulnerability to developmental shifts in middle aged and older husbands. Paper presented at the International Conference on Gender and the Family, Brigham Young University, Provo, Utah, February.

Hackel, L. S. and Ruble, D. N. (1992). Changes in the marital relationship after the first baby is born: Predicting the impact of expectancy disconfirmation. *Journal of Personality and Social Psychology*, **62**, 944–957.

Hagestad, G. O. (1985). Continuity and connectedness. In V. L. Bengtson and J. F. Robertson (eds), *Grandparenthood* (pp. 31–48). Beverly Hills, Calif.: Sage.

Hagestad, G. O. (1988). Demographic change and the life course: Some emerging trends in the family realm. *Family Relations*, **37**, 405–410.

Hansson, R. (1986). Relational competence, relationships and adjustment in old age. *Journal of Personality and Social Psychology*, **50**, 1050–1058.

Hansson, R. and Carpenter, B. (1986). Coping with fear of crime among the elderly. *Clinical Gerontologist*, **4**, 38–40.

Hansson, R. O. and Carpenter, B. N. (1994). *Relationships in Old Age: Coping with the Challenge of Transition*. New York: Guilford Press.

Harlton, S. V., Keating, N. and Fast, J. (1998). Defining eldercare for policy and practice: Perspectives matter. *Family Relations*, **47**, 281–288.

Hartley, R. and de Vaus, D. (1997). Young people. In D. de Vaus and I. Wolcott (eds), *Australian Family Profiles: Social and Demographic Patterns* (pp. 25–36). Melbourne, Australia: Australian Institute of Family Studies.

Hartup, W. W. (1970). Peer interaction and social organization. In P. H. Mussen (ed.), *Carmichael's Manual of Child Psychology* (Vol. 2, pp. 361–456). New York: John Wiley & Sons.

Hartup, W. W. (1987). The developmental significance of close relationships. Paper presented at China Satellite International Society for Behavioural Development Conference, Beijing.

Harvey, D. M., Curry, C. J. and Bray, J. H. (1991). Individuation and intimacy in intergenerational relationships and health: Patterns across two generations. *Journal of Family Psychology*, **5**, 204–236.

Hatfield, E. and Rapson, R. L. (1996). Stress and passionate love. In C. D Speilberger and I. G. Sarason *et al.* (eds), *Stress and Emotion: Anxiety, Anger and Curiosity* (Vol 16, pp. 29–50). Washington, DC: Taylor & Francis.

Hatfield, E., Utne, M. and Traupmann, J. (1979). Equity theory and intimate relationships. In R. L. Burgess and T. L. Huston (eds), *Social Exchange in Developing Relationships*. New York: Academic Press.

Hazan, C. and Shaver, P. R. (1987). Romantic love conceptualized as an attachment process. *Journal of Personality and Social Psychology*, **52**, 511–524.

Hazan, C. and Shaver, P. R. (1994). Attachment as an organizational framework for research on close relationships. *Psychological Inquiry*, **5**, 1–22.

Hazan, C. and Zeifman, D. (1994). Sex and the psychological tether. In K. Bartholomew and D. Perlman (eds), *Advances in Personal Relationships*. Vol. 5: *Attachment Processes in Adulthood* (pp. 151–178). London: Jessica Kingsley.

Heaton, T. B. (1990). Marital stability throughout the child-rearing years. *Demography*, **27**, 55–63.

Henderson-King, D. H. and Veroff, J. (1994). Sexual satisfaction and marital well-being in the first years of marriage. *Journal of Social and Personal Relationships*, **11**, 509–534.

Hiedemann, B., Suhomlinova, O. and O'Rand, A. M. (1998). Economic independence, economic status and empty nest in midlife marital disruption. *Journal of Marriage and the Family*, **60**, 219–231.

Hill, C. D., Thompson, L. W. and Gallagher, D. (1988). The role of anticipatory bereavement in older women's adjustment to widowhood. *The Gerontologist*, **28**, 792–796.

Hill, R. (1949). *Families Under Stress*. New York: Harper & Row.

Hinde, R. A. (1979). *Towards Understanding Relationships*. New York: Academic Press.

Hinde, R.A. (1992). Human social development: An ethological/relationship perspective. In H. McGurk (ed.), *Childhood Social Development: Contemporary Perspectives* (pp. 191–207). Hillsdale, N.J.: Lawrence Erlbaum Associates.

Hobfoll, S. E. (1988). *The Ecology of Stress*. Washington, DC: Hemisphere.

Hobfoll, S. E. (1996). Social support: Will you be there when I need you? In N. Vanzetti and S. Duck (eds), *A Lifetime of Relationships* (pp. 46–74). Pacific Grove, Calif.: Brooks/Cole.

Hobfoll, S. and Stokes, J. (1988). The process and mechanics of social support. In S. W. Duck (ed.), *Handbook of Personal Relationships* (pp. 497–517). Chichester, UK: John Wiley & Sons.

Holahan, C. K. (1984). Marital attitudes over 40 years: A longitudinal and cohort analysis. *Journal of Gerontology*, **38**, 49–57.

Holahan, C. J., Moos, R. H. and Bonin, L. (1997). Social support, coping, and psychological adjustment: A resource model. In G. R. Pierce, B. Lakey, I. G. Sarason and B. R. Sarason (eds), *Sourcebook of Social Support and Personality* (pp. 169–186). New York: Plenum Press.

Holman, T. B. and Li, B. D. (1997). Premarital factors influencing perceived readiness for marriage. *Journal of Family Issues*, **18**, 124–144.

Horowitz, A. V. and White, H. R. (1998). The relationship of cohabitation and mental health: A study of a young adult cohort. *Journal of Marriage and the Family*, **60**, 505–514.

Howes, C. (1985). Sharing fantasy: Social pretend play in toddlers. *Child Development*, **56** (5), 1253–1258.

Huston, T. L. (1983). Power. In H. Kelley, E. Berscheid, A. Christensen, J. Harvey, T. Huston, G. Levinger, E. McClintock, L. A. Peplau and D. Peterson (eds). *Close Relationships* (pp. 169–218). New York: Freeman.

Huston, T. L. and Vangelisti, A. L. (1995). How parenthood affects marriage. In M. A. Fitzpatrick and A. L. Vangelisti (eds), *Explaining Family Interactions* (pp. 147–176). Thousand Oaks, Calif.: Sage.

Huyck, M. H. (1995). Marriage and close relationships of the marital kind. In R. Blieszner and V. H. Bedford (eds), *Handbook of Aging and the Family* (pp. 181–199). Westport, Conn.: Greenwood Press.

Huyck, M. H. and Gutmann, D. L. (1992). Thirtysomething years of marriage: Understanding experiences of men and women in enduring family relationships. *Family Perspective*, **26**, 249–265.

Hymel, S. (1983). Preschool children's peer relations: Issues in sociometric assessment. *Merrill-Palmer Quarterly*, **19**, 237–260.

Ingersoll-Dayton, B. and Antonucci, T. C. (1988). Reciprocal and nonreciprocal social support: Contrasting sides of intimate relationships. *Journal of Gerontology*, **43**, 565–573.

Irvine, A. B., Biglan, A., Smolkowski, K., Metzler, C. W. and Ary, D. V. (1998). The effectiveness of a parenting skills program for parents of middle school students in small communities. Unpublished manuscript, Oregon Research Institute.

Jacobsen, T., Edelstein, W. and Hofmann, V. (1994). A longitudinal study of the relation between representations of attachment in childhood and cognitive functioning in childhood and adolescence. *Developmental Psychology*, **30** (1), 112–124.

Jendrek, M. P. (1993). Grandparents who parent their grandchildren: Effects of lifestyle. *Journal of Marriage and the Family*, **55**, 609–621.

Jenkins, J. M. and Astington, J. W. (1996). Cognitive factors and family structure associated with theory of mind development in young children. *Developmental Psychology*, **32** (1), 70–78.

Johnson, C. L. and Bahrer, B. M. (1987). Marital instability and the changing kinship networks of grandparents. *The Gerontologist*, **27**, 330–335.

Johnson, C. L. and Troll, L. E. (1994). Constraints and facilitators to friendship in late late life. *The Gerontologist*, **34**, 79–87.

Johnson, E. M. and Huston, T. L. (1998). The perils of love, or why wives adapt to husbands during the transition to parenthood. *Journal of Marriage and the Family*, **60**, 195–204.

Kahana, B. and Kahana, E. (1970). Grandparenthood from the perspective of the developing grandchild. *Developmental Psychology*, **3**, 98–105.

Kahn, R. L. (1975). The mental health system and the future aged. *Gerontologist*, **15**, 24–31.

Karney, B. R. and Bradbury, T. N. (1997). Neuroticism, marital interaction, and the trajectory of marital satisfaction. *Journal of Personality and Social Psychology*, **72**, 1075–1092.

Kaufman, G. and Uhlenberg, P. (1998). Effects of life course transitions on the quality of relationships between adult children and their parents. *Journal of Marriage and the Family*, **60**, 924–938.

Kayser, K. (1993). *When Love Dies: The Process of Marital Dissatisfaction*. New York: Guilford Press.

Keating, N. C. and Cole, P. (1980). What do I do with him 24 hours a day? Changes in the housewife role after retirement. *The Gerontologist*, **20**, 84–89.

Kelley, H. H. (1983). Love and Commitment. In H. H. Kelley, E. Berscheid, A. Christensen, J. H. Harvey, T. L. Huston, G. Levinger, E. McClintock, L. A. Peplau and D. R. Peterson (eds), *Close Relationships* (pp. 265–314). New York: W. H. Freeman.

Kelley, J. (1995). Dating: Social patterns in Australia [15 paragraphs]. *Worldwide*

Attitudes [On-line serial], 1995/11/27. Canberra: Australian National University, November. Available http://coombs.anu.edu.au/Depts/RSSS/NSSS/ WWA.html

Kelly, E. and Conley, J. (1987). Personality and compatibility: A prospective analysis of marital stability and satisfaction. *Journal of Personality and Social Psychology*, **52**, 27–40.

Kerig, P. K. (1995). Triangles in the family circle: Effects of family structure on marriage, parenting and child adjustment. *Journal of Family Psychology*, **9**, 28–43.

King, T. (1993). The experiences of midlife daughters who are caregivers for their mothers. *Health Care for Women International*, **14**(5), 419–426.

Kivett, V. R. (1985a). Consanguinity and kin level: Their relative importance to the helping networks of older adults. *Journal of Gerontology*, **40**, 228–234.

Kivett, V. R. (1985b). Grandfathers and grandchildren: Patterns of association, helping and psychological closeness. *Family Relations*, **34**, 565–571.

Kivnick, H. Q. (1983). Dimensions of grandparenthood meaning: Deductive conceptualisation and empirical derivation. *Journal of Personality and Social Psychology*, **44**, 1056–1068.

Kleban, M. H., Brody, E. M., Schoonover, C. B. and Hoffmann, C. (1989). Family help to the elderly: Perceptions of sons-in-law regarding parent care. *Journal of Marriage and the Family*, **51**, 303–312.

Koss, M. P. (1993). Rape: Scope, impact, interventions and public policy responses. *American Psychologist*, **48**, 1062–1069.

Kovacs, A. L. (1992). Introduction: Gender issues at midlife. In B. R. Wainrib (ed.), *Gender Issues Across the Life Cycle* (pp. 105–106). New York: Springer Publishing Company.

Krause, A. and Haverkamp, B. (1996). Attachment in adult–child older parent relationships: Research, theory, and practice. *Journal of Counselling and Development*, **75**, 83–92.

Kupersmidt, J. B. and Coie, J. D. (1990). Preadolescent peer status, aggression and school adjustment as predictors of externalizing problems in adolescence. *Child Development*, **61**, 1350–1362.

Ladd, G. W. (1999). Peer relationships and social competence during middle childhood. *Annual Review of Psychology*, **50**, 333–360.

Lamborn, S. D., Mounts, N., Steinberg, L. and Dornbusch, S. (1991). Patterns of competence and adjustment among adolescents from authoritative, authoritarian, indulgent, and neglectful families. *Child Development*, **62** (5), 1049–1065.

Lamme, S., Dykstra, P. A. and Broese Van Groenou, M. I. (1996). Rebuilding the network: New relationships in widowhood. *Personal Relationships*, **3**, 337–349.

Langlois, J. H. and Downs, A. C. (1979). Peer relations as a function of physical attractiveness: The eye of the beholder or behavioural reality. *Child Development*, **50**, 409–418.

Larson, R. W. (1997). The emergence of solitude as a constructive domain of experience in early adolescence. *Child Development*, **68**, 80–93.

Larson, R. and Richards, M. (1994). *Divergent Realities: The Emotional Lives of Mothers, Fathers and Adolescents*. New York: Basic Books.

Larson, R., Zuzanek, J. and Mannell, R. (1985). Being alone versus being with people: Disengagement in the daily experience of older adults. *Journal of Gerontology*, **3**, 375–381.

Lawrence, B. M. (1984). Conversation and cooperation: Child linguistic maturity, parental speech and helping behavior of young children. *Child Development*, **55**, 1926–1935.

Leaper, C. and Holliday, H. (1995). Gossip in same-gender and cross-gender friends' conversations. *Personal Relationships*, **2**, 237–246.

Lee, G. R. (1988). Marital satisfaction in later life: The effects of nonmarital roles. *Journal of Marriage and the Family*, **50**, 775–783.

Lee, G. R., Mancini, J. A. and Maxwell, J. W. (1990). Sibling relationships in adulthood: Contact patterns and motivations. *Journal of Marriage and the Family*, **52**, 431–440.

Lerner, R. M. and Spanier, G. B. (1978). *Child Influences on Marital snd Family Interaction: A Lifespan Perspective*. New York: Academic Press.

Levitt, M. J., Antonucci, T., Clark, M.C. and Rotton, J. (1985). Social support and well-being: Preliminary indicators based on two samples of the elderly. *International Journal of Aging and Human Development*, **21**, 61–77.

Levy-Shiff, R. (1994). Individual and contextual correlates of marital change across the transition to parenthood. *Developmental Psychology*, **30**, 591–601.

Lieberman, M., Doyle, A. and Markiewicz, D. (1999). Developmental patterns in security of attachment to mother and father in late childhood and early adolescence: Associations with peer relations. *Child Development*, **70**, 202–213.

Lilliard, A., Brien, M. J. and Waite, L. J. (1995). Premarital cohabitation and subsequent marital dissolution: A matter of self-selection. *Demography*, **32**, 437–456.

Livesley, W. J. and Bromley, D. B. (1973). *Person Perception in Childhood and Adolescence*. London: John Wiley & Sons.

Lock, M. (1998). Deconstructing the change: Female maturation in Japan and North America. In R. A. Shweder (ed.), *Welcome to Middle Age!* (pp. 45–75). Chicago: University of Chicago Press.

Luescher, K. and Pillemer, K. (1998). Intergenerational ambivalence: A new approach to the study of parent–child relationships in later life. *Journal of Marriage and the Family*, **60**, 413–425.

McDavid, John-W. and Harari, Herbert. (1966). Stereotyping of names and popularity in grade-school children. *Child Development*, **37**(2), 453–459.

McGoldrick, M., Heiman, M. and Carter, B. (1993). The changing family cycle: A perspective on normalcy. In F. Walsh (ed.), *Normal Family Processes*, 2nd edn (pp. 405–443). New York: Guilford Press.

McGrath, E. (1992). New treatment strategies for women in the middle. In B. R. Wainrib (ed.), *Gender Issues Across the Life Cycle* (pp. 124–136). New York: Springer Publishing Company.

McLanahan, S. and Sorensen, A. B. (1985). Life events and psychological well-being. In G. H. Elder, Jr. (ed.), *Life Course Dynamics* (pp. 217–238). Ithaca, N.Y.: Cornell.

Maccoby, E.E. and Martin, J.A. (1983). Socialization in the context of the family: Parent–child interaction. In E.M. Hetherington (ed.), *Handbook of Child Psychology* (pp. 1–101). New York: John Wiley & Sons.

Main, M. and Solomon, J. (1990). Procedures for identifying infants as disorganized/disoriented during the Ainsworth Strange Situation. In M.T. Greenberg, D. Cicchetti and E.M. Cumming (eds), *Attachment in the Preschool Years: Theory, Research and Intervention* (pp. 121–160). Chicago: University of Chicago Press.

Mancini, J. and Blieszner, R. (1989). Aging parents and adult children: Research themes in intergenerational relations. *Journal of Marriage and the Family*, **51**, 275–290.

Marcia, J. (1980). Identity in adolescence. In J. Adelson (ed.), *Handbook of Adolescent Psychology* (pp. 159–187). New York: John Wiley & Sons.

Mares, M. L. (1995). The aging family. In M. A. Fitzpatrick. and A. L. Vangelisti (eds), *Explaining Family Interactions* (pp. 344–374). New York: Sage Publications.

Martin, B. (1990). The transmission of relationship difficulties from one generation to the next. *Journal of Youth and Adolescence*, **19**, 181–199.

Martin, T. C. and Bumpass, L. L. (1989). Recent trends in marital disruption. *Demography*, **26**, 37–51.

Mattessich, P. and Hill, R. (1987). Life cycle and family development. In M. B. Sussman and S. K. Steinmetz (eds), *Handbook of Marriage and the Family* (pp. 437–469). New York: Plenum Press.

Matthews, S. H. (1986a). Friendships in old age: Biography and circumstance. In V. W. Marshall (ed.), *Later Life: The Social Psychology of Aging* (pp. 233–269). Beverly Hills, Calif.: Sage.

Matthews, S. H. (1986b). *Friendships Through the Life Course: Oral Biographies in Old Age*. Beverly Hills, Calif.: Sage.

Matthews, S. H. (1996). Friendships in old age. In N. Vanzetti and S. Duck (eds), *A Lifetime of Relationships* (pp. 406–430). Pacific Grove, Calif.: Brooks/Cole.

Matthews, S. H. and Rosner, T. T. (1988). Shared filial responsibility: The family as the primary caregiver. *Journal of Marriage and the Family*, **50**, 185–195.

Matthews, S. H. and Sprey, J. (1984). The impact of divorce on grandparenthood: An exploratory study. *The Gerontologist*, **24**, 41–47.

Meins, E., Fernyhough, C., Russell, J. and Clark-Carter, D. (1998). Security of attachment as a predictor of symbolic and mentalising abilities: A longitudinal study. *Social Development*, **7**, 1–25.

Menaghan, E. (1983). Marital stress and family transitions: A panel analysis. *Journal of Marriage and the Family*, **45**, 371–386.

Metzler, C. W., Biglan, A., Ary, D. V. and Li, F. (1998). The stability and validity of early adolescents' reports of parenting constructs. *Journal of Family Psychology*, **12**, 600–619.

Meyerhoff, B. (1980). *Number Our Days*. New York: Simon & Schuster.

Mickelson, K. D., Helgeson, V. S. and Weiner, E. (1995). Gender effects on social support provision and receipt. *Personal Relationships*, **2**, 211–224.

Mikulincer, M. and Florian, V. (1998). The relationship between adult attachment styles and emotional and cognitive reactions to stressful events. In J. A. Simpson and W. S. Rholes (eds), *Attachment Theory and Close Relationships* (pp. 143–165). New York: Guilford Press.

Miller, B. (1987). Gender and control among spouses of the cognitively impaired. *Gerontologist*, **27**, 447–453.

Miller, B. (1990a). Gender differences in spouse caregiver strain: Socialization and role expectations. *Journal of Marriage and the Family*, **52**, 311–321.

Miller, B. (1990b). Gender differences in spouse management of the caregiver role. In E. K. Abel and M. K. Nelson (eds), *Circles of Care: Work and Identity in Women's Lives* (pp. 92–104). Albany: State University of New York Press.

Miller, B. C. and Sollie, D. L. (1980). Normal stresses during the transition to parenthood. *Family Relations*, **29**, 459–465.

Mitchell, C. A. (1977). The differences between male and female joke telling as exemplified in a college community. *Dissertation Abstracts International*, **37**.

Mitchell, P. (1997). *Acquiring a Concept of Mind: A Review of Psychological Research and Theory*. Hove, UK: Psychology Press.

Miyake, K., Chen, S. and Campos, J. (1985). Infant temperament, mother's mode of interaction and attachment in Japan. *Monographs of the Society for Research in Child Development*, **50**, 276–297.

Montemayor, R. (1983). Parents and adolescents in conflict: All families some of the time and some families most of the time. *Journal of Early Adolescence*, **3**, 83–103.

Montgomery, B. M. (1988). Quality communication in personal relationships. In S. Duck (ed.), *Handbook of Personal Relationships* (pp. 343–359). New York: John Wiley & Sons.

Montgomery, B, M. (1993). Relationship maintenance versus relationship change: A dialectical dilemma. *Journal of Social and Personal Relationships*, **10**, 205–224.

Moreno, J.L. (1934). *Who Shall Survive?* Washington, DC: Nervous and Mental Diseases Publishing Co.

Moss, E., Gosselin, C., Parent, S., Rouseau, D. and Dumont, M. (1997). Attachment and joint problem-solving experiences during the preschool period. *Social Development*, **6** (1), 1–17.

Nadelson, C., Polonsky, D. and Matthews, M. A. (1981). Marriage problems and marital therapy in the middle-aged. In J. Howells (ed.), *Modern Perspectives in the Psychiatry of Middle Age* (pp. 337–352). New York: Brunner-Mazel.

Neugarten, B. (1968). The awareness of middle age. In B. Neugarten (ed.), *Middle Age and Aging* (pp. 93–98). Chicago: University of Chicago Press.

Neugarten, B. and Neugarten, D. (1987). The changing meanings of age. *Psychology Today*, **21**, 29–33.

Neugarten, B. L. and Weinstein, K. K. (1964). The changing American grandparent. *Journal of Marriage and the Family*, **26**, 199–204.

Newcomb, M. D. and Keefe, K. (1997). Social support, self-esteem, social conformity, and gregariousness: Developmental patterns across 12 years. In G. R. Pierce, B. Lakey, I. G. Sarason and B. R. Sarason (eds), *Sourcebook of Social Support and Personality* (pp. 303–333). New York: Plenum Press.

Newman, P. and Smith, A. (1997). *Social Focus on Families*. London: The Stationery Office.

NICHD (National Institutes of Child Health and Development) (1997). The effects of infant child care on infant–mother attachment security: Results of the NICHD study of early child care. *Child Development*, **68**, 860–879.

Nolan, M., Grant, G. and Keady, J. (1996). *Understanding Family Care: A Multidimensional Model of Caring and Coping*. Buckingham, UK: Open University Press.

Noller, P. and Bagi, S. (1985). Parent–adolescent communication. *Journal of Adolescence*, **8**, 125–144.

Noller, P. and Callan, V. J. (1986). Adolescent and parent conceptions of family cohesion and adaptability. *Journal of Adolescence*, **9**, 97–106.

Noller, P. and Callan, V. J. (1990). Adolescents' perceptions of the nature of their communication with parents. *Journal of Youth and Adolescence*, **19**, 349–362.

Noller, P. and Callan, V. J. (1991). *The Adolescent in the Family*. London: Routledge.

Noller, P., Feeney, J. A. and Blakeley-Smith, A. (2000). Handling pressures for change in marriage: Making attributions for relational dialectics. In V. Manusov and J. Harvey (eds), *Attributions, Communication Behaviour and Close Relationships* (pp. 153–172). Cambridge, UK, Cambridge University Press.

Noller, P., Feeney, J. A., Bonnell, D. and Callan, V. J. (1994). A longitudinal study of conflict in early marriage. *Journal of Social and Personal Relationships*, **11**, 233–252.

Noller, P., Feeney, J. A., Peterson, C. and Atkin, S. (1999). Conflict in adolescent families: An analogue study. Paper presented at the annual conference of The Society of Australasian Social Psychologists, Coolum, April.

Noller, P., Feeney, J. A., Peterson, C. and Sheehan, G. (1996). Learning conflict patterns in the family: Links between marital, parental and sibling relationships. In T. Socha and G. Stamp (eds), *Parents, Children and Communication: Frontiers of Teaching and Research* (pp. 273–298). Hillsdale, N.J.: Lawrence Erlbaum Associates.

Noller, P. and Fitzpatrick, M. A. (1993) *Communication in Family Relationships*. Englewood Cliffs, N.J.: Prentice-Hall.

Noller, P., Seth-Smith, M., Bouma, R. and Schweitzer, R. (1992). Parent and adolescent perceptions of family functioning: A comparison of clinic and non-clinic couples. *Journal of Adolescence*, **15**, 101–114.

Norris, J. E. (1990). Peer relationships of the never married. Paper presented at the annual meeting of the Canadian Association on Gerontology, Victoria, BC.

Norris, J. E. and Forbes, S. J. (1987). Cohesion and adaptability in caregiving families. Paper presented at the Annual Meeting of the Gerontological Society of America, Washington, DC.

Norris, J. E. and Tindale, J. A. (1994). *Among Generations: The Cycle of Adult Relationships*. New York: Freeman.

Notman, M. (1979). Midlife concerns of women and implications of menopause. *American Journal of Psychiatry*, **136**, 1270–1274.

O'Connor, D. (1992). *Males will be . . . A Report on the Survey of Year Nine Males and their Attitudes to Forced Sex*. Brisbane, Australia: Domestic Violence Resource Centre.

Offer, D. and Sabshin, M. (1984). *Normality and the Life Cycle*. New York: Basic Books.

Olson, D. H., McCubbin, H., Barnes, H. L., Larsen, A., Muxen, M. and Wilson, M. (1983). *Families: What Makes Them Work?* Beverly Hills, Calif.: Sage.

O'Neil, J. M. and Egan, J. (1992). Men's and women's gender role journeys: A metaphor for healing, transition and transformation. In B. R. Wainrib (ed.), *Gender Issues Across the Life Cycle* (pp. 107–136). New York: Springer Publishing Company.

Osofsky, H. J. and Culp, R. E. (1989). Risk factors in the transition to fatherhood. In S. H. Cath, A. Gurwitt and L. Gunsberg (eds), *Fathers and their Families* (pp. 145–165). Hillsdale, N.J.: Analytic Press.

Osofsky, J. D. and Culp, R. (1993). A relationship perspective on the transition to parenthood. In G. H. Pollock and S. I. Greenspan (eds), *The Course of Life*. Vol. 5: *Early Adulthood* (pp. 75–98). Madison, Conn.: International Universities Press.

Oyserman, D., Gant, L. and Ager, J. (1995). A socially contextualized model of African American identity: Possible selves and school persistence. *Journal of Personality and Social Psychology*, **69**, 1216–1232.

Parke, R. D. and Beitel, A. (1988). Disappointment: When things go wrong in the transition to parenthood. *Marriage and Family Review*, **12**, 221–265.

Parker, J. G. and Asher, S. R. (1987). Peer relations and later personal adjustment: Are low-acceptance children at risk? *Developmental Psychology*, **28**, 231–241.

Parker, S. and de Vries, B. (1993). Patterns of friendship for women and men in same and cross-sex friendships. *Journal of Social and Personal Relationships*, **10**, 617–626.

Parks, S. H. and Pilisuk, M. (1991). Caregiver burden: Gender and the psychological costs of caregiving. *American Journal of Orthopsychiatry*, **61**(4), 501–509.

Patterson, G. R., Debaryshe, B. and Ramsey, E. (1989). A developmental perspective on antisocial behaviour. *American Psychologist*, **44**, 1–7.

Patterson, G. R., Reid, J. B. and Dishion, T. J. (1992). *Antisocial Boys: A Social Interactional Approach* (Vol. 4). Eugener, Oreg.: Castalia.

Patton, W. and Mannison, M. (1995). Sexual coercion in high school dating. *Sex Roles*, **33**, 447–457.

Pears, J. and Noller, P. (1995). Youth homelessness: Abuse, gender and the process of adjustment to life on the streets. *Australian Journal of Social Issues*, **30**, 405–424.

Pearson, J., Cowan, P., Cowan, C. and Cohn, D. (1993). Adult attachment and adult child older parent relationships. *American Journal of Orthopsychiatry*, **63**, 606–613.

Pearson, J. C. (1996). Forty-forever years? Primary relationships and senior citizens. In N. Vanzetti and S. Duck (eds), *A Lifetime of Relationships* (pp. 383–405). Pacific Grove, Calif.: Brooks/Cole.

Peevers, B. H. and Secord, P. F. (1973). Developmental changes in attribution of descriptive concepts to persons. *Journal of Personality and Social Psychology*, **27**(1), 120–128.

Perner, J., Ruffman, T. and Leekam, S. (1994). Theory of mind is contagious: You catch it from your sibs. *Child Development*, **65**, 1228–1238.

Perry, D.G. and Bussey, K. (1984). *Social Development*. Englewood Cliffs, N.J.: Prentice-Hall.

Peterson, C. (1999). Grandfathers' and grandmothers' satisfaction with the grand-parenting role: Seeking new answers to old questions. *International Journal of Aging and Human Development*, **49**(1), 61–78.

Piaget, J. (1952). *The Origins of Intelligence in Children*. New York: International Universities Press.

Piaget, J. (1970). Piaget's theory. In P. H. Mussen (ed.), *Carmichael's Manual of Child Psychology*. New York: John Wiley & Sons.

Pillemer, K. (1985). The dangers of dependence: New findings on domestic violence against the elderly. *Social Problems*, **33**, 148–158.

Pillemer, K. (1993). The abused offspring are dependent. In R. J. Gelles and D. Loeseke (eds), *Controversies in Family Violence* (pp. 237–249). Newbury Park, Calif.: Sage.

Pillemer, K. and Finkelhor, D. (1988). The prevalence of elder abuse: A random sample survey. *Gerontologist*, **28**, 51–57.

Pillemer, K. and Suitor, J. J. (1991). 'Will I ever escape my children's problems?' Effects of adult children's problems on elderly parents. *Journal of Marriage and the Family*, **53**, 585–594.

Porter, B. and O'Leary, D. (1980). Marital discord and childhood behavior problems. *Journal of Abnormal Child Psychology*, **8**(3), 287–295.

Pratt, M. W. and Norris, J. E. (1994). *The Social Psychology of Aging: A Cognitive Perspective*. Oxford: Blackwell.

Putallaz, M. (1983). Predicting children's sociometric status from their behaviour. *Child Development*, **54**, 1417–1424.

Putallaz, M. and Gottman, J.M. (1981). Social skills and group acceptance. In S.R. Asher and J.M. Gottman (eds), *The Development of Children's Friendships* (pp. 189–216). Cambridge: Cambridge University Press.

Quirouette, C. and Gold, D. (1992). Spousal characteristics as predictors of well being in older couples. *International Journal of Aging and Human Development*, **34**, 257–269.

Raschke, H. (1987). Divorce. In M. Sussman and S. Steinmetz (eds), *Handbook of Marriage and the Family* (pp. 597–624). New York: Plenum Press.

Reis, H. T. (1998). Gender differences in intimacy and related behaviors: Context and process. In D. J. Canary and K. Dindia (eds), *Sex Differences and Similarities in Communication* (pp 203–233). Mahwah, N.J.: Lawrence Erlbaum Associates.

Rempel, J. (1985). Childless elderly: What are they missing? *Journal of Marriage and the Family*, **47**, 343–348.

Rexroat, C. and Shehan, C. (1987). The family life cycle and spouses' time in housework. *Journal of Marriage and the Family*, **49**, 737–750.

Rheingold, H. (1982). Little children's participation in the work of adults, a nascent prosocial behavior. *Child Development*, **53**, 114–125.

Rholes, W. S., Simpson, J. A. and Blakely, B. S. (1995). Adult attachment styles and mothers' relationships with their young children. *Personal Relationships*, **2**, 35–54.

Rholes, W. S., Simpson, J. A. Blakely, B. S., Lanigan, L. and Allen, E. A. (1997). Adult attachment styles, the desire to have children, and working models of parenthood. *Journal of Personality*, **65**, 357–385.

Rice, K. G. (1990). Attachment in adolescence: A narrative and meta-analytic review. *Journal of Youth and Adolescence*, **19**, 511–538.

Richards, M. H., Crowe, P. A., Larson, R. and Swarr, A. (1998). Developmental patterns and gender differences in the experience of peer companionship during adolescence. *Child Development*, **69**, 154–163.

Riedmann, A. and White, L. (1996). Adult sibling relationships: Racial and ethnic comparisons. In G. H. Brody (ed.), *Sibling Relationships: Their Causes and Consequences. Advances in Applied Developmental Psychology*, Vol. 10 (pp. 105–126). Norwood, N.J.: Ablex Publishing Corporation.

Roberto, K. A. and Scott, J. P. (1986). Equity considerations in the friendships of older adults. *Journal of Gerontology*, **41**, 241–247.

Roberts, R. E. L. and Bengtson, V. L. (1996). Affective ties to parents in early adulthood and self-esteem across 20 years. *Social Psychology Quarterly*, **59**, 96–106.

Rolland, J. S. (1993). Mastering family challenges in serious illness and disability. In F. Walsh (ed.), *Normal Family Processes*, 2nd edn (pp. 444–473). New York: Guilford Press.

Rollins, B. C. (1989). Marital quality at midlife. In S. Hunter and M. Sundel (eds), *Midlife Myths: Issues, Findings and Practical Implications* (pp. 184–194). Newbury Park, Calif.: Sage.

Rook, K. S. (1987). Reciprocity of social exchange and social satisfaction among older women. *Journal of Personality and Social Psychology*, **52**, 145–154.

Rook, K. S. (1990). Stressful aspects of older adults' social relationships:

Current theory and research. In M. A. P. Stephens, J. H. Crowther, S. E. Hobfoll and D. L. Tennenbaum (eds), *Stress and Coping in Later-life Families* (pp. 173–192). New York: Hemisphere.

Rook, K. S. and Pietromonaco, P. (1987). Close relationships: Ties that heal or ties that bind? In W. H. Jones and D. Perlman (eds), *Advances in Personal Relationships* (Vol. 1, pp. 1–35). Greenwich, Conn.: JAI.

Rosenthal, D. A. and Moore, S. M. (1991). Risky business: Adolescents and HIV/AIDS. *Youth Studies*, **10**, 20–25.

Ross, H. G. and Milgram, J. I. (1982). Important variables in adult sibling relationships: A qualitative study. In M. E. Lamb and B. Sutton-Smith (eds), *Sibling Relationships: Their Nature and Significance Across the Life Span* (pp. 225–249). Hillsdale, N.J.: Lawrence Erlbaum Associations.

Rossi, A. S. (1968). Transition to parenthood. *Journal of Marriage and the Family*, **30**, 26–39.

Rubin, K. H. (1998). Social and emotional development from a cultural perspective. *Developmental Psychology*, **34**, 611–615.

Rubin, K., Hastings, P., Chen, X., Stewart, S. and McNichol, K. (1998). Intrapersonal and maternal correlates of aggression, conflict, and externalizing problems in toddlers. *Child Development*, **69**(6), 1614–1629.

Rubin, K., Coplan, R., Nelson, L, Cheah, C. and Lagace-Seguin, D. (1999). Peer relationships in childhood. In M. Bornstein, H. Marc, M. Lamb *et al.* (eds), *Developmental Psychology: An Advanced Textbook* (4th edn) (pp. 451–501). Mahwah, N.J.: Lawrence Erlbaum Associates.

Ruble, D. N., Fleming, A. S., Hackel, L. S. and Stangor, C. (1988). Changes in the marital relationship during the transition to first time motherhood: Effects of violated expectations concerning division of household labor. *Journal of Personality and Social Psychology*, **55**, 78–87.

Rusbult, C. E. and Buunk, B. P. (1993). Commitment processes in close relationships: An interdependence analysis. *Journal of Social and Personal Relationships*, **10**, 175–205.

Ruvolo, A. P. (1998). Marital well-being and general happiness of newlywed couples: Relationships across time. *Journal of Social and Personal Relationships*, **15**, 470–489.

Salokangas, R. K., Mattila, V. and Joukamaa, M. (1988). Intimacy and mental disorder in late middle age. *Acta Psychiatrica Scandinavia*, **78**, 555–560.

Samter, W., Whaley, B. B., Mortenson, S. T. and Burleson, B. R. (1997). Ethnicity and emotional support in same-sex friendship: A comparison of Asian-Americans, African-Americans, and Euro-Americans. *Personal Relationships*, **4**, 413–430.

Sanchez, L. and Thomson, E. (1997). Becoming mothers and fathers: Parenthood, gender, and the division of labor. *Gender and Society*, **11**, 747–772.

Sanderson, C. A. and Cantor, N. (1997). Creating satisfaction in steady dating relationships: The role of personal goals and situational affordances. *Journal of Personality and Social Psychology*, **73**, 1424–1433.

Sarantakos, S. (1992). *Modern Families*. Melbourne, Australia: Macmillan.

Sarason, I. G., Pierce, G. R. and Sarason, B. R. (1990). Social support and interactional processes: A triadic hypothesis. *Journal of Social and Personal Relationships*, **7**, 495–507.

Schaffer, H. R. (1996). *Social Development*. Oxford: Blackwell.

Schaffer, H. R. and Emerson, P. (1964). Patterns of response to physical contact in early human development. *Journal of Child Psychology and Psychiatry*, **5**, 1–13.

Schaie, W. K. (1994). The course of adult intellectual development. *American Psychologist*, **49**(4), 304–313.

Scott, J. P. (1983). Siblings and other kin. In T. H. Brubaker (ed.), *Family Relationships in Later Life* (pp. 47–62). Beverly Hills, Calif.: Sage.

Selman, R. (1981). The child as a friendship philosopher. In S. R. Asher and J. M. Gottman (eds), *The Development of Children's Friendships*. Cambridge: Cambridge University Press.

Shanas, E. (1973). Family-kin networks and aging in cross-cultural perspective. *Journal of Marriage and the Family*, **35**, 505–511.

Shanas, E. (1980). Older people and their families: The new pioneers. *Journal of Marriage and the Family*, **42**, 9–15.

Shapiro, T. and Stern, D. (1989). Psychoanalytic perspectives of the first year of life: The establishment of the object in an affective field. In S. J. Greenspan and G. H. Pollock (eds), *The Course of Life*. Vol 1: *Infancy* (pp. 271–293). Madison: International Universities Press.

Shifflett-Simpson, K. and Cummings, M. (1996). Mixed message resolution and children's responses to interadult conflict. *Child Development*, **67**(2), 437–448.

Siegal, M. (1997). *Knowing Children: Experiments in Conversation and Cognition* (2nd edn). Hove, UK: Psychology Press.

Siegal, M. and Peterson, C.C. (1994). Children's theory of mind and the conversational territory of cognitive development. In C. Lewis and P. Mitchell (eds), *Children's Early Understanding of Mind: Origins and Development*. Hove, UK: Lawrence Erlbaum Associates.

Sillars, A. L. and Scott, M. D. (1983). Interpersonal perception between intimates: An integrative review. *Human Communication Research*, **10**, 153–176.

Silverberg, S. B. (1992). Adolescence and family interaction. In V. Van Hasselt and M. Hersen (eds), *Handbook of Social Development: A Lifespan Perspective* (pp. 93–102). New York: Plenum Press.

Silverstein, M. and Bengston, V. L. (1991). Do close parent–child relations reduce the mortality risk of older parents? *Journal of Health and Social Behaviour*, **32**, 382–395.

Simpson, J. A. (1990). Influence of attachment styles on romantic relationships. *Journal of Personality and Social Psychology*, **59**, 971–980.

Simpson, J. A., Rholes, W. S. and Nelligan, J. S. (1992). Support seeking and support giving within couples in an anxiety-provoking situation: The role of attachment styles. *Journal of Personality and Social Psychology*, **62**, 434–446.

Singer, D. and Rummo, J. (1973). Ideational creativity and behavioral style in kindergarten-age children. *Developmental Psychology*, **8**(2), 154–161.

Skolnick, A. (1981). Married lives: Longitudinal perspectives on marriage. In D. H. Eichorn, J. A. Clausen, N. Haan, M. P. Honzik and P. H. Mussen (eds), *Present and Past in Middle Life* (pp. 269–298). New York: Academic Press.

Small, S. A. and Luster, T. (1994). Adolescent sexual activity: An ecological, risk-factor approach. *Journal of Marriage and the Family*, **56**, 181–192.

Smart, R. and Smart, M. (1980). Complexity of preadolescents' social play and games. *New Zealand Journal of Educational Studies*, **25**, 81–92.

Smetana, J. (1988). Adolescents' and parents' conceptions of parental authority. *Child Development*, **59**(2), 321–335.

Smetana, J. G. and Asquith, P. (1994). Adolescents' and parents' conceptions of parental authority and personal autonomy. *Child Development*, **65**, 1147–1162.

Smetana, J. G., Yau, J., Restrepo, A. and Braeges, J. L. (1991). Adolescent–parent conflict in married and divorced families. *Developmental Psychology*, **27**, 1000–1010.

Smith, C. A. (1997). Factors associated with early sexual activity among urban adolescents. *Social Work*, **42**, 334–346.

South, S. and Spitze, G. (1986). Determinants of divorce over the marital life course. *American Sociological Review*, **51**, 583–590.

Spitze, G. and Logan, J. (1990). More evidence on women (and men) in the middle. *Research on Aging*, **12**, 182–198.

Spitze, G. and Logan, J. R. (1991). Sibling structure and intergenerational relations. *Journal of Marriage and the Family*, **53**, 871–884.

Sprecher, S. and McKinney, K. (1993). *Sexuality*. Newbury Park, Calif.: Sage.

Sroufe, L. (1985). Generational boundary dissolution between mothers and their preschool children: A relationship systems approach. *Child Development*, **56**(2), 317–325.

Sroufe, L. A. and Waters, E. (1977). Attachment as an organizational contruct. *Child Development*, **48**, 1184–1199.

Stafford, L. and Bayer, C. L. (1993). *Interaction Between Parents and Children*. Newbury Park, Calif.: Sage.

Stark, K. D., Humphrey, L. L., Crook, K. and Lewis, K. (1990). Perceived family environments of depressed and anxious children: Child's and maternal figure's perspectives. *Journal of Abnormal Child Psychology*, **18**, 527–547.

Starrels, M. E., Ingersoll-Dayton, B., Dowler, D. W. and Neal, M. B. (1997). The stress of caring for a parent: Effect of the elder's impairment on an employed child. *Journal of Marriage and the Family*, **59**, 860–872.

Stein, C. H. (1992). Ties that bind: Three studies of obligation in adult relationships with family. *Journal of Social and Personal Relationships*, **9**, 525–547.

Stein, C. H., Wemmerus, V. A., Ward, M., Gaines, M. E., Freeberg, A. L. and Jewell, T. C. (1998). 'Because they're my parents': An intergenerational study of felt obligation and parental caregiving. *Journal of Marriage and the Family*, **60**, 611–623.

Steinberg, L. (1991). Autonomy, conflict and harmony in the family relationship. In S. S. Feldman and G. R. Elliott (eds), *At the Threshold: The Developing Adolescent* (pp. 255–276). Cambridge, Mass.: Harvard University Press.

Steinberg, L., Lamborn, S. D., Darling, N., Mounts, N. S. and Dornbusch, S. M. (1994). Over-time changes in adjustment and competence among adolescents from authoritative, authoritarian, indulgent and neglectful families. *Child Development*, **65**, 754–770.

Steinberg, L., Mounts, N., Lamborn, S. and Dornbusch, S. (1991). Authoritative parenting and adolescent adjustment across varied ecological niches. *Journal of Research on Adolescence*, **1**(1), 19–36.

Stephens, M. A. P. and Clark, S. L. (1996). Interpersonal relationships in multi-generational families. In N. Vanzetti and S. Duck (eds), *A Lifetime of Relationships* (pp. 431–454). Pacific Grove, Calif.: Brooks/Cole.

Stern, D. (1976). A microanalysis of mother–infant interaction: Behavior regulating social contact between a mother and her 3½ month old twins. In E. Rexford, L. Sanders and T. Shapiro (eds), *Infant Psychiatry* (pp. 113–126). New Haven, Conn.: Yale University Press.

Stewart, R. B., Verbrugge, K. M. and Beilfuss, M. C. (1998). Sibling relationships in early adulthood: A typology. *Personal Relationships*, **5**, 59–74.

Stocker, C. and McHale, S. M. (1992). The nature and family correlates of pre-adolescents' perceptions of their sibling relationships. *Journal of Social and Personal Relationships*, **9**, 179–195.

Stocker, C., Dunn, J. and Plomin, R. (1989). Sibling relationships: Links with child temperament, maternal behaviour, and family structure. *Developmental Psychology*, **63**, 1–19.

Stoller, E. P. (1985). Exchange patterns in the informal support networks of the elderly: The impact of reciprocity on morale. *Journal of Marriage and the Family*, **47**, 335–342.

Stone, L. G. and Church, J. (1968). *Childhood and Adolescence: A Psychology of the Growing Person*, 2nd edn. New York: Random House.

Strahan, B. J. (1995). Predictors of depression: An attachment theoretical approach. *Australian Journal of Marriage and Family*, **12**, 12–26.

Suitor, J. J. and Pillemer, K. (1988). Explaining intergenerational conflict when adult children and elderly parents live together. *Journal of Marriage and the Family*, **50**, 1037–1047.

Suitor, J. and Pillemer, K. (1992). Status transitions and marital satisfaction: The case of adult children caring for elderly parents suffering from dementia. *Journal of Social and Personal Relationships*, **9**(4), 549–562.

Sullivan, H. S. (1953). *The Interpersonal Theory of Psychiatry*. New York: W. W. Norton.

Swenson, C. H., Eskew, R. W. and Kohlhepp, K. A. (1981). Stage of family life cycle, ego development, and the marriage relationship. *Journal of Marriage and the Family*, **43**, 841–853.

Taylor, J. E. and Norris, J. E. (1993). The response of midlife women to maternal death. Manuscript submitted for publication.

Terry, D. J. (1991a). Stress, coping, and adaptation to new parenthood. *Journal of Social and Personal Relationships*, **8**, 527–547.

Terry, D. J. (1991b). Transition to parenthood. In P. C. Heaven (ed.), *Lifespan* (pp. 184–211). Sydney, Australia: Harcourt, Brace, Jovanovich.

Terry, D. J., McHugh, T. A. and Noller, P. (1991). Role dissatisfaction and the decline in marital quality across the transition to parenthood. *Australian Journal of Psychology*, **43**, 129–132.

Thomas, J. L. (1986a). Age and sex differences in perceptions of grandparenting. *Journal of Gerontology*, **41**, 417–423.

Thomas, J. L. (1986b). Gender differences in satisfaction with grandparents. *Psychology and Aging*, **1**, 215–219.

Thompson, R. A. and Limber, S. P. (1990). Social anxiety in infancy: Stranger and separation anxiety. In H. Leitenberg (ed.), *Handbook of Social Anxiety* (pp. 85–137). New York: Plenum Press.

Thompson, L. and Walker, A. J. (1990). Gender in families: Women and men in marriage, work and parenthood. *Journal of Marriage and the Family*, **51**, 845–871.

Thompson, S., Medvene, L. and Freedman, D. (1995). Caregiving in the close relationships of cardiac patients: Exchange, power, and attributional perspectives on caregiver resentment. *Personal Relationships*, **2**(2), 125–142.

Thornton, A., Orbuch, T. L. and Axinn, W. G. (1995). Parent–child relationships during the transition to adulthood. *Journal of Family Issues*, **16**, 538–564.

Tizard, B. and Hughes, M. (1984). *Young Children Learning*. London: Fontana.

Traupmann, J. and Hatfield, E. (1983). How important is marital fairness over the lifespan? *International Journal of Aging and Human Development*, **17**, 89–101.

Trevarthen, C. (1980). The foundations of intersubjectivity: Development of interpersonal and cooperative understanding in infants. In D. Olson (ed.), *The Social Foundations of Language and Thought* (pp. 179–204). New York: W.W. Norton.

Trevarthen, C. (1992). An infant's motives for speaking and thinking in the culture. In A. Wold *et al.* (eds), *The Dialogical Alternative: Towards a Theory of Language and Mind* (pp. 99–137). Oslo: Scandinavian University Press.

Trinke, S. J. and Bartholomew, K. (1997). Hierarchies of attachment relationships in young adulthood. *Journal of Social and Personal Relationships*, **14**, 603–625.

Van Ijzendoorn, M. H. and DeWolff, M. S. (1997). In search of the absent father: Meta-analyses of infant–father attachment. *Child Development*, **68**, 604–609.

Van Lieshout, C. and Van Aken, M. A. G. (1987). Peer acceptance and rejection and the structure of children's self concept. Paper presented at the 9th Biennial International Society for the Study of Behavioural Development Meetings, Tokyo.

Vandell, D. L., Minnett, A. M. and Santrock, J. W. (1987). Age differences in sibling relationships during middle childhood. *Journal of Applied Developmental Psychology*, **8**, 247–258.

Vanzetti, N. and Duck, S. (1996). *A Lifetime of Relationships*. Pacific Grove, Calif.: Brooks/Cole.

Vaux, A. (1988). *Social Support: Theory, Research, and Intervention*. New York: Praeger.

Vemer, E., Coleman, M., Ganong, L. H. and Cooper, H. (1989). Marital satisfaction in remarriage: A meta-analysis. *Journal of Marriage and the Family*, **51**, 713–725.

Walker, A. and Thompson, L. (1983). Intimacy and intergenerational aid and contact among mothers and daughters. *Journal of Marriage and the Family*, **45**(4), 841–849.

Walsh, F. (1982). *Normal Family Processes*. New York: Guilford Press.

Walsh, F. (1993). *Normal Family Processes*. New York: Guilford Press.

Ward, R. A. (1993). Marital happiness and household equity in later life. *Journal of Marriage and the Family*, **55**, 427–438.

Weber, M. T. (1998). Identity construction in the interview narratives of self-abusive women. *Dissertation Abstracts International* (Section B: The Sciences and Engineering), **59**(2-B).

Weishaus, S. and Field, D. (1988). A half century of marriage: Continuity or change? *Journal of Marriage and the Family*, **50**, 763–774.

Weiss, R. S. (1986). Continuities and transformations in social relationships from childhood to adulthood. In W. W. Hartup and. Z. Rubin (eds), *Relationships and Development* (pp. 95–110). Hillsdale, N.J.: Lawrence Erlbaum Associates.

Weiss, R. S. (1991). The attachment bond in childhood and adulthood. In C. M. Parkes, J. Stevenson-Hinde and P. Marris (eds), *Attachment Across the Life Cycle* (pp. 66–76). London: Tavistock/Routledge.

Wellman, H. (1990). *The Child's Theory of Mind*. Cambridge, Mass.: Bradford Books.

Wenar, C. (1982). On negativism. *Human Development*, **25**, 1–23.

Wentowski, G. J. (1985). Older women's perceptions of great-grandparenthood: A research note. *The Gerontologist*, **25**, 593–596.

Whitbeck, L. B., Hoyt, D. R. and Huck, S. M. (1993). Family relationship history, contemporary parent–grandparent relationship quality, and the grandparent–grandchild relationship. *Journal of Marriage and the Family*, **55**, 1025–1035.

Whitbeck, L. B., Simons, R. L. and Conger, R. D. (1991). The effects of early family relationships on contemporary relationships and assistance patterns between adult children and their parents. *Journal of Gerontology*, **46**, 330–337.

Whiting, J. and Whiting, B. (1975). Aloofness and intimacy of husbands and wives: A cross-cultural study. *Ethos. Sum*, **3**(2), 183–207.

Winemiller, D. R., Mitchell, M. E., Sutliff, J. and Cline, D. J. (1993). Measurement strategies in social support: A descriptive review of the literature. *Journal of Clinical Psychology*, **49**, 638–648.

Winstead, B. (1986). Sex differences in same-sex friendships. In V. Derlega and

B. Winstead (eds), *Friendship and Social Interaction* (pp. 81–99). Heidelberg: Springer.

Wolf, R. and Pillemer, K. (1989). *Helping Elderly Victims: The Reality of Elder Abuse*. New York: Columbia University Press.

Wright, P. H. (1982). Men's friendships, women's friendships and the alleged inferiority of the latter. *Sex Roles*, **8**, 1–20.

Young, C. (1987). *Young People Leaving Home in Australia: The Trend Towards Independence*. Melbourne: Australian Institute of Family Studies.

Zajonc, R. and Hall, E. (1986). Mining new gold from old research. *Psychology Today*, **19**, 46–51.

Zal, H. M. (1992). *The Sandwich Generation: Caught Between Growing Children and Aging Parents*. New York: Plenum Press.

Zarit, S., Todd, P. and Zarit, J. (1986). Subjective burden of husbands and wives as caregivers: A longitudinal study. *Gerontologist*, **26**(3), 260–266.

Zietlow, P. H. and Sillars, A. L. (1988). Life-stage differences in communication during marital conflicts. *Journal of Social and Personal Relationships*, **5**, 223–245.

Zietlow, P. H. and Van Lear, C. A. (1991). Marriage duration and relational control: A study of developmental patterns. *Journal of Marriage and the Family*, **53**, 773–785.

Author index

Subject index